THE QUIET PINT

**A
GUIDE
TO
QUIET PUBS**

THE QUIET PINT

Compiled and Edited by
Derek and Josephine Dempster

"Q" Publications Limited
3 Harnet Street
Sandwich
Kent CT13 9ES
Tel: 01304 613547   Fax: 01304 613548

Cover Design

Concept by Derek and Josephine Dempster
Graphic Design by Clare Limbrey – *Buckland Press Ltd.*
Computer Graphics by John Harvey – *Buckland Press Ltd.*
Watercolour of King's Arms, Blakeney, Norfolk, by Janet Beckett

The contents of this book were believed to be correct at the time of going to press. However, because public houses and wine bars are subject to changes of ownership, management and policy, the publishers accept no responsibility for any differences that may occur between the information given in this Guide and the actuality.

ISBN 0 9526349 0 2

Directors: Edwin Peat, Derek Dempster, Josephine Dempster, Roger Viner, Nicolas Irwin.

Printed by Buckland Press Ltd. London and Dover, Kent.

THE QUIET PINT is affiliated to the Pipedown Campaign,
6 Kingsley Mansions, London W14 9SG. Tel/Fax: 0171 385 5811

CONTENTS

FOREWORD

By Julian Lloyd Webber

Never has a Guide like THE QUIET PINT been so urgently needed.

Piped music has spread like an insidious cancer in our society so that it is now incredibly difficult to find any indoor public place where we can be peaceful. In these hectic times it is important that we should at least be able to have a drink in peace if that's what we want. But, all too often, finding ourselves in a strange city, town or village, every pub or hotel we go into will be blasting out canned music we have not chosen and do not want to hear.

Now, at long last, THE QUIET PINT will steer you towards the haven of peace you may crave! And I hope it is a huge, raging success, and that more landlords, hoteliers, restaurateurs and shopkeepers etc. etc. will take notice. We deserve to have a say in whether we want somebody else's 'muzak' inflicted on us or not. If music is any good, it deserves to be listened to, not to drivel away in the background as a constant aural pollutant. The idea that 'muzak' is hugely influential in persuading people to buy more products is a myth encouraged by 'Psycho-Acoustic Consultants', 'Sound Designers' and 'Mood Engineers' for their own profitability. It has been proved that people don't want 'muzak'. Look at the Gatwick Airport survey. And Marks & Spencers and W.H. Smith (oases of muzak-free tranquillity in our High Streets) don't exactly do too badly.

Vote with your feet and go to the wonderful, individual establishments in this Guide and watch the tide begin to turn at last!

Julian Lloyd Webber

INTRODUCTION

It all started in August 1994, when the *Daily Telegraph* published a letter in which I congratulated Nigel Rodgers for starting the Pipedown Campaign in protest at the proliferation of background music in public places, and I suggested that readers send me the names and addresses of any muzak-free pubs they knew so that I might include them in a Pop-Free Pub Guide.

The response, from both the public and the licensed trade, was astounding. Regrettably, about one third of the nominated establishments had to be eliminated on closer scrutiny. In all probability they had been visited by our correspondents during a natural break between tapes, while a broken tape-deck was being repaired or the landlord had not bothered to switch on. When we checked, it was disappointing and sometimes surprising to discover how many had to be eliminated. A well-known television chef's West Country inn had rock playing so loudly that it was pointless asking the barman to fetch him to the telephone to answer our routine set of questions.

It was amazing how many failed to differentiate between piped "easy-listening", soft-rock, pop and classical music. "Oh no, we don't have piped music - only classical!" was a typical response - as though classical music was the smart way of attracting up-market customers and giving them the illusion of value for money. To quote freelance writer Oliver Bennett, "You don't expect to pay £2.99 for a burger if you have been listening to 'expensive' music."

While some pubs are not fully wired for sound, they do have CD players - which begs the question: do they have a licence to play music and are they paying their dues to the Performing Rights Society? Others claim to be sponsored by local radio stations to switch on and tune in permanently to their rocking wave-bands.

Some landlords answer complaints by explaining "that the staff like listening to music!" to which one of our more vociferous correspondents acidly retorts, "If you hadn't driven all the customers away by playing music, you'd be so busy the staff wouldn't have time to listen to it!"

A public house is a community centre where people usually go to be sociable. It's a place where patrons need to be mindful of their fellow customers' varying ages, persuasions and tastes. The whole idea of going to a pub is to have a drink, seek company if you're on your own, exchange a few jokes with your friends, talk to the barman, nurse your depressions in a quiet corner, if that's how you feel, play darts or shove h'apenny, eat perhaps, and generally relax. If there's background music it's bound to irritate if you have not chosen it yourself, and as so often happens, it's too damned loud.

To emphasise this, another of our correspondents tells of being in a musically noisy pub with a crowd of leather-clad bikers when one of the loud-speakers in the bar packed up. Gradually, all the bikers, clutching their pints, drifted over to the quiet end of the bar - under the dead speaker.

From the stream of letters we received, there emerged a number that gave me an understanding of the stress, frustration and isolation hearing disorders can inflict on its victims. Typical of these was a retired aero-engine fitter who neglected to wear ear defenders when he worked on jet engine test rigs; he now suffers from tinnitus and finds piped music in pubs quite intolerable. Another tinnitus victim described how the moment he sat down for a pub meal one evening, loud pop music started to reverberate throughout the building. After explaining his problem, the staff turned off the music in the restaurant, but he could still hear it coming from the foyer and the bar. Then, seeing that he was stuffing his ears with cotton wool, they took pity on him and turned off the music completely.

They're not all as considerate as that, though, which makes the availability of THE QUIET PINT all the more important.

Complaints about muzak have been going on for years. As long ago as 1986 Pipedown patron and *Daily Mail* columnist Keith Waterhouse marked pubs down as by far the worst offenders. "It is now practically impossible to find a pub that is not as enveloped in noise as its cold sausages are encased in grease," he wrote. "More than any other malign influence - more than video games, more than the over-priced keg lager, more than the squalor and the plastic tat, more than the microwaved pub grub, more than the brewers greed and stupidity, more than the licensing laws - the non-stop, stereophonic, eardrum-piercing blare is what is destroying the British pub."

It's almost ten years since Keith Waterhouse wrote that. Has anything changed? Well, yes. Thanks to CAMRA, we've almost got rid of keg beer. Let's hope that ten years from now most pubs will be havens of peace.

"Clever" designers try persuading one that music is hugely influential to the profitability of public houses. They say it relaxes you and persuades you to spend more. Conversely, others say that if you play the music too loudly, people will leave. (Several publicans we have questioned admit to putting on some very loud music to clear the pub at closing time.) But what these hidden persuaders do not consider is how totally offensive some music can be - loud or not. Someone else's choice can make a pub uncongenial. A key reason for having music, say the acoustic designers, is that the public are scared of the void. They can't cope with silence. Therefore, if you have to have noise coming through loud-speakers, what about wallpaper conversation; in other words, the recorded sound of chat, laughter, beer engines, clinking glasses - the sound of a busy pub. No one could argue about that!

Derek Dempster

COMMENTS

We believe that all the pubs listed in this Guide will be welcoming and the licensees will offer you good, friendly service. Some are eccentric, as are their establishments, which adds to their charm. Convention does not feature in their vocabulary. As you can imagine with any disparate group of people, we did find that some of the licensees were so extraordinarily rude and charmless that we have had to exclude them from the Guide. Only a handful, but I am seriously thinking of having a category next year headed "Charm School failures", giving you the name and address of the pub and allowing you to make up your own mind.

We are not judging a pub for the quality of its food, we are just reporting what we have been told. Our aim is to give you a list of pubs with none of the dreaded canned music. If the wiring has suddenly sneaked in and all is blaring forth DO LET US KNOW (stickers available from either ourselves or Pipedown). Live music you have to accept, in any case you are usually given ample warning. Juke boxes are an unfortunate fact of life - but somewhere you'll find an on/off switch.

With our existing (and growing) list we hope you can be sure of a decent drink, food, friendly service, conversation and nobody else's choice of music - personally, I'm into choral works and opera, but I wouldn't be so arrogant as to assume that you are too. The Chief is into South American music and good jazz - not my cup of tea! - or glass of beer I should say!

Up to now counties we would have expected to have a larger number of piped-music free pubs have been a disappointment. One county we did think would have a preponderance of quiet pubs was Surrey, but it turned out to be one of the least well served. The Isle of Wight has none - as far as we know! Dorset was another disappointment; it also had the rudest landlords. Kent came close; the rest were up North (rude landlords). Apart from Sussex, the South-East corner is not yet well served; we are convinced the quiet pubs are out there somewhere - and when word gets around that an entry in THE QUIET PINT is FREE, we know numbers will grow.

One thing that did surprise us is the amount paid to the Performing Rights Society every year to get rid of the customers! £500 on average - which must cut into the profits a bit - it's a high price to pay to keep the staff entertained. Landlords ought to bear in mind just who is paying their way.

NOTES

There are no prices for the food mentioned. We found that prices seemed to average out, and you can choose what you want to spend. Food is a very subjective thing: we have found that in gathering all this information we have gained an insight into pub catering. In more than three quarters of the pubs there was a distinct similarity in the menus. Truly original menus are few and far between; but that does not suggest that you will not be adequately fed, even though not imaginatively. Treasure those establishments where the soup is freshly made, the ham is really off-the-bone, and the sandwiches are properly filled. (What is this with 'doorstep' sandwiches: don't they have a proper breadknife, or has the reason escaped me?) Expect bar-meal times to be 12 to 2 and 7 to 9.

Virtually all pubs close on December 25th. If you haven't anything better to do and you're desperate for a drink we suggest you telephone - no one at home, no drink!

We have rarely included directions; we do give the full address and telephone number and hope that if you're fairly local you will know how to find the pub; travelling, you're bound to have a map. The human voice is quite useful: you wind down the window and hail a friendly native.

Because we have a dog and hate leaving him in the car - and won't on a hot day - we've made a point of asking all licensees their attitude towards dogs - and obviously children. If they offer accommodation a note is made of that but with no other details. Prices can change, it is far better to telephone and be completely up to date. When we know there is an outside seating area we have said so, mostly in a rather cryptic way, but at least you know there is a garden/terrace/courtyard and on a lovely sunny day nothing could be nicer than sitting with your drink in congenial surroundings.

Finally a word about publicans: contacting them has made us realise how much hard work goes into running an establishment: keeping the ales in good condition, feeding the customers and making them feel at home. Some double the effort and have exceptional places, wonderful gardens, memorable food and all those extras which make a pub stand out. All deserve an accolade, particularly as they have all kept their pubs free of piped music.

Josephine Dempster.

THE PIPEDOWN CAMPAIGN

by Nigel Rodgers
Honorary Secretary

The majority of British pubs have been ruined by piped music. A sweeping statement, but one millions of people throughout Britains would agree with. Until recently, however, they have felt they were fighting a losing battle. Twenty years ago CAMRA, the Campaign for Real Ale, did wonders in saving real ale - although the big brewers at the time insisted there was no market for it. But CAMRA has been far less successful at saving real pubs. And this is where **The Quiet Pint** comes in.

What is a pub? Pubs surely are places where you go to drink what you choose, eat what you choose and talk to the people you choose, or sit quietly in a corner relaxing with a drink. But you cannot talk or relax in most pubs these days with being deafened by someone else's choice of music. Go to what seems like a quiet corner away from the bar and piped music follows you, pouring out of speakers above your head, destroying conversation. Little wonder that pubs are often half empty. The brewers in despair, seduced by the piped music industry's smooth (and unproved) sales talk, compound their mistake by upping the volume - and pay for the privilege. Piped music costs a pub money. And the person who just wants a quiet pint or glass of wine, is driven out yet again, longing for something that used to be commonplace but is now a comparative rarity: a muzac-free pub.

So I warmly welcome **The Quiet Pint**, the much-needed guide to muzac-free pubs and wine-bars. No further need to poke your head in through the door looking for a quiet pub - and finding, after you have bought a drink, that the quiet was merely the pause between tapes.

Pipedown Supporters: Kingsley Amis, Alfred Brendel, John Drummond, Stephen Fry, Tom Conti, Christopher Hogwood, Gwyneth Jones, John Lill, Julian Lloyd Webber, Joanna Lumley, Miriam Margolyes, Peter Maxwell Davies, George Melly, Yehudi Menuhin, Spike Milligan, Tony Parsons, Simon Rattle, Prunella Scales, Claire Tomalin, Keith Waterhouse, Gillian Weir, A. N. Wilson.

ACKNOWLEDGEMENTS

We are grateful to the many people who wrote to us initially, nominating pubs they thought ought to be listed in THE QUIET PINT and then went to the trouble of getting our questionnaires answered. They are listed here. Many asked to remain anonymous. There were a lot of unsigned nominations. Many licensees also responded. We thank all of them.

Viv Adcock, John Alston, J. Bains, Dorothy Barnard, P. Gerald Barnet, Cmdr. Gerald Barnett, R.N., Derek Beaumont, Raymond Berger, L. Bewley, N. Binns, Terence Boxall, M. W. Bradley, Charles Brodie, David Brockensha, J. Buckby, James Busvine, Hector Carter, Neil Charman, P. J. Chester, Stan Coates, Frank Coffey, Brian Cook, Mrs. Shirley Cosgrave, Paul Crane, Andrew Cruikshank, Dr. A. C. Daniel, Godfrey Dann, Hugh Denham, W. A. Dixon, J. Dodds, Kenneth Downs, Dr. Frank Duckworth, Clive Dussek, David Dutton, Denis Dutton, Grace Ellis, Jack Emblow, Joan Evans, Laurence Fagan, R. Farran, John Fawthrop, R. H. Ffitch, James I. C. Flint, Dr. P. J. Fraser, Alan Friswell, Denis Gale, Peter Gill, Diana Griffith, O. Griffiths, J. Haffey, Arthur Hall, Mrs. J. Hall, David Hancock, Paula Harris, E. C. Harrison, Anthony Harvey, Mrs. P. Hawes, Mrs. M Haydock, Mr. & Mrs. Helmer, Norman Higget, F. H. Honnor, Helen Howels, P. O. & B. B. Howland, D. S. Hughes, John James, Walter Jenkins, R. Johnson, K. S. Jones, Leslie M. Jones, J. D. Kaye, Andrew Keener, Prof. W. E. Kershaw, Mr. & Mrs. A. B. King. Chris Kitcherer, J. C. P. Lansley, Ivan Lawrence, D. H. Letcher, Gareth Lewis, Graham Lovell, Douglas Lowndes, A. & K. Lulman, William March, Chris Marwood, Michael & Anne Marwood, M. E. Mason, P. McDonald, P. D. Michel, Rosie Miller, Harry Montgomery, Dr. Hilda Morgan, Owen Mortimer, M. Morris, Bruce Munroe, Mrs. William Nation, Stuart Neale, Gerard Noel, John C. H. Nunn, Jean Oak, Chris Owen, David Oxford, John Painter, Rev. A. M. Parker, Mrs. M. L. H. Parker, Mrs. W. Parker, Eric Pointing, Rachel Polity,

Douglas Pollack, Bryn Clayton Poulter, P. H. Ranson, M. C. Rawbone, Mrs. Deborah Reader, N. F. Richardson, D. Roberts, Martin Roberts, Mrs. Norval Rodgers, C. P. Ryall, B. M. Sane, Maxwell Savage, Nigel Savage, Leslie Scott, Mr. & Mrs. P. A. Scruton, V. G. Sherwin, Mrs. D. Smith, Mrs. E. M. Smith, David L. O. Smith, Leslie Smith, Robert Innes-Smith, R. Neil, W. Smith, Mrs. Jo Smithies, Dr. John Stabler, T. B. Standen, David Stead, Prof. P. M. Stell, David Stonex, David Sumbler, Vernon Sweeny, Bill & Frances Taylor, Peter Thompson, Mrs. M. Thraves, Prof. John Treble, Alan Trueman, Mrs. Jean Trussell, D. W. Turvey, Brian Vaughton, Tom Walsh, D. J. Watson, M. H. Watson, M. T. Warwood, Gerry Webb, G. R. Weston, Maurice Whitehouse, Gordon J. Williams, B. Williamson, Capt. Robert Haywood-Willis, Col. Tony Willman, Caroline & Richard De Wolf, Don Woodman, H. Yates, Mrs. R. Zeitler.

Thanks are also due to those who helped with our research, in particular, Audrey Lang, Trevor Love and Juliet Morris.

ENGLAND

AVON & SOMERSET

BATH

Old Green Tree
Tel: 01225 462357

12 Green Street, Bath, Avon
Free House. Nick Luke, licensee

Small, very popular town pub with three panelled rooms, all of them no smoking. Being small, it can get very crowded, particularly at lunchtime, which incidentally is the only time food is available. The short menu includes well filled rolls, good sized ploughmans, several pasta dishes, omelettes and a daily special. The five ales come from mainly local breweries and the choice varies considerably. There are also a number of unusual wines. Pimms is served during the summer and mulled wine in winter.

OPEN: 11 - 11 (closed Sun morning winter).
Real Ale. Lunchtime meals and snacks (not Sun).
Children over 10 if eating lunchtime only. No dogs.

BRISTOL

Highbury Vaults
Tel: 0117 9733203

164 St Michael's Hill, Kingsdown, Bristol BS2 8DE
Smiles. Brad Francis, manager

Being near the university, this pub is understandably very popular in term time. Fundamentally a Georgian building with a late Victorian/Edwardian interior. It has a small front bar and a bigger bar at the back. Reasonably priced traditional bar food. The main ales stocked come from Smiles; they also have Brains SA, Fullers London Pride and two changing guests, plus local Long Ashton cider. During the summer they have a weekend barbecue in the pub courtyard.

OPEN: 12 - 11.
Real Ale. No food Sat/Sun eves.
Dogs and children in garden.

COMBE HAY

Wheatsheaf   Tel: 01225 833504

Combe Hay, Nr Bath, Avon BA2 7EG
Free House. M G Taylor, licensee

Unless you have a reason for exploring the lovely countryside surrounding the city of Bath, you wouldn't usually venture along the narrow, twisting, wonderfully overgrown lanes that lead from one hidden village to the next. Clinging to the side of the hill in this charming village, the Wheatsheaf is one good reason for venturing forth. On a clear day the views from the pub garden are of the English countryside at its best. Inside are cosy, low-ceilinged rooms, country furnishings, a big log fire in winter and a huge blackboard menu. Interesting, imaginative choice of dishes including the familiar bar snacks. The specials board might include: king prawns in garlic butter, venison in red wine sauce, game in season and several fish dishes. Courage Best and Hook Norton plus two guest beers. Seats in the garden.

OPEN: 11 - 3; 6.30 - 10.30 (Fri & Sat 11).
Real Ale. Restaurant.
Children away from bar. Dogs on leads.

COMPTON MARTIN

Ring O'Bells   Tel: 01761 221284

Compton Martin, Nr Bath, Avon BS18 6JE
Free House. Roger Owen, licensee

Close to the Mendip Hills and Chew Valley Lake, this village pub is popular with walkers and locals alike. Stone walls, flagstoned floors and big log fires make it wonderfully inviting in winter. Usual sandwiches, ploughmans, grills and lasagne plus imaginative specials. A roast lunch is available on Sundays. Bass, Wadworths 6X and Butcombe Bitter plus a guest ale. Local cider on draught. Seats in the garden amidst the apple trees - there is also a play area for children

OPEN: 11.30 - 3; 6 - 11.
Real Ale. Restaurant (not Sun eve).
Children in family room. Dubious about dogs.

CRANMORE

Strode Arms   Tel: 01749 880450

Cranmore, Nr Shepton Mallet, Somerset BA4 4QT
Free House. Rodney & Dora Phelps, licensees

Originally a 14th century farmhouse, then a coaching inn, now the village pub. Situated opposite the duck pond and not far from the East Somerset Railway, it houses an interesting collection of railway memorabilia. Country furnishings, big log fires in winter and a smart restaurant. Bar food includes the usual range of sandwiches, ploughmans, filled baked potatoes, venison sausages, fish dishes plus daily specials. Marstons Pedigree, Wadworths 6X and Flowers IPA. Farm cider. Seats on the terrace at the front of the pub overlooking the village pond.

OPEN: 11.30 - 2.30; 6.30 - 11. Closed Sun eve Oct-Feb.
Real Ale. Restaurant.
Children in restaurant. Dogs in bar on leads.

CROSCOMBE

Bull Terrier
Tel: 01749 343658

Croscombe, Nr Wells, Somerset BA4 4QJ
Free House. Barry Vidler, licensee

There's a Medieval Cross next to this old building which was originally a priory, the home of the Abbot of Glastonbury. First licensed early in the 17th century, it has three bars: the lounge - called the "Inglenook" - which still has its original beamed ceiling - the "Snug" and the "Common Bar"; there is also a family room. Home-made food, which ranges from ploughmans and vegetarian dishes to specials such as turkey ham and mushroom pie or ginger chicken with noodles. Good puddings. Varying ales but mainly Bull Terrier Best Bitter brewed for the pub, also Butcombe Bitter, Greene King Abbot, Hook Norton Old Hooky, Palmers IPA and Smiles Best. Local cider, brandy and good list of wines. The attractive walled garden backs onto the village church and - continuing the ecclesiastical theme - there is a footpath from the village to the Bishop's Palace in Wells.

OPEN: 12 - 2.30; 7 - 11 (closed Mon winter).
Real Ale. No food winter Sun eve or all day Mon.
Children in family room. Dogs if they like the look of them.
Bedrooms.

DUNSTER

Luttrell Arms
Tel: 01643 821555

High Street, Dunster, Somerset TA24 6SG
Free House (Forte). Mrs M Coffey, manager

Built in the 15th century, the Luttrell Arms was originally the guesthouse for the monks of Cleeve Abbey. They created a Gothic hall with a wonderful hammer beam roof, a window of exceptional size for the time and a truly immense fireplace. Originally "The Ship," it was renamed the Luttrell Arms in 1779 - a gesture of respect for the Luttrells, owners of Dunster Castle. An historic, medieval village, with its 16th century yarn market dominating the high street, it was built when Dutch craftsmen arrived to take advantage of the prosperous cloth weaving industry already established in the area. It was probably the Dutch who were responsible for the ornate moulded plasterwork found in the Luttrell Arms. Now an elegant, well run hotel, there is nevertheless a good pubby atmosphere in the timbered back bar. They serve a buffet at lunchtime and also during the evening in the old kitchen next to the Gothic hall. Usual bar snacks on offer, with more formal meals in the Luttrell Restaurant. Flowers IPA, Bass and John Smiths ales. Extensive wine list. Good walks and lots of places to explore.

OPEN: 10.30 - 11.
Real Ale. Restaurant.
Children in eating areas. Dogs on leads.

EXFORD

Crown Hotel   Tel: 01643 831554

Exford, Somerset TA24 7PP
Free House. Matthew Shadbolt, manager

In the picturesque heart of the Exmoor National Park, the 17th century Crown, with its later additions, offers elegant accommodation as well as an informal public bar atmosphere. Here they serve freshly prepared, imaginative bar meals and pints of traditional ale. There is a separate restaurant with well chosen seasonal menus, plus a carefully selected wine list. Brakspear Bitter and Flowers Original on hand pump.

OPEN: 11 - 2.30; 6 - 11 (12-3, 7-10.30 Sun).
Real Ale. Restaurant.
Children welcome. Dogs on leads.
Bedrooms.

FAULKLAND

Tuckers Grave
Tel: 01373 834230

Faulkland, Nr Bath, Somerset BA3 5XF
Free House. Ivan & Glenda Swift, licensees

Poor Tucker, hanged himself at a nearby farm back in the mists of time and was buried at the crossroads where this old stone pub now stands. Think of a pub that has been serving the small local community for centuries and you have a picture of this unspoilt little place. Casks of Bass and Butcombe Bitter; also Cheddar Valley cider. A skittle alley for fun, seats in the garden for relaxation and a ploughmans or sandwich for lunchtime sustenance.

OPEN: 11.30 - 3; 6 - 11.
Real Ale.
Children welcome. No dogs.

KELSTON

Old Crown
Tel: 01225 423023

Bath Road, Kelston, Nr Bath, Avon BA1 9AQ
Free House. Richard Jackson & Michael Steele, licensees

On the old Bath to Bristol road you might be forgiven for thinking that time has stood still if you arrive at night and find candle-light flickering inside the pub. Traditionally furnished, with polished flagstone floors, it has two bars and two small, attractive dining rooms, lunchtime bar food and an evening restaurant for serious eating. Well kept ales include Bass, Butcombe, Wadworths 6X and Smiles Best plus a regular guest ale. Tables under the fruit trees in the orchard at the back. The car park is on the opposite side of the busy road.

OPEN: 11.30 - 2.30; 5 - 11.
Restaurant (not Sun) Thurs, Fri & Sat eves.
Lunchtime meals and snacks (not Sun).
No children. Dogs on leads.

LUXBOROUGH

Royal Oak Tel: 01984 640319

Luxborough, Nr Dunster, Exmoor National Park, Somerset TA23 0SH
Free House. Robin & Helen Stamp, licensees

Situated by a stream - at the bottom of a valley near the Exmoor National Park at Dunkery Beacon - it is about as idyllic as you can get. Add a 14th century thatched country pub with heavily beamed bars complete with flagged floors, inglenook fireplaces, and an assortment of country furniture, and what more could you want, but well kept local ales and good, hearty country cooking? The choice ranges from sandwiches to rabbit stew or roast wild boar. Sunday lunches. Cotleigh Tawny, Exmoor Gold, Thatchers Cheddar Valley, Flowers IPA are among the ales you may find; also Rich's Farmhouse Cider. Good list of wines by the bottle and a few by the glass. Seats outside in the garden.

OPEN: 11 - 2.30; 6 - 11 (6.30 - 11 winter).
Real Ale. Restaurant.
Children in dining room and rear bar. Dogs in bar.
Folk Music Friday. Bedrooms.

MARSHFIELD

Catherine Wheel Tel: 01225 892220

High Street, Marshfield, Wilts SN14 8LC
Free House. Royston & Carole Elms, licensees

This pub has a Georgian frontage behind which lies a much older Elizabethan building. The attractive interiors, particularly the dining room, reflect more of the Georgian than the Elizabethan. The beamed main bar with big fireplace, pine tables and country chairs is friendly and welcoming. Traditional bar food, plus imaginative additions and daily specials. Wadworths IPA and 6X, Courage Bitter, farm cider and a good wine list.

OPEN: 11 - 3; 6 - 11. Closed Mon lunch except Bank Holidays.
Real Ale. Restaurant. No meals Sunday.
Children in eating area until 8.30.
Dogs on leads.
Thurs eve Sing-alongs.

MONTACUTE

Kings Arms Inn   Tel: 01935 822513

Bishopston, Montacute, Somerset TA15 6UU
Free House. Michael Harrison, licensee

A handsome 16th century inn, once a staging post where the
horses were changed before the long pull up Ham Hill on the main
road from Plymouth to London. Now a popular beauty spot with
tremendous views to the Mendips and Quantocks to the north,
and the Dorset hills to the south. In the centre of the village, the
Kings Arms is a popular meeting place for locals and visitors alike.
Bar food includes an impressive cold buffet and daily hot dishes
plus sandwiches and soup. Wadworths 6X, Bass and probably a
guest beer. Farmhouse cider and good wine list. Montacute
House, owned by the National Trust, is worth a visit.

OPEN: 11 - 11.
Real Ale. Restaurant.
Children in eating areas.
No dogs. Bedrooms.

OLDBURY ON SEVERN

Anchor   Tel: 01454 413331

Church Road, Oldbury on Severn, Avon BS12 1QA
Free House. Alex de la Torre, licensee

In a quiet village not far from the river and tidal flats of the Severn
Estuary, the Anchor Pub - with its beamed bar, window seats,

traditional furnishings and big log fires - is a welcome haven if you are walking the area in a bracing westerly. The bar food - all cooked by the landlord - uses lots of local produce and changes daily in both the bar and restaurant. A selection of good cheeses, a plate of rare roast beef and locally produced sausages are always available. Bass from the cask, Marstons Pedigree, Butcombe Bitter, Theakstons Best Bitter and Old Peculiar on hand pump. Seats outside in the attractive garden.

OPEN: 11.30 - 2.30; 6.30 - 11 (11.30 - 3; 6 - 11 Sat).
Real Ale. Restaurant.
Children in restaurant. Dogs on leads.
Occasional live entertainment.

PORLOCK

Ship Inn
Tel: 01643 862507

High Street, Porlock, Somerset TA24 8QD
Free House. Mark & Judy Robinson, licensees

Porlock village, set in a natural bowl, is surrounded by wooded hills and has spectacular views. At the bottom of Porlock Hill sits the small, partially-thatched, 13th century Ship Inn. Inside, it's heavily beamed, flagstoned, traditionally furnished and serves well-chosen bar food. Familiar favourites: soups, ploughmans, paté, local sausages, daily specials and fresh fish when available. Children's menu. Cotleigh Old Buzzard, Bass, Courage Best and a local guest beer. Steep garden at the back of the pub, with a children's play area. Not far from the sea and open moor.

OPEN: 10.30 - 3; 5.30 - 11.
Real Ale. Restaurant (not Sun eve).
Children welcome away from bar. Dogs on leads.
Morris dancing and occasional folk. Bedrooms.

STANTON WICK

Carpenters Arms   Tel: 01761 490202

Stanton Wick, Nr Pensford, Bristol, Avon BS18 4BX
Free House. Nigel Pushman, licensee

In a hamlet overlooking the Chew Valley, this stonebuilt pub was originally a row of miners' cottages. Lots of beams and warming fires inside. Two dining areas: the restaurant, and another, less formal one for bar meals. Well chosen bar food, with daily specials written on the blackboard. A more elaborate menu features in the restaurant. Bass, Butcombe Bitter, Wadworths 6X and Boddingtons. Ten wines by the glass and a well priced wine list. Seats in the flowery garden.

OPEN: 11 - 11.
Real Ale. Restaurant (not Sun eve).
Children welcome. Dogs on leads.
Occasional live pianist in restaurant.
Bedrooms.

WEST HUNTSPILL

Cross Ways Inn   Tel: 01278 783756

West Huntspill, Nr Highbridge, Somerset TA9 3RA
Free House. Michael Ronca & Tony Eyles, licensees

On the A38 and 3 miles from Exit 22 on the M5, is not the usual way to introduce an easily accessible pub, but anyone travelling on boring motorways and wanting peace and quiet plus good food and a pint is usually desparate for this sort of information. The 17th century Cross Ways Inn has a low beamed, traditionally furnished interior, log fires and friendly, welcoming atmosphere. Extensive menu with something for everyone, including children's meals. Pub specials include broccoli, chicken and ham mornay, moussaka and salad, a vegetable bake and its own beef curry.

Friday night is fish night and on Saturdays there is a three course dinner. Flowers IPA, Original and Royal Oak plus varying guest ales - could be Smiles Best, Butcombe Bitter, Bass, Oakhill. Choice of malt whiskies and Rich's farmhouse cider. Seats in the large garden among the fruit trees.

OPEN: 12 - 3; 5.30 - 11 (6 - 11 Sat).
Real Ale. Restaurant Fri & Sat only.
Children welcome (except in main bar). Dogs on leads.
Occasional live music. Bedrooms.

WINCANTON

Stags Head Inn   Tel: 01963 440393

Yarlington, Wincanton, Somerset BA9 8DG
Free House. Andy & Ann Sugg, licensees

Without the inn sign hanging from the side of the pub and stag's horns fixed above the front door, you would hesitate even to think that this was a pub. At first glance it would seem to be a solid, stone built village house, with a long low garden wall and front gate. But inside the small very friendly pub there are two bars with pine serving counters, traditional furnishings and wholesome varied bar food. There is an à la carte menu in the restaurant and special Sunday lunches. Butcombe Bitter, Castlemaine XXXX, Tetleys and Lowenbrau; also Inch's farm cider. Seats in the garden.

OPEN: 12 - 2.30; 7 - 11.
Real Ale. Restaurant (no food Monday).
No dogs.

WINSFORD

Royal Oak Inn
Tel: 01643 851455

Winsford, Exmoor National Park, Somerset TA24 7JE
Free House. Charles Steven, licensee
(NB After a disastrous fire, inn re-opening late summer '95)

In a picturesque village on the edge of the Exmoor National Park, among stone and thatched cottages, you will find the smart, cream-washed, thatched 12th century Royal Oak. Inside are fine oak beams, panelling and big open fires. Light bar meals include sandwiches, jacket potatoes, ploughmans, game terrine, paté, various filled pies. There are daily specials and everything is home-cooked, including the bread. There is also a full restaurant menu. Flowers Original and IPA on hand pump. The River Winn, on which the Royal Oak has its own beat, runs through the village and fishing can be arranged.

OPEN: 11 - 2.30; 6 - 11.
Real Ale. Restaurant (not Sun eve).
Children welcome except in front bar. Dogs on leads.
Bedrooms.

WITHYPOOL

Royal Oak
Tel: 01643 831506

Withypool, Somerset, TA24 7QP
Free House. Michael Bradley, licensee

Not a haunt of the anti-hunting brigade: stags' antlers and fox masks nailed to the walls make a very positive statement. Fishing memorabilia in another room. Filling, well-chosen and extensive bar snacks range from sandwiches and soups to steaks and a choice of fish in season. The blackboard menu is more adventurous and may offer you lamb casserole, poached salmon or half a crispy duck. There's a table d'hote and an à la carte menu in the restaurant. Very busy, particularly on Sundays and in the hunting, shooting season. Flowers IPA, Castle Eden and Bentleys Yorkshire. Farm ciders and malt whiskies. Interesting wine list. Lots of walks, wonderful views, and if you're really keen, you can hunt, shoot or fish by arrangement.

OPEN: 11 - 2.30; 6 - 11.
Real Ale. Restaurant.
No children. Dogs on leads.

BEDFORDSHIRE & CAMBRIDGESHIRE

BOLNHURST

Olde Plough   Tel: 01234 376274

Kimbolton Road, Bolnhurst, Beds MK44 2EX
Free House. M J Horridge, licensee

Not only is there a good choice of home-made food and real ales
in this 500 year old pub, but also the added bonus of a lovely
garden and long terrace - where you can sit and look over the
pond - and a landlady who (it is rumoured) will let all you keen
gardeners take cuttings of anything you fancy. Let's hope there
isn't too much demand; one has visions of a denuded garden. The
restaurant upstairs and the bar share the same menu which
changes weekly and could include filled rolls, soup, paté, local
sausages, vegetarian pasta, fillet of salmon in green peppercorn
sauce, steaks, interesting puds. Ruddles Best, Courage Directors,
John Smiths Magnet on hand pump. Buck's Fizz in summer - so
civilised! Two resident cats, two dogs. No cats up trees, please,
so watch your dogs!

OPEN: 12 - 2.30 (3 Sat); 7 - 11.
Real Ale. Restaurant Fri, Sat eve & Sun lunch only.
Well behaved children until 9. Dogs on leads.

BYTHORN

White Hart Tel: 01832 710226

Bythorn, Nr Huntingdon, Cambs CB2 3QN.
Free House. Bill & Pam Bennett, licensees

This 17th century village inn is really more of a restaurant than a pub. Having said that, you don't need to have more than a beer or a glass of wine with a nut or a crisp. Food is served in the bar as well as the restaurant and a no-smoking dining room. The menu is very creative and popular: home-made soup, ploughman's, duck liver terrine, fresh scallops, venison casserole, game in season, loin of pork in orange sauce, steaks, home-made puddings. Big Sunday lunches. Greene King IPA and Abbot ales. Wines by the glass. Seats and tables outside in the garden.

OPEN: 11 - 3; 6 - 11. Closed Sun eve and all day Mon.
Real Ale.
Restaurant. No-smoking dining room.
Children welcome. No dogs.
Morris dancers occasionally.

CAMBRIDGE

Eagle Tel: 01223 301286

Bene't Street, Cambridge, Cambs CB2 3QN
Greene King. Peter & Carol Hill, licensees

A lively rambling 16th century town pub with a lot of the interior still intact: 17th century fireplaces, some mullioned windows, wall paintings and original pine panelling. More up to date are the names of British and American airmen written on the ceiling in lipstick or whatever else came to hand during World War Two. They have been left intact although the ceiling has been given a little wash. Simple, good range of bar food: a variety of salads, quiches, pasties, roast lamb, chicken, etc. Greene King ales on hand pump. Many wines by the glass. There are seats and tables in the cobbled, galleried yard at the entrance to the pub.

OPEN: 11 - 11; Meal/snacks 12-2.30; 5.30-8 not Fri, Sat, Sun.
Real Ale.
Children welcome. No dogs.

CAMBRIDGE

Free Press   Tel: 01223 68337

Prospect Row, Cambridge, Cambs CB1 1QU
Greene King. Debbie & Christopher Lloyd, tenants

No need to fear you'll be press-ganged into training for the next University boat race when you enter this totally non-smoking pub, which is registered as a boat club and has walls covered in rowing blades and appropriate photographs. Originally a terraced house, it became a pub in 1840 and was named after a failed local paper of the same name *(I am quoting Jill, the jolly barmaid)* which, as you can see, has nothing to do with boats! There are five home-made soups daily, one of which is vegetarian, hot chilli, lamb casserole, several vegetarian dishes and home-made puddings. Ales are Greene King and there is a range of malt whiskies. Seats in the sunny, sheltered garden which is a home to the extras from Watership Down.

OPEN: 12 - 2.30; 6 - 11.
Real Ale.
Children welcome. Dogs on leads.

FEN DRAYTON

Three Tuns
Tel: 01954 230242

High Street, Fen Drayton, Cambs CB4 5SJ
Greene King. Michael & Eileen Nugent, tenants

Exceptional 15th Century carvings on the tie beams suggests this was an important local building. It is thought to have been Fen Drayton's guildhall. (Known as Fenny Dreiton in 1285). The pub has been considerably altered and extended over the years. The present bar was built onto the side of the original building. Heavily beamed and with inglenook fireplaces, it is filled with interesting bric à brac and old photographs. Food is cooked to order - short varied menu offering: fried whitebait, chicken satay, grills, fish, home-cured ham, chicken curry, salads, sandwiches and choice of puddings. Greene King IPA, Abbot and Rayments Special Bitter. Range of malt whiskies. Tables on the lawn at the back of the pub amongst the fruit trees.

OPEN: 11 - 2.30; 6.30 - 11.
Real Ale.
Children in eating area until 8. Dogs in garden only.

FOWLMERE

Chequers
Tel: 01954 230242

High Street, Fowlmere, Cambs. SG8 7SR
Pubmaster. Norman Rushton, lease

How to be in two places at once: depending on which address you read, this pub is either in Cambridgeshire or near Royston, Hertfordshire. You may be forgiven for thinking this is the reason the inn sign is one colour one side, another on the reverse - confusion is everywhere - the answer is all to do with Foulmere Aerodrome and the proprietor will be only too pleased to tell you all about it. A very civilised old coaching inn which has a considerable reputation for an interesting variety of food: home-made soups, mussels in garlic butter, duck and pork paté, cassoulet, vegetarian dishes and home-made puddings. Two cosy rooms and a galleried restaurant. Tetleys and Tolly Cobbold Original. Good choice of wines, ports and brandies. Seats in the pretty, flowery garden.

OPEN: 12 - 2.30; 6 - 11.
Real Ale. Restaurant.
Children welcome. No dogs.

HORNINGSEA

Plough & Fleece   Tel: 01223 860795

High Street, Horningsea, Cambs. CB5 9JG
Greene King. Kenneth Grimes, tenant

This small, lively 200 year old pub is a great favourite with locals and visitors alike. It has a beamed public bar with oak settles and tables and a no-smoking dining room. There is a good choice of bar food: sandwiches, home-made soups, omelettes, Suffolk Hot Pot, etc., good puddings. Always a roast at weekends. Greene King ales; choice of malt whiskies and vintage ports. Tables in the garden.

OPEN: 11.30 - 2.30; 7 - 11. No food Sun or Mon eves
Real Ale: No-smoking restaurant.   Children over 5 in restaurant only. Dogs on leads.

KEYSTON

Pheasant   Tel: 01832 710241

Village Loop Road, Keyston, Nr Bythorn, Cambs PE18 0RE
Free House. John Hoskins & Roger Jones, licensees

There's just one room in this well kept, pretty thatched pub. Used to be the village blacksmiths and still has some horsey artefacts hanging around the walls. Heavily beamed and comfortable, it has a no-smoking area in the restaurant. Using the best local produce, like fresh fish, game in season, it has an interesting menu which changes every couple of weeks. The menu includes an extensive list of starters and light snacks - wild boar sausages, breast of pigeon, poached fillet of hake, etc. Over ten puddings to choose from. Roast sirloin on Sundays. British cheeses. Adnams Best and three guest beers. Good wine list, a considerable number by the glass. Tables outside.

OPEN: 12 - 3; 6 - 11.
Real Ale.
Children welcome. No dogs.

MADINGLEY

Three Horseshoes   Tel: 01954 210221

High Street, Madingley, Cambs CB3 8AB
Free House. R Stokes & John Hoskins, licensees

Try not to ask for anything flambé here. This whitewashed, thatched pub, with a single bar has been burnt down three times, so they say. It was last rebuilt in 1911. The menu emphasises Mediterranean style food, both in the restaurant and on the blackboard menu in the bar. Home-made soup, tomato and basil tart, fresh crab salads, boeuf en daube, duck breast with mint and caper dressing. Interesting British cheeses. Good puddings. Wide ranging wine list, 75% of the customers are wine buffs. Adnams Best and three guest beers are on hand pump. Tables in the flowery garden during the summer.

OPEN: 11.30 - 2.30; 6 - 11. No restaurant Sun eve.
Real Ale.
Children welcome. No dogs.

NEWTON

Queens Head
Tel: 01223 870436

Newton, Nr Cambridge, Cambs CB2 5BG
Free House. David & Juliet Short, licensees

This is a charming, traditional 17th century village inn. A painting of the goose on the pub sign depicts poor Belinda, keeper of the car park, now in residence in the public bar - stuffed. One beamed, main bar with a big log fire in winter and a smaller cosy saloon. Simple good bar food complements the fine ales and country wines. Sandwiches, home-made soup, filled baked potatoes. Evenings and Sunday lunchtime there is a selection of cold meats, salads, etc. Adnams Bitter and Broadside with Adnams Old Ale in winter - all tapped from the cask. Country fruit wines, farm cider. Seats at the front of the pub or on the green.

OPEN: 11.30 - 2.30; 6 - 11.
Real Ale.
Children in Games Room. Dogs on leads.

PULLOXHILL

Cross Keys
Tel: 01525 712442

High Street, Pulloxhill, Beds MK45 5HB
Charles Wells. Peter & Sheila Meads, tenants

Typical English country pub; architecturally pleasing, white painted and flower-bedecked. Heavily beamed interior with large log-filled fireplaces. Dating back to the 15th century, there is a legend that the ghost of a slain Cavalier stalks the pub by night. A satisfying lunchtime bar snack menu provides soups, ploughman's, salads, scampi, trout and Virginia ham. Daily specials and more substantial dishes are on offer in the restaurant: steaks, mixed grills, chicken Kiev and a variety of fish. Good choice of wines. Charles Wells and Adnams ales. Seats in the garden. Serious jazz sessions on Sunday nights with the likes of Kenny Baker, Charlie Galbraith, Acker Bilk and that ilk.

OPEN: 11 - 3; 6 - 11.
Real Ale. Restaurant. Specially priced lunches for senior citizens Mon-Fri.
Children in own room. No dogs.
Jazz every Sun eve.

SLAPTON

Carpenter's Arms   Tel: 01525 220563

Slapton, Nr Leighton Buzzard, Beds LU7 9DB
Free House. Jim & Anne Vogler, licensees

Only half a mile from the Grand Union Canal - in the rolling Bedfordshire countryside - this delightful 16th century village pub and restaurant not only provides good cask ales and an extensive menu to choose from, but - next door in the Maltings, keeping pub hours - a large, second-hand bookshop in which to browse while waiting for your lunch to turn up. Large home-made pies with fillings such as pigeon breasts in red wine, salmon, cod and scallops, aubergine and mushroom with fresh coriander are a speciality of the house. Lots of salads, steaks, poached salmon, home-made soups, paté and Italian cold meats. Greene King IPA and one guest cask bitter. There are tables and chairs on the terrace.

OPEN: 12 - 3; 7 - 11 (closed Sat lunchtime).
Real Ale.
Quiet children welcome. Quiet dogs on leads.

TODDINGTON

Sow & Pigs   Tel: 01525 873089

19 Church Square, Toddington, Nr Dunstable, Beds LU5 6AA
Greene King. Roger Martin, licensee

Just down the road from territory closely guarded until last year by the Terror of Toddington - a Muscovy duck of uncertain temper, now retired for his own good - is the unpredictable Sow & Pigs Pub. A notice pinned to the doors stating "No footballers" encourages any lingerer to enter and find out why. Not many concessions to comfort in the minute public bar - nor in the lounge either. Bar snacks are freshly prepared. There is a Victorian style dining room which is used for special occasions. As the name suggests, you will find plenty of pigs - some even flying. A sense of humour is useful. The landlord is a splendid and ebullient man, popular with the local eccentrics and farmers discussing their poverty. There are occasional poetry or jazz evenings upstairs. The ales come from Greene King and there are some guest beers.

OPEN: 11 - 11.
Real Ale.
Children welcome. Dogs on leads.

WANSFORD

Haycock   Tel: 01780 782223

Wansford, Peterborough, Cambs PE8 6JA
Free House. Richard Neale, licensee

Situated next to the river and more of a hotel than others on our list, it is nevertheless a well-run, friendly and appealing place for a drink and a meal. The Haycock has a flagstoned hall, an attractively panelled main bar, sitting room at the front with a big log fire and a garden room opening out onto a sunny terrace. There are two no-smoking areas. Good choice of bar food: grilled sardines in garlic butter, vegetable stroganoff, open sandwiches, home-made soup, grilled salmon with herb butter, home-made puddings. A reasonably priced three-course lunch is available during the week. The regular ales are Bass, Ruddles Best and County, Banks & Taylors Sheffords Bitter, also Adnams ale together with a guest. Choice of wines and vintage ports. There is a boules and cricket pitch if you're feeling energetic and can muster a team.

OPEN: All day 10.30 onwards.
Real Ale. Restaurant.
Children welcome. Dogs on leads. Bedrooms.

BERKSHIRE

ALDWORTH

Bell
Tel: 01635 578272

Aldworth, Nr Reading, Berks RG8 9SB
Free House. H E Macaulay, licensee

This 14th century pub is a popular stop for locals and energetic people walking the Ridgeway. Grade 1 listed, it has been in the same family for two centuries. Nothing much has changed over the years; heavily beamed, with panelled walls and traditional furnishings - no bar counter, just a hatch through which you are served. Food is limited to crusty rolls filled with ham, cheese, smoked salmon, salt beef or Devon crab; home-made soup during the winter. Ales are: Badger Best, Hook Norton Best, Arkells BBB and Kingsdown. Some wines by the glass. Seats in the attractive garden next to the cricket pitch.

OPEN: 11 - 3; 6 - 11. Closed Mon (Open Bank Holiday Mon).
Real Ale. Children in Tap Room. Dogs on leads.
Occasional Morris Dancing.

COOKHAM

Bel & The Dragon
Tel: 01628 521263

High Street, Cookham Village, Berks SL6 9SQ
Free House. Mr & Mrs F E Stuber & Mr & Mrs H Schlatter

Licensed since the 15th century, the Bell was established as a house of refreshment for people attending Cookham Church, parts of which date back to 1040. It has three rooms, one of which is no-smoking. Lots of beams and a friendly atmosphere. Bar food - served in the lounge bar - includes sandwiches, quiche, toasties, omelettes, steak & kidney pie and other hot dishes - all home-made. Full meals are served in the restaurant. Brakspears ale, tapped from the cask. Choice of wines. Seats in the garden and on the terrace. The Stanley Spencer Gallery is virtually opposite and well worth a visit.

OPEN: 11 - 2.30; 6 - 10.30 (11 Sat).
Real Ale. Restaurant closed Sun eve. Sandwiches only.
Children welcome. Dogs on leads in bar only.

CRAZIES HILL

Horns   Tel: 01734 401416

Crazies Hill, Wargrave, Berks RG10 8LY
Brakspears. David & Patsy Robinson, tenants

Originally a Tudor hunting lodge - but that's not why there are stags' antlers above the front door. Antlers, Horns - get it? It's a friendly country pub with lots of beams and big open fires. Typical lunchtime menu includes filled rolls, soup, salads, pasta and other hot dishes which vary daily. Meals are served in the restaurant on Friday and Saturday evenings. The rest of the week, evenings are devoted to conversation, pub games and a friendly drink. Brakspears ales and lots of malt whiskies. Good choice of wines. There is a big garden of several acres.

OPEN: 11 - 2.30 (3 Sats); 5.30 - 11.
Real Ale. Lunchtime food only. No food Sun or Mon. Brasserie meals Friday and Saturday evenings - Must book.
Children in pub barn. Dogs on leads.
Live Music Mon eves.

FRILSHAM

Pot Kiln
Tel: 01635 201366

Frilsham, Nr Hermitage, Berks RG16 0XX
Free House. Philip Gent, licensee

It's unspoilt, old-fashioned, tucked away down a country lane, and popular with the locals and passing ramblers. No counter, just a hatch for your orders in the tiny entrance hall. A good fire keeps the customers warm in winter and a simple bar menu sustains them. Home-made soup, filled rolls, ploughmans and daily specials. Ales are: Morlands Original, Old Speckled Hen, Morrells Mild and Arkells BBB. Tables in the big, sheltered garden. Good walks nearby.

OPEN: 12 - 2.30; 6.30 - 11.
Real Ale. Limited food Sun & Tues.
Children in dining room. Dogs on leads.
Live Music 3rd Sun of month.

HAMSTEAD MARSHALL

White Hart
Tel: 01488 658201

Hamstead Marshall, Nr Newbury, Berks RG15 0HW
Free House. Mr Nicola Aromando, licensee

Deep in the Berkshire countryside, this pleasant Georgian country inn is set in a pretty walled garden and surrounded by flowers. Inside there is an L-shaped bar, seats built into the bow windows and a double-sided log fire. Renowned for its food, the White Hart has an Italian licensee who does most of the cooking and places the emphasis on meals, rather than on bar snacks, although there will usually be a soup of the day, freshly made pasta dishes and other daily specials. Home-made puddings. Badger Best and Wadworth 6X are the ales. There are seats in the lovely garden.

OPEN: 12 - 2.30; 6 - 11. Closed Sun.
Real Ale.
Children in eating area. No dogs. Bedrooms.

HOLYPORT

Belgian Arms   Tel: 01628 34468

Holyport Street, Holyport, Maidenhead, Berks SL6 2JR
Brakspears. Alfred Morgan, tenant

To give meaning to this pub's name, illustrations of Belgian army uniforms and other military prints adorn the low-ceilinged bar. The pub has a restaurant in the conservatory, used as an overflow for the busy lunchtime trade. It reverts to a proper restaurant in the evening. Bar food includes sandwiches, plain and toasted, pizzas with various toppings, ham and eggs and other daily specials. Brakspears ales and several malt whiskies are available. Seats in the garden overlook the pond and village green.

OPEN: 11 - 3; 5.30 - 11 (6 Sat).
Real Ale. No food Sun eve.
Children in restaurant. Dogs on leads.

HURLEY

Dew Drop Inn   Tel: 01638 824327

Nr Hurley, Berkshire SL6 6RB
Brakspears. Michael Morris, tenant

Golf pictures feature here. The friendly landlord is a very keen player. The main bar in this remote and unpretentious country pub has blazing log fires at each end in winter. Food varies from filled French sticks and salads in the summer to ploughmans and curries. Occasional summer barbecues are set in the pleasantly natural garden. Brakspear ales and a choice of malt whiskies.

OPEN: 11 - 2.30 (3 Sat); 6 - 11.
Real Ale. No food Sun eve or Mon.
Children in eating area. Loves dogs.

KINTBURY

Dundas Arms   Tel: 01488 658263

53 Station Road, Kintbury, Nr Newbury, Berks RG15 0UT
Free House. David A Dalzell Piper, licensee

A pub for over 200 years, the Dundas Arms enjoys an enviable situation by the Kennett & Avon Canal. Its attractive terrace is very popular during the summer and the dining room overlooks the canal. The menu reflects the skill and enthusiasm of the owner/chef who offers a three course luncheon menu and an à la carte dinner. But you can eat less ambitiously in the small bar: fish soup with croutons, crab au gratin, paté, smoked eel and bacon salad, leek and gruyère pie and lots of other dishes. A wide variety of wines come from the cellar. Morlands Bitter, Charles Wells Bombardier, Fullers London Pride are among the ales kept.

OPEN: 11 - 2.30; 6 - 11.
Restaurant.
Children to stay. No dogs. Bedrooms.

KNOWL HILL

Seven Stars   Tel: 01628 822967

Knowl Hill, Berks RG10 9UR
Brakspear. Robin & Lyn Jones, tenants

There is a picture in the saloon bar showing the Seven Stars as it was before the imposition of the Window Tax in the early 18th Century. The Tax caused many a building to change radically in appearance: to reduce the tax bill, inessential windows were blocked up. One of the oldest licensed houses on the Old Bath Road, it was thought to have started out as a hunting lodge in what was then part of Windsor Forest. It was the haunt of several notorious highwaymen who found travellers on the Bath Road a very profitable target. Welcoming and friendly, it has beams, panelling, log fires and traditional furnishings. Bar food ranges from sandwiches, ploughmans and vegetarian dishes to daily specials. Brakspears ales; choice of wines. Seats in the large garden. Go on the right night and you may be lucky enough to see one of the four ghosts said the haunt the area. You have the choice of a headless woman, a white lady, a white dog and last, but not least, a phantom horseman.

OPEN: 11 - 2.30; 5 - 11. (12-3; 7-10.30 Sun).
Real Ale.
Children welcome. Dogs on leads.

MAIDENHEAD

Hand & Flowers   Tel: 01628 23800

15 Queen Street, Maidenhead, Berks SL6 1NB
Brakspear. Jane Page & Keith Warner, tenant

===

A small, one-bar Victorian pub in the middle of the town. Very popular at lunchtime; all the food is home-made: spicy sausage casserole, roast beef and other dishes, sandwiches have up to twenty five different fillings. They make a point of not serving any frozen food, chips or jacket potatoes. Beers are Brakspears Bitter, Special and Old.

OPEN: 10.30 - 3; 5 - 11.
Real Ale.
Children welcome. Dogs on leads.

YATTENDON

Royal Oak   Tel: 01635 201325

The Square, Yattendon, Nr Newbury, Berks RG16 0UF
Free House. Jeremy Gibbs, manager

===

This popular creeper-clad pub - with its pretty panelled bar and comfortable lounge with big log fire - has gained a reputation for serving high quality, imaginative food. Home-made soups, poached mussels in creamy garlic and chive sauce, spicy vegetable and mushroom ravioli, and patés, complement the daily specials and home-made pies. Wadworths 6X, Badgers Tanglefoot, Adnams and Farmers Glory are on hand pump. Normally, the attractive garden is reserved for residents, but comes into general use as the bar overflow in summer.

OPEN: 12 - 3; 6.30 - 11.
No smoking restaurant. Closed Sun eve.
Children welcome. Dogs on leads.

BUCKINGHAMSHIRE

BEACONSFIELD

Old Hare   Tel: 01494 673380

41 Aylesbury End, Beaconsfield, Bucks HP9 1LU
Allied. Peter Tye, Manager. Samantha Wilks, Asst Manager

An attractive, rambling pub that dates back to 1723. Pictures of hares (what else?), photographs and prints of the pub decorate the rooms. Interestingly varied food with varying daily specials shown on the blackboard; home-made puddings. The beers are well kept and include Ind Coope, Burton, Benskins Best, Tetleys Yorkshire and other guest beers. Selection of whiskies and house wines. There is a large sunny garden.

OPEN: 11 - 3; 5.30 - 11. Real Ale. No food Sun eve.
Children in eating area. Dogs on leads.
Occasional Morris Dancing.

BLEDLOW

Lions of Bledlow   Tel: 01844 343345

Church End, Bledlow, Bucks GP27 9PE
Free House. F J McKeow, licensee

Ideally situated in good walking country; in fact, all the best used tracks seem to converge on this sixteenth century pub, making it an ideal place to start or finish a long walk. In summer you can relax on the sheltered terrace and admire the views; in winter, warm by the fire in the comfortable beamed bars. On the menu are home-made soup, filled rolls, steak pie, some fish dishes and daily specials. John Smiths, Courage Directors, Gales HSB, Tolly Cobbold and Wadworths 6X on hand pump.

OPEN: 11 - 3; 6 - 11.
Real Ale. No food Sun eve. Restaurant open Wed-Sat eve.
Children in side room & restaurant. Dogs on leads.

BOLTER END

Peacock   Tel: 01494 881417

Lane End, Bolter End, Bucks HP14 3LU
Allied. Peter Hodges, lease

Located opposite the common, the 17th Century Peacock is popular and friendly. Traditionally furnished, its heavily-beamed bar was redecorated last year. The imaginative bar food ranges from ploughmans, with a choice of interesting cheeses, to Aberdeen Angus steaks and daily specials. The poultry is free range. Fresh fish on Fridays. Bass, Ansells Mild, Tetleys and ABC Bitter are complemented by guest beers and wines. Seats in the garden during summer.

OPEN: 11.45 - 2.30; 6 - 11.
Real Ale. No food Sun eve.
No children.
Dogs on leads.

CHALFONT ST PETER

Greyhound   Tel: 01753 883404

High Street, Nr Chalfont St Peter, Bucks SL9 9RA
Courage. John Harriman, lease

Named The Greyhound in 1490, this creeper-covered old coaching inn is actually a century older than its name. It has low beams, dark panelling and a big log fire. Bar food ranges from sandwiches to filled baked potatoes and a choice of three roasts from the carvery. Part of the restaurant is no-smoking. John Smiths, Marstons Pedigree, Courage Best and Directors, Ruddles County and Wadworths 6X. There are seats in the courtyard at the front of the pub and on the grass by the river.

OPEN: 11 - 11.
Real Ale. No food Sun eve.
Children in eating area & restaurant. Dogs on leads.

COLESHILL

Red Lion   Tel: 01494 727020

Village Road, Coleshill, Bucks HP7 0LN
Allied Lyons. Christine & John Ullman, managers

Tucked away down a country lane about two miles from Amersham, The Red Lion - which at first glance looks like a 1930's villa - is very popular with all age groups, not only for its well kept beers, but also for its reliable bar food: freshly made sandwiches, ploughmans, salads (real ham - off the bone), creamed sardines on toast, daily specials such as chicken and mushroom pie, meatballs in red wine and tomato sauce and salmon quiche. There will be a roast on Sundays. Good selection of puddings. Summer barbecues. Flowers IPA, Tetleys and Wadworths 6X, and sometimes Morrells Oxford ales. Some wines by the glass. Tables at the front of the pub during the summer.

OPEN: 11 - 3.30; 5.30 - 11 (all day Sat).
Real Ale. Only bar snacks Sun eve.
Children welcome. Dogs on leads.

FINGEST

Chequers   Tel: 01491 638335

Fingest, Nr Henley-on-Thames, Bucks RG9 6QD
Brakspears. Bryan Heasman, tenant

During the winter there is a huge log fire warming up this attractive 15th century brick and flint village pub. The comfortable lounge has french windows leading into the garden, which has a lovely view of the Hambleden valley. You can eat in a small no-smoking room and the popular bar food ranges from: sandwiches and soup to freshly caught trout, steaks, salmon and vegetarian dishes. A more ambitious menu features in the restaurant. Brakspears PA, SB and Old Ale. Varied wine list, some by the glass. Seats in the garden amongst the flowers. This is a good walking area.
OPEN: 11 - 3; 6 - 11 (12 - 3; 7 - 10.30. Sun).
Real Ale. No food Sun eve.
Children in eating areas. Dogs in garden only.

FORD

Dinton Hermit   Tel: 01296 748379

Ford, Nr Aylesbury, Bucks HP17 8XH
Free House. John & Jane Tompkins, licensees

The hermit was a local man who lived at Dinton Hall. He was clerk to one of the Judges who was responsible for condemning Charles I to death. The rest of his life was one of repentance for the part he played in the death of the King. Set in attractive countryside, this 15th century stone inn is a busy local, attractive not only for its well kept ales but for the above average home-cooked food. Soups, sandwiches, saucy mushrooms, kidneys in cognac sauce, chicken curry, veggy hotpot, fruit pies and bread and butter pudding. There is a greater choice of fish and grills in the evening. (You must book.) ABC Best Bitter, Tetleys and

Wadworths 6X. Lovely views of the surrounding countryside from here and lots of walks nearby.

OPEN: 11 - 2.30; 6 - 11.
Real Ale. No food Sun or Mon, nor for three weeks in July.
Well behaved children welcome. No dogs.

FORTY GREEN

Royal Standard of England
Tel: 01494 673382

Forty Green, Nr Beaconsfield, Bucks HP9 1XT
Free House. Philip Eldridge and Peter & Gill Carroll, licensees

Renamed in 1651 when Charles II, fleeing after the battle of Worcester, hid in the pub rafters to escape the Parliamentarians. Interesting interiors with splendid oak panelling, fireplaces and magnificent oak beams. There is a splendid buffet of cooked ham, beef, turkey, salmon and various salads, pies, quiches and a choice of hot dishes. All the bread is home baked. Marstons Pedigree and Owd Roger (originally brewed at the Inn), Morlands Old Speckled Hen and regular guest beers. Good choice of malt and Irish whiskies; also fruit wines.

OPEN: 11 - 3; 5.30 - 11.
Real Ale.
Children in eating area. No dogs.

FRIETH

Prince Albert
Tel: 01494 881683

Mores End, Nr Henley-on-Thames, RG9 6PX
Brakspears. Frank & Joss Reynolds, licensees

Surrounded by attractive, wooded countryside with lots of wonderful walks, this tiny, 250 year old pub has built a reputation for serving quality bar food. Brown rolls with lots of different fillings, ham and eggs and other hot dishes - really good well-made food. Brakspears Bitter, Special, Mild, Old and OBJ on hand pump. Good choice of wines and decent whiskies.

OPEN: 11 - 3; 5.30 - 11. Mon opens half an hour later.
Real Ale. Food available lunchtime only.
No children. Dogs on leads.

GREAT MISSENDEN

George   Tel: 01494 862084

94 High Street, Great Missenden, Bucks HP16 0BG
Greenalls. Guy & Sally Smith, tenants

A pleasing pub that was built towards the end of the 15th century as a hospice for the nearby Abbey. Listed Grade II, the bars still have their original heavily beamed ceilings. Home-made soup, deep fried mushrooms and steak and kidney pies and just a few of the dishes on the menu. Adnams, Wadworths 6X and two guest beers. Sangria in summer and mulled wine in winter. They have a lovely large garden.

OPEN: 11 - 11. Real Ale. Food served all day. No-smoking restaurant.
Children in eating areas. Dogs on leads. Bedrooms.

LITTLEWORTH COMMON

Blackwood Arms   Tel: 01753 642169

Common Lane, Littleworth Common, Bucks SL1 8PP
Free House. Graham & Alison Titcombe licensees

This is a beer drinkers' paradise - over 900 ales last year. Every Friday there are approximately 16 different beers to try and two days to sober up! To soak up this embarras de richesse, there is a good choice of home-made food: filled rolls, omelettes, home-cured ham, steak and ale pies, etc. Evening extras could include: lamb aux fine herbes and salmon in champagne and cream sauce. There is always a Sunday roast. Among the beers you may try are Black Sheep Special, Hambleton, Mauldons Black Adder, Orkney Skull Splitter and Woodfordes Nelson's Revenge. Belgian beers, farm ciders and a choice of malt whiskies. Good head-clearing country walks nearby.

OPEN: 11 - 2.30; 5.30 - 11. Fri & Sat 11 - 11.
Real Ale, lots of it!
Children if well behaved. Dogs on leads.

MARSH GIBBON

Greyhound   Tel: 01869 277365

Marsh Gibbon, Nr Bicester, Ox/Bucks OX6 0HA
Free House. Richard Kaim, licensee

Four hundred years old, extended two hundred and fifty years ago, this old stone pub has seen some changes in its lifetime. Now, someone with a love of Thai cooking is orchestrating the food and it is becoming a favourite meeting place for those interested in South East Asian food. There are a few traditional bar snacks, but you will be more likely to find: spring roll or spare ribs in a special sauce, chicken satay, beef in oyster sauce and entrecote teriyaki among others. Fullers London Pride, Greene King Abbot and IPA, Hook Norton Best and McEwans 80/- on hand-pump. Seats in the pretty small front garden - more room at the back.

OPEN: 12 - 3; 6 - 11.
Real Ale.
Children if well behaved. No dogs.

NORTHEND

White Hart   Tel: 01491 638353

Northend, Henley-on-Thames RG9 6LE
Brakspears. Andrew Hearn, tenant

Very much a foody pub, the emphasis here being on the quality of
the food, but if you just want a drink and bar snack you will be
more than welcome.
An attractive 16th century pub with low ceilings, panelling and a
big log fire. The landlord is a very keen golfer, so tales from the
links are highly acceptable. All the food is home-made, even the
pickle accompanying the ploughmans. Greek salad, pasta with
tomato, mushroom, parmesan, basil and cream, roast duckling in
raspberry sauce and home-made puddings, are just a few of the
dishes on offer. Daily specials. Brakspears PA, SB, Old and Mild
on hand pump. Lots of walks in the beech woods.

OPEN: 11.30 - 2.30; 6 - 11 (6.30 winter).
Real Ale. No food Sun eve.
Children in eating area. Dogs on leads (if pub not too busy).

SKIRMETT

Old Crown   Tel: 01491 638435

Skirmett, Nr Henley-on-Thames RG9 6TD
Brakspears. Peter Mumby, tenant

A charming 17th century village pub. Three heavily beamed
rooms, one of which is a no-smoking tap room; open fires, lots of
paintings, antiques and interesting bric-à-brac. The pub does get
extremely busy so you need to book to be sure of a table in the
evenings and at weekends. All the food is home-made: from
soups, steak-kidney and mushroom pie, poached Scottish salmon
with a prawn and dill sauce, to fresh sea bass. Beer from the

barrel and served through a hatch: Brakspear PA and SB. Moderately priced wines. Pretty flower tubs on the terrace. There are seats in the garden which has a fish pond.

OPEN: 11 - 2.30; 6 - 11. Closed Mon except Bank Holiday Mondays.
Real Ale.
No children under 10. No dogs.

WEST WYCOMBE

George & Dragon   Tel: 01494 464414

West Wycombe, Nr High Wycombe, Bucks HP14 3AB
Courage. Philip Cass Todd, lease

Dating back to the 15th century, this former coaching inn on the old London Oxford road, was added to and modernised in 1720. Full of atmosphere, it has huge beams, sloping walls and big log fires. The ghost of a servant girl is reputed to haunt the handsome staircase. Well prepared food: soup, herby mushrooms, duck or pigeon pies, potted stilton, steaks, game from Wycombe Park and home-made puddings. Courage Best and Directors plus a guest beer on hand pump. Good wine list and a selection of malt whiskies. Culture at West Wycombe Park (Hellfire Caves and all that). Interesting walks nearby.

OPEN: 11 - 2.30; 5.30 - 11. 11 - 11 Sats.
Real Ale.
Children in own room. Dogs on leads. Bedrooms.

CORNWALL

ALBASTON

Queen's Head   Tel: 01822 832482

Albaston, Nr Gunnislake, Cornwall PL18 9AJ
Inntrepreneur. Messrs. F E & P F May, managers

It's not often you find father and son as joint managers of a pub.
But that's just what you have at the Queen's Head which has been
under May family management since 1961. Advertised as "just a
pub", it contains a large collection of mineral specimens -
examples of the rich deposits of zinc, tin, copper and arsenic found
in Cornwall and mined during the 19th century. There is one large
and one small bar - both with open fires. Food is limited but pasties
and various pies always available. Courage BB, Ruddles County,
Bass from the cask and a keg mild. Several New World wines.
Cotehele House, a wonderful 15th century example of a medieval
squire's house, surrounded by the most lovely grounds, and
Cotehele Quay on the River Tamar, are near and well worth a visit.

OPEN: 11 - 3; 6 - 11.
Real Ale.
Children in eating rooms. Dogs on leads.
Live music fortnightly. RNLI Collection.

SUNDAY OPENINGS

The new law allowing all-day Sunday opening came into force too
late for us to check every pub. However, it can be taken that tied
houses are open all-day Sunday, whereas free houses depend on the
inclinations of their licensees. Some are putting all-day-opening to the
test; others are sticking to the old licensing hours.

CONSTANTINE

Trengilly Wartha   Tel: 01326 40332

Nancenoy Constantine, Nr Helston, Cornwall TR11 5RP
Free House. Nigel Logan & Michael Maguire, licensees

Situated in a valley close to the Helford River, this charming old farmhouse has only been licensed since 1950. The unusual pub name means the settlement above the trees. The farmhouse, now the pub, dates back to the 18th century. There is one low-beamed main bar, lounge, an eating area off the bar and a no-smoking family conservatory. A pretty garden, with picnic tables during the summer. Lots of home-made bar food: soups, filled baked potatoes, paté, vegetable pie or lasagne, ploughmans with home-made pickles, salads and daily specials. Fresh fish when available. Also an imaginative blackboard menu. Furgusons Dartmoor, Tetleys and St Austell XXXX Mild on hand pump and constantly changing guests from Sharks new Cornish brewery and other small independents. Ciders, big selection of malt whiskies, and good choice of wines by the bottle or glass.

OPEN: 11 - 2.30; 6 - 11 (6.30 in winter).
Real Ale. Restaurant.
Children welcome. Dogs on leads. Bedrooms.
Occasional live music.

HELSTON

Blue Anchor   Tel: 01326 562821

50 Coinagehall Street, Helston, Cornwall
Own Brew. Kim & Simon Corbett, licensees

Strong own-brew Spingo Ale is the feature in this granite and thatched 15th century pub. It is thought that beer has been brewed here for the past 400 years. Brewing was originally started by the local monks and continued after the dissolution of the monasteries. Locally very popular, the Blue Anchor has two bars and a family room. Filled rolls, pasties and a changing selection of hot meals make up the menu. Ales here are in-house so to speak: Medium, Best, Spingo Special and Extra Special. You can see around the brewery some lunchtimes by arrangement.

OPEN: All day.
Real Ale.
Children in family room. Dogs on leads.
Live bands Fri eve.

LUDGVAN

White Hart   Tel: 01736 740574

Ludgvan, Nr Penzance, Cornwall TR20 8EY
Devenish. Dennis Churchill, tenant

Unspoilt, quiet and appealing, this friendly 14th century village pub has small beamed rooms, full of interesting objects, pictures and photographs. Rugs on the floor; two big wood burning stoves for warmth; fine old seats and tables. Good, reasonably priced bar food: sandwiches, home-made soup and real Cornish pasties, salads, omelettes, steaks, daily specials and fresh fish. There is a no-smoking section in the eating area. Devenish, Cornish Original, Flowers IPA and Marstons Pedigree from the barrel.

OPEN: 11 - 2.30; 6 - 11.
No food Mon eve, Nov-May.
Real Ale.
Children in restaurant. Dogs on leads.

MORWENSTOW

Bush Inn   Tel: 01288 331242

Morwenstow, Nr Bude, Cornwall EX23 9SR
Free House. J H Gregory, licensee

One of the oldest pubs in Britain, and thought to date back to the 10th century, the Bush Inn is in a hamlet near the coastal path and spectacular Vicarage Cliff. The ship's figurehead in the churchyard, surrounded by the graves of 40 unknown men, bears witness to the fierce weather that can attack this part of the Cornish coast. Once a monastic guesthouse, this little pub is full of fascinating items including a propeller from an old De Havilland Gypsy Moth aeroplane. The landlord, Mr Gregory, now well over pensionable age, tells us he is carrying on until he is carried off! Lunchtime bar food only - home-made soup, pasties, ploughmans with home-made pickle, stews and good school puddings such as Spotted Dick. Beers include St Austell HSB and Winter Brew (January and February only) on hand pump; guest beers i.e. Cotleigh Old Buzzard and Farmers Glory from the barrel.

OPEN: 12 - 3; 7 - 11. Closed Mon Oct-Apr except Bank Holidays.
Real Ale.
Lunchtime food only but not Mon.
No children. No dogs.

MYLOR BRIDGE

Pandora   Tel: 01326 372678

Restronguet Creek, Mylor Bridge, Nr Falmouth, Cornwall TR11 5ST
St Austell. Roger & Helen Hough, tenants

There aren't many pubs where you can sail straight in - not quite into the bar except on a very high spring tide - but certainly up to the jetty. A very pretty 15th century thatched pub, which even has showers for visiting yachtsmen. There will be a permanent audience in good weather, sitting at the front of the pub, waiting for you to make a hash of tying up. Having found your land legs, the pub offers a choice of three bars, a restaurant and two no-smoking areas. Bar food includes home-made soup, wholemeal pancakes, fish pie, crab thermidor and daily specials. St Austells ales and Bass on hand pump. Malt whiskies and a large selection of wines. If you are coming by road, remember parking can be a bit tight at the height of the summer.

OPEN: 11 - 11 summer; 12 - 2.30 (3 Sun); 7 - 11 winter.
Real Ale. Food till 10pm summer; restaurant closed winter eves and winter Suns.
Children in eating area. Dogs on leads.

PELYNT

Jubilee   Tel: 01503 220312

Pelynt, Nr Looe, Cornwall PL13 2JZ
Free House. Frank Williams, licensee

The crowns on the pillars outside this handsome 16th century inn give an indication of the royal memorabilia that can be found inside the pub. Renamed the Jubilee to celebrate the first 50 years of Queen Victoria's reign, you will find old prints, Staffordshire figures of the Queen and Prince Albert, also Windsor armchairs! Big log fires in winter, lots of flowers during the summer. Here you can get some of the best Cornish cooking, the emphasis being on the fresh fish and shellfish straight off the boats at nearby Looe. The wood-panelled bar has an extensive selection of bar snacks from traditional pasties and ploughmans, to steak & kidney pies. The very attractive restaurant offers an impressive choice of dishes and afternoon Cornish teas. Locally brewed Jubilee Special, Furgusons Dartmoor Strong and Tetleys on hand pump. Choice of malt whiskies and a good wine list. There is a flowery courtyard for sitting in during the summer. Barbecues, children's play area.

OPEN: 11 - 3; 6 - 11.
No restaurant Sun eve.
Real Ale.
Children welcome. Dogs on leads. Bedrooms.

PHILLEIGH

Roseland　　　　　　　　　　　　　Tel: 01872 580254

Philleigh-in-Roseland, Truro, Cornwall TR2 5NB
Greenalls. Graham Hill, tenant

Home to the Roseland Rugby Club during the winter months, the pub also has a choir practice twice a week. You could say there was a very varied repertoire on the song front. Just don't argue with the Rugby club's choice of music - they are always bigger than you. One low-ceilinged bar with a big log fire in the winter. During the summer you can sit in the sunny courtyard. Home-made food includes soup, pasties and filled baked potatoes, ratatouille and stuffed peppers. There is a greater selection in the evenings: sirloin steak with cream and whisky sauce and local fish dishes. Devenish Cornish Original, Flowers Original and Marstons Pedigree on hand pump. Farm cider in the summer; a good range of malt whiskies.

OPEN: 11 - 3; 6 - 11 (11.30 - 3; 6.30 - 11 winter).
Real Ale.
Children welcome. Dogs on leads.

ST AGNES

Railway　　　　　　　　　　　　　Tel: 01872 552310

10 Vicarage Road, St Agnes, Cornwall TR5 0TJ
Greenalls. Christopher O'Brien, tenant

St Agnes was once a tin mining village which has since become a thriving holiday centre. The Railway has seen changes too. This little terraced pub used to be the local blacksmith until 1850 when it became the Smith's Arms. Around 1900 it was renamed The Railway. The trains have long gone but the pub remains. Tremendous collection of horse brasses, shoes, naval memorabilia, including the Admiralty announcement of the cease fire at the end of the First World War. Usual bar food: soups, sandwiches, ploughmans, daily specials and fresh fish. Boddingtons Best,

Flowers IPA and Marstons Pedigree on hand pump. There is a juke box in the rear bar. Stay in the front bar for peace and quiet.

OPEN: 11 - 3; 6 - 11.
Real Ale.
Children in eating area. Dogs on leads.

ST BREWARD

Old Inn   Tel: 01208 850711

St Breward, Bodmin, Cornwall PL30 4PP
Free House. Ann & Iain Cameron, licensees

Parts of this friendly old pub date back to the 12th century; it is reputed to have been the beer hall for the masons who built the church in 1072. It has a two-roomed bar with flagstoned floors and low oak beams; an inner room with a log fire and a games room where children are allowed. Generous home-made bar food includes soup, sandwiches, fresh fish, pie of the day, vegetarian dishes, mixed grills and various puddings. Large range of malt whiskies. Bass, John Smiths Best, Ruddles County and a guest beer on hand pump. Seats outside in the low stone-walled garden - the walls protecting you from the free range sheep and cattle.

OPEN: 12 - 3; 6 - 11 (winter may close 2.30).
Real Ale. Restaurant.
Children in eating area, children's room & one bar.
Dogs on leads.
Sometimes live groups.

ST JUST IN PENWITH

Star   Tel: 01736 788767

1 Fore Street, St Just in Penwith, Cornwall TR19 7LL
St Austell. Rosie & Peter Angwin, tenants

Near to the coastal path, this welcoming 18th century pub has remained unchanged for years. The L-shaped bar with its mining memorabilia reminds the visitor that you are in what was once a prosperous tin mining area. Through the bar there is a separate snug, with a toy box for the children. No piped music, but there is a jukebox - just hope no one plays it. Food is served all day, but only pasties and rolls between 3 and 6. Food includes soups, pasties, French bread topped with chilli or garlic mushrooms, ploughmans, vegetable curry and daily specials such as chicken in wine and cream sauce. St Austell Tinners, HSD and XXX Mild from the cask. Mulled wine in winter, cider in the summer. Pretty back terrace for sitting on during the summer months.

OPEN: 11 - 11.
Real Ale.
Food served all day but only rolls & pasties 3 - 6.
Children in Snug. Dogs on leads. Bedrooms.
Celtic folk music Mon eves.

ST KEVERNE

White Hart   Tel: 01326 280325

St Keverne, Nr Helston, Cornwall TR12 7NP
Greenalls. Vicki Blake, tenant

The square in this old village is dominated by the church, a place of worship for over 1200 years. The spire was used as a warning to ships that they were approaching the dangerous Manacles Reef - an early form of lighthouse without the light. Not far from the sea, this friendly 14th century pub is well known for its variety of fish dishes. King Prawns in garlic, crab salad, scallops, plaice or bass and lobster. Soups and sandwiches too. Devenish Cornish Original, Flowers IPA and Original on hand pump. Seats outside the front of the pub on the small terrace.

OPEN: 11 - 3; 6.30 - 11.
Real Ale.
Restaurant. No food in winter on Sun eves.
Children welcome. Dogs on leads. Bedrooms.

ST KEW

St Kew Inn   Tel: 01208 841259

St Kew, Nr. Wadebridge, Cornwall PL30 3HB
St Austell. Steve & Joan Anderson, tenants

This stone built 15th century inn is situated in an attractive wooded valley. There are two bars and a public lounge. A friendly, efficient pub with very popular bar food. Soups, sandwiches, lasagne, smoked salmon, steaks and King Prawns in garlic. Sunday roast and children's menu. (They pride themselves on a secret recipe for their sirloin steaks.) The beers are St Austell Tinners and HSD served from casks behind the counter.

OPEN: 11 - 2.30; 6 - 11.
Real Ale. Restaurant.
Children (well behaved, in restaurant & own room; none under 6 in eves). No dogs.

ZENNOR

Tinners Arms   Tel: 01736 796927

Zennor, Cornwall TR26 3BY
Free House. David Care, licensee

Over 400 years old, this stone built pub used to be the tin miners' local. The landlord took over from his father twenty years ago as "custodian" and promised to keep it very much as it had always been. It is thought to have been built as a hostelry to house masons working on the church in the 13th century. Continuing the tradition of feeding and watering the populace, this comfortable old pub offers good simple bar food: smoked mackerel, lasagne, ploughmans, chicken and ham pie, vegetarian dishes. The menu changes with the season. St Austells ales from the barrel - Hicks Special during the winter and Tinners Ale in the summer.

OPEN: 11 - 3; 6.30 - 11. Summer 11 - 11.
Real Ale.
Children. Dogs on leads.

CUMBRIA

AMBLESIDE

Golden Rule Tel: 015394 33363

Smithy Brow, Ambleside, Cumbria LA22 9AS
Hartleys (Robinsons). John Lockley, tenant

If you are out for one of those character-building walks, this pub is in just the right place for a welcoming, refreshing drink and sustaining snack. Popular with walkers, climbers and paragliders - the landlord being a paragliding instructor - the Cumbria Soaring Club meets here. Hang gliders take off from the ridges around the pub, but whether you fly or walk in, you will find: Hartleys Ale, Robinsons Best Bitter and Stockport Bitter, light snacks and meals. There was a brew house on the site in 1630. Seats outside in the pretty garden.

OPEN: 11 - 11.
Real Ale.
Children welcome. Dogs on leads. Parking difficult.

APPLEBY

Royal Oak Tel: 017683 51463

Bongate, Appleby-in-Westmoreland, Cumbria CA16 6UN
Free House. Colin & Hilary Cheyne, licensees

Opposite an old church, and close to the River Eden with its gently wooded valleys, you'll find the long, low, white-painted Royal Oak. In the summer there are seats among the flower-filled tubs at the front of the pub. Inside, you will find beamed and panelled rooms where you can enjoy a well-kept pint, or choose a dish from the imaginative menu: home-baked bread to go with the soup, home-cooked ham and beef to go in the sandwiches, filled crêpes, pork fillet in cream and madeira sauce, fresh fish, steaks and daily specials. Children's menu. There are two restaurants, one of which is non-smoking. Ten beers are kept on hand pump and, in summer, a traditional cider. Local beers such as Yates are always available and the Hesket Newmarket Brewery brew ales especially for The Royal Oak. Guests include interesting beers from small breweries in the north of England and Scotland that perhaps are not too well known. Lots of lovely walks nearby and you are also near the wonderful Settle/Carlisle Railway which is well worth a trip.

OPEN: 11 - 3; 6 - 11.
Real Ale.
Non-smoking Restaurant.
Well behaved children welcome. Dogs on leads. Bedrooms.

BROUGHTON MILLS

The Blacksmiths Arms   Tel : 01229 716824

Broughton Mills, Broughton-in-Furness Cumbria
Free House. Andrew Wood, licensee

Situated in the Lickie Valley, one of the prettiest valleys in the Lakes, the Blacksmiths Arms is an out-of-the-way, basic, traditional pub, serving the local farming community and everyone else nearby. However, it has tremendous character - 300 years old with beams and flagstone floors. Very popular with climbers and walkers as well as ordinary travellers. Not smart, but a good pint and sandwich is all you will need to sustain you. If you can stand a bit of ribbing from the locals, an evening here can be an entertaining and rewarding experience. Theakstons range of ales.

OPEN: Extremely flexible hours.
Real Ale.
Children tolerated.
Dogs - depends on the Landlord. Bedrooms.

BUTTERMERE

Bridge Hotel   Tel: 017687 70252

Buttermere, Nr Cockermouth, Cumbria CA13 9UZ
Free House. Bill Raftery, manager

Originally a simple, two-storey ale house, it has over the years
been extended and improved, resulting in the attractive and
comfortable hotel you find today. Very much geared up to walkers
and the erratic Cumbrian weather - it even has a drying room!
Muddy boots? - then make for the walkers' bar and its flagstoned
floor. If they're really muddy, it's best to stop where the carpet
begins. Good selection of bar food from the walkers' snack
corner: from simple soup, sandwiches and ploughmans to the
cosmopolitan - prawns, smoked salmon in seafood spicy sauce,
Cumbrian hotpot, mad stag and bobtail pie (hare, venison and
rabbit topped with puff pastry), chicken breast cooked in herbs
and garlic, chef's daily specials and vegetarian dishes. Sunday
roast. The restaurant is no-smoking. Youngers Best, Theakstons
Ales and a couple of guest beers. Wines by the glass. A selection
of malt whiskies. Seats outside on the terrace and wonderful
walks.

OPEN: 10.30 - 11.
Real Ale. Evening restaurant.
Children welcome. Dogs on leads.

DENT

Sun Inn   Tel: 0153 96 25208

Main Street, Dent, Sedbergh, Cumbria LA10 5QL (village off
A683)
Own Brew. Martin Stafford, licensee

A charming, typical Dales village inn within the Yorkshire Dales
National Park. The cobbled streets of Dent are lined with
cottages, some of which date back to the 15th century. There is

the added attraction of the Dent Brewery not far away, which provides the Sun with its own beer - Bitter, Ramsbottom and T'Owd Tup. Inside the pub there are lots of beams, comfortable furnishings and home-cooked bar food. This includes the stalwarts, plus pasties, chicken curry, chilli, steak & kidney pie, Cumberland sausage, salads and a changing variety of puds. Seats outside in summer.

OPEN: 11 - 11 (11 - 3; 7 - 11 winter).
Real Ale.
Children welcome until 9 pm. Dogs on leads. Bedrooms.

ELTERWATER

Britannia Inn   Tel: 0153 94 37210

Ambleside, Cumbria, LA22 9HP
Free House. David Fry, licensee

Opposite the village green, and in the very heart of the Lake District, the Britannia Inn is ideally situated to sustain you whilst you admire the magnificence of the surrounding countryside, or recover from walking the peaks and fells. Small friendly bars with beams and log fires. There is a wide-ranging menu with the usual favourites: soups, filled baps, baked potatoes, ploughmans, some unusual alternatives and daily specials. Jennings Bitter, Boddingtons Bitter and Wadworths 6X plus guest ales. Lots of garden chairs and tables on the terrace in front of the pub.

OPEN: 11 - 11.
Real Ale.
Restaurant.
Children welcome. Dogs on leads. Bedrooms.

ESKDALE GREEN

Bower House Inn   Tel: 0194 6723244

Eskdale, Holmrook, Cumbria CA19 1TD (on Santon Bridge Road)
Free House. Derek Connor, licensee

Old, rambling, comfortable, friendly; all a traditional country inn should be, complete with cosy log fires, good ales and imaginative food. Usual bar snacks plus daily specials which could be: pork in cider, fillet of beef in red wine sauce, wild duck or guinea fowl, locally smoked mackerel and trout, good choice of cheeses and a range of puddings. Hartleys XB, Courage Directors, Theakstons Best and various guest beers. Seats outside in the garden. No need to tell you that there are lots of wonderful walks.

OPEN: 11 - 11.
Real Ale. Restaurant.
Children at lunchtime and early eve. No dogs.

GRASMERE

Dove & Olive Branch   Tel: 015394 35592

Wordsworth Hotel, Grasmere, Cumbria
Free House. R M Lees, manager

The Dove and Olive Branch is an "in-house pub", attached to the very elegant, smart, Wordsworth Hotel. In the centre of Grasmere, and next to the churchyard where the poet William Wordsworth is buried, the Dove is the drinking place for all appreciative locals and visitors. Tasty bar snacks, lots of filled baguettes, ploughmans, savoury baked potatoes and daily specials. Bass, Stones Best Bitter and Mitchells Ales. There are seats and tables on the veranda, from where you can watch the world go by.

OPEN: 11 - 3; 6 - 11.
Real Ale.
No children under 14. No dogs.

HAWKSHEAD

Drunken Duck   Tel: 015394 36347

Barngates, Ambleside, Cumbria LA22 0NG (off B5286 Hawkshead-Ambleside)
Free House. Stephanie Barton, licensee

At a crossroads, set in its own 60 acres and the magnificent scenery of the Lake District, The Drunken Duck has been a haven for the traveller for over 400 years. How the Barn Gates Inn became the Drunken Duck is worth a journey for the telling alone. Cosy, beamed rooms with good winter fires, good ales and a daily changing menu. Food includes sandwiches, many home-made patés, smoked trout (very local), Cumberland sausage casserole, game pie, pastas and puddings of the jam rolypoly, spotted dick genre. Jennings Best Bitter, Marstons Pedigree, Tetley Bitter, Theakstons Old Peculiar and XB, Yates and other guest beers. Over 60 malt whiskies. A pretty pub, with a veranda at the front on which there are seats and opulent hanging baskets in summer.

OPEN: 11.30 - 3; 6 - 11.
Real Ale.
Children in eating area. Dogs on leads.
Bedrooms.

INGS

Watermill Inn   Tel: 01539 821309

Ings, Nr Stavely, Kendal, Cumbria LA8 9PY (E of Windermere)
Free House. Alan Coulthwaite, licensee

Originally a wood mill which made shuttles and bobbins for the Lancashire cotton mills, the watermill is now a traditional, family-run, Lakeland inn only two miles from Windermere. Comfortable, friendly bars with log fires, and the interesting use of old, wooden church fittings to create a "gothicky" bar counter. All bar favourites here; a constantly changing chef's special on the blackboard and vegetarian dishes. Up to 15 real ales on hand pump. Also a traditional cider, plus continental and English bottled beers. The River Gowan, which used to power the old mill, runs through the grounds.

OPEN: 12 - 2.30 (3 Sat); 6 - 11.
Real Ale.
Children in lounge. Dogs on leads. Bedrooms.

KIRKBY LONSDALE

Snooty Fox   Tel: 0152 4271308

Main Street, Kirkby Lonsdale, Cumbria LA6 2AH
Free House. Jack Shone, licensee

An imposing, listed, white-painted Jacobean town inn, in what is known as the "capital" of the lovely Lune Valley. Two traditional bars, hung about with lots of interesting objets d'art; birds and animals - stuffed and mounted - uniforms, bugles, swords and china, and an attractive dining room. All the dishes are freshly prepared using the best local produce where possible. Chicken liver mousse with redcurrant and orange sauce, quenelles of smoked mackerel, poached salmon in champagne and herb sauce, Hungarian goulash with smoked bacon and rosemary, salads and lunchtime daily specials. A gourmet menu is available in the evening restaurant. This could include smoked salmon roulade with fresh asparagus, cream cheese and a yoghurt and dill sauce; pan-fried mignons of Angus fillet, served with potato and chive pancake and a cognac and pink peppercorn sauce - and much more. Sunday roast too, for which you need to book. Hartleys XB, Theakstons Best and Timothy Taylors Landlord on hand pump. The chef/manager was head chef at Sharrow Bay Hotel, so expect something really exciting to come from the kitchens. Tables on the terrace and in the garden. Walks along the River Lune from the medieval Devil's bridge.

OPEN: 11 - 11. Meals & snacks all day.
Real Ale.
Children in eating area.
Dogs in bar only. Bedrooms.

LANGDALE

Old Dungeon Ghyll   Tel: 015394 37272

Gt Langdale, Ambleside, Cumbria LA22 9JY
Free House. Neil Walmsley, licensee

This is one place where you can be sure of peace and quiet, inside and out. At the foot of the Langdale Pikes, the road from Chapel Style on the Great Langdale beck, comes to an abrupt end at the Old Dungeon Ghyll Hotel. Here it really is "on with your boots" to climb the steep path that leads you to the spectacular Dungeon Ghyll waterfall which drops into an abyss 100 feet below. Back at the hotel the Hikers Bar has refreshing beer and food: home-cooked meals and snacks - soups, sandwiches, Cumberland sausages, chicken dishes, local trout, steaks, etc. A four-course dinner is served in the no-smoking restaurant. Jennings Cumberland, Theakstons XB, Old Peculiar and Mild plus some guest beers. The pub is owned by the National Trust, who also own the campsite opposite, which can get very jolly and busy over the weekends.

OPEN: 11 - 11.
Real Ale.
Evening restaurant.
Children welcome. Dogs on leads. Bedrooms.
Occasional live music.

SEATHWAITE

Newfield Inn   Tel: 01229 716208

Duddon Valley, Broughton-in-Furness, Cumbria LA20 6ED
Free House. Chris Burgess, licensee

In a small hamlet in the Duddon Valley, this old lakeland pub is a popular stopping place for fell walkers. There is an interesting slate floor in the main bar, showing different levels of volcanic activity, and legend has it that the old beams in the pub came from ships of the Spanish Armada. Homely bar food - soups, sandwiches, Cumberland sausages, home-cooked gammon and steaks, plus a vegetarian dish or two. There is a more extensive evening menu. Theakstons ales, and during the summer, guest ales, i.e. Morlands Old Speckled Hen or Charles Wells Bombardier. Tables in the garden, from where you can admire the dramatic scenery.

OPEN: 11 - 3; 6 - 11 (11 - 11 Sat).
Real Ale.
Restaurant.
Children welcome if well behaved. Dogs on leads.
Self-catering flats available.
Occasional folk music.

WASDALE HEAD

Wasdale Head Inn   Tel: 0194 67 26229

Gosforth, Seascale, Cumbria CA20 1EX (NE of Lake)
Free House. Jaspar & Sue Carr, licensees

One of the more remote taverns in the Lake District, situated at the head of the dramatic Wast Water - the deepest lake in England. Understandably popular with travellers and climbers alike as Wasdale Head is approximately eight miles from the nearest habitation. Someone described the area as a collection of sheep pastures and an inn. This particular inn is a wonderfully sturdy, handsome, three-storey building with a good range of well-prepared bar food and well-kept ales. Theakstons Best and Old Peculiar, Jennings and Yates Bitter on hand pump, plus a summer guest beer. Dramatic scenery. No need to say there are wonderful walks round here because that is what you probably came to enjoy, anyway.

OPEN: 11 - 11 (closed mid-Nov - Dec 28, mid Jan - mid Feb).
Real Ale.
Restaurant.
Children in own room. No dogs.
Bedrooms (10).

WINSTER

Brown Horse
Tel: 0153 9443443

Winster, Nr Bowness-on-Windermere, Cumbria LA23 3WR
(S of Windermere)
Free House. Rudolph Schaeffer & Steven Doherty, licensees

Not quite so many of the big boots and hairy socks brigade here, but that's not to say you wouldn't be welcome for a pint in this appealing lakeside pub if you were so attired, but you will find the food on offer has gone up a few notches - beyond the merely sustaining. There is a reasonably priced, very imaginative and creative menu and such is the popularity of the pub, that you need to book to be sure of a table. Sandwiches are available if they are not too busy. Beers are all guests, and change periodically. Bittburger Pils on draught, Carlsberg Hof, Murphys Stout. Good short wine list.

OPEN: 12 - 3; 6 - 11.
Real Ale.
Children welcome.
Dogs on leads if pub not too busy.

DERBYSHIRE & STAFFORDSHIRE

BEELEY

Devonshire Arms   Tel: 01629 733259

Beeley, Nr Matlock, Derbyshire DE4 2NR
Free House. J A Grosvenor, licensee

Originally three separate cottages, they were converted in 1726 and during the early 18th century became a prosperous coaching inn on the road between Bakewell and Matlock. Now a popular, charming, well-kept village inn, catering for locals and visitors to the lovely Derbyshire Peak District. There is an interesting bar menu, ranging from sandwiches, ploughmans and vegetarian dishes plus salads to mushrooms in a tarragon, mustard and sour cream sauce, trout with lemon and herb stuffing, gammon and pineapple and breast of chicken in a stilton sauce. Dishes of the day on the blackboard; also a wide range of home-made puds. Theakstons Best, Old Peculier, Boddingtons, Black Sheep and a guest beer. An outstanding area for walking and cycling. Also very near Chatsworth House.

OPEN: 11 - 3; 6 - 11 (11 - 3; 7 - 10.30 Sun).
Real Ale.
Restaurant.
Children welcome, upstairs family room. No dogs.

BIRCHVALE

Waltzing Weasel
Tel: 01663 743402

New Mills Road, Birchvale, Derbyshire SK12 5BT
Free House. Michael Atkinson, licensee

There are wonderful views towards Kinderscout from the restaurant in this appealing English country inn, which was considerably extended in 1992. The bar is as popular as ever, but it is the cooking that has been attracting particular attention, the chef, George Benham, having come here from the Lamb Inn in Oxfordshire. Very comfortable, well decorated bars with open fires and interesting pieces of furniture. Bar food includes soups, pies, salads and a hot and cold carvery which is available at lunchtime. In the evening you could choose an individual cheese soufflé, crayfish tails with garlic mayonnaise, gravadlax, poussin stuffed with leeks and ham, wrapped in bacon in a madeira sauce or pork fillet sautéed with peppers and mushrooms in ginger and white wine. There is a separate pudding menu. Marstons Pedigree and draught cider. Good wine list, some by the glass.

OPEN: 12 - 3; 6 - 11 (7 - 10.30 Sun).
Real Ale.
Restaurant.
Children under tight control. Dogs on leads.

BRASSINGTON

Ye Olde Gate
Tel: 01629 540448

Well Street, Brassington, Derbys DE4 4HJ (NE of Ashbourne)
Marstons. Paul Burlinson, tenant

An unchanging, old country pub dating back to the 17th century. Very jolly atmosphere in the beamed bars, which have big log fires during the winter. Bar food changes by the day, but large open sandwiches, home-made curries, roasts, steaks and good puds available. No chips with anything! No-smoking dining room.

Marstons Pedigree and Owd Roger plus lots of malt whiskies.

Open: 12 - 2.30 (3 Sat); 6 - 11.
Closed Mon lunchtime.
Real Ale.
Children over 10 in dining room. Dogs on leads.

BRETTON

Barrel   Tel: 01433 630856

Bretton, Nr Eyam, Sheffield S30 1QD (between Eyam & Hathersage)
Free House. Derek Smith, licensee

A totally unspoilt historic inn, 1300 feet above sea level, with the reputation of being the highest pub in Derbyshire, and having views, (on a good day), over five counties. You don't need to be Einstein to work out that at that height it can be a bit cold in winter, so you need to know there are good log fires in this pub. Also reasonably priced bar food. There could be soups, sandwiches with various fillings, double decker sandwiches, filled baps, salads, chicken, ham and mushroom pie, all freshly prepared to order. Bass and Boddingtons Ales. Seats outside so you can admire the view. But be warned - at this high altitude you get very cool stiff breezes.

Open: 12 - 3; 6.30 - 11 (12 - 11 Summer Sats).
Real Ale.
Children welcome. Dogs on leads.

BURTON-ON-TRENT

Burton Bridge Inn   Tel: 01283 536596

24 Bridge Street, Burton-on-Trent, Staffs DE14 1SY
Own Brew. Kevin McDonald, tenant

Burton Bridge Brewery tap. The beer is brewed on site - Tuesday is viewing day but you must book your place. Lots of bits and pieces relating to brewery - notices, awards, etc. Quite a range of bar snacks: filled cobs and filled oatcakes, Yorkshire puddings with faggots and peas, roasts and hot bacon and egg rolls. A skittle alley, which seems to be booked months ahead, is available for private parties. Burton Bridge Bitter, XL Bitter, Porter and Festival plus seasonal varieties. Selection of malt whiskies and fruit wines.

Open: 11.30 - 2.15; 5.30 - 11. (Sun: 12 - 2; 7 - 10.30.)
Real Ale. No food Sunday.
Children over 10 in eating area. Dogs on leads.

DERBY

The Flower Pot   Tel: 01332 204955

25 King Street, Derby DE1 3DZ
Free House. Michael John Evans, licensee

Close to the centre of Derby, and within walking distance of the Cathedral and shopping centre, The Flower Pot, built in the early eighteenth century as a private house, was first licensed in about 1750. Not only do they provide refreshment for the inner man, but there is also the opportunity to improve the mind - they have a small library of books - mostly donated by the customers - with which you can while away the time, or even take home to read. Bar food is limited to filled rolls at the moment, as they are having a big think as to the direction the pub food should take. Rolls, a crisp and nut should see you through. Timothy Taylors Landlord, Bass and Marstons Pedigree are the regular ales; there are also guest beers. Quite a selection of malt whiskies. Small walled garden at the back of the pub, where there is also a children's play area.

Open: 11 - 11.
Real Ale.
Dogs on leads.

DERBY

Brunswick   Tel: 01332 290677

1 Railway Terrace, Derby
Free House. Trevor Harris, licensee

Built to accommodate the railway workers, this pub is now a magnet for those appreciating a comfortable, busy, friendly tavern which also offers an extensive range of ales - including their own brew. A beer festival is held on their anniversary in October: fourteen ales on hand pump and guests from the cask. Their own brew includes: First Brew, Railway Porter, Old Accidental and Owd Abusive. One roomy serving bar and a no-smoking room with an open fire. Traditional bar food: soup, filled rolls, beef and onion pie and other hot dishes. Seats outside on the terrace behind the pub.

OPEN: 11 - 11.
Real Ale.
Lunchtime meals/snacks. Filled rolls only Sun. Restaurant closed Sun.
Children in family parlour. Dogs on leads.
Jazz Thurs eves. Folk Club.

DERBY

Ye Olde Dolphin Inn   Tel: 01332 349115

6/7 Queen Street, Derby DE1 3DL
Bass. Tony Williams, manager

Ye Olde Dolphin dates back to 1540 and has been a drinking and eating house throughout most of its history, although a doctor's surgery took some space - nothing sinister in that, we hope. A traditional period building with beamed interiors, comfortable bars and welcoming fires. Situated near the cathedral, it is popular with visitors and locals alike. The pub aims to provide the best traditional pub food with the addition of some continental specialities. Draught Bass, Worthingtons Bitter, Highgate Mild and other guest ales. There is a small, paved rear garden.

OPEN: 10.30 - 11.
Restaurant.
No children. Dogs on leads.

EYAM

Miners Arms   Tel: 01433 630853

Water Lane, Eyam, Derbyshire S30 1RG
Free House. Nicholas & Ruth Cook, licensees

Built in 1630 before the village was struck by the plague, the original inn's stones can be seen over the lintel. The pub also boasts a couple of ghosts, thought to be two unfortunate girls who perished in a fire on the same site before the inn was built. There are three unghostly, quiet rooms in the pub and a very good choice of home-made dishes, a lot of them prepared from local seasonal produce. Bar lunches might include home-made soups, lamb and mint sausages in onion gravy, haddock mornay, quiche, ploughmans and sandwiches. There is also an evening à la carte menu when the selection of dishes goes up a notch. No bar snacks on Sunday, but there is a traditional roast. Boddingtons Ales.

OPEN: 12 - 3; 7 - 11.
Real Ale. Evening Restaurant.
No food Sun or Mon except Sun lunch in restaurant.
Children welcome.
No Dogs.

HASSOP

Eyre Arms   Tel: 01629 640390

Hassop, Nr Bakewell, Derbys DE45 1NS
Free House. Nick & Lynne Smith, licensees

===

A fifteenth century village pub serving popular good wholesome food and well kept ales. Spacious public bar. Tables are laid in the roomy lounge bar for dinner in the evenings. Extensive menu of traditional English fare. Morlands Old Speckled Hen, John Smiths Pedigree ales.

OPEN: 11 - 11.
Real Ale.
Children at lunchtime only. Dogs on leads & well behaved.

HAYFIELD

Lantern Pike Inn   Tel: 01663 747590

Glossop Road, Little Hayfield, Via Stockport SK12 5NG
Free House. Gerry McDonald, licensee

===

Unpretentious, welcoming, and on the hillwalkers' route to the Lantern Pike; nothing is too much trouble here, whatever it may be. It has a traditional interior with a good fire, home-made bar snacks and well kept ales. Food includes: soups, sandwiches, ploughmans, curries, steak, steak & kidney pie and a choice of vegetarian dishes. Timothy Taylors Landlord, Flowers IPA, Boddingtons and guest beers. Seats on the terrace looking towards the Peaks.

OPEN: 11.30 - 3; 6 - 11. (All day Sat.)
Real Ale. Restaurant open all day Sun.
No dogs. Bedrooms.

KIRKIRETON

Barley Mow   Tel: 01335 370306

Main Street, Kirkireton, Ashbourne, Derbyshire DE6 3JP
Free House. Mary Short, licensee

On the edge of the Peak District, the imposing 17th century Barley Mow, which was built at the top of the village street, has been catering for villagers and visitors for nearly 200 years. There is an unspoilt interior with open fires and a small bar. Only filled rolls are available at lunchtime. Evening meals are served, but only for residents. Well kept beers from the cask: Hook Norton Best, Old Hooky, Marstons Pedigree and Timothy Taylors Landlord. These can do a quick change with Adnams, Courage Directors, Greene King and Wadworths. Seats in the garden and at the front of the pub.

OPEN: 12 - 2; 7 - 11.
Real Ale. Rolls at lunchtime.
Children welcome by arrangement. Dogs on leads.
Bedrooms (Five en suite).

LICHFIELD

Queens Head   Tel: 01543 410932

Queen Street, Lichfield, Staffs WS13 6QD
Marstons. John P Ketley & Sue Midgley, tenants

"The art of conversation is not dead at the Queens Head" is the slogan thought up by the landlord when he took over last year. Deciding he wanted a "talking" pub, the wiring for the muzak was somewhat trimmed back! Recently redecorated, the pub is to be Marston's first real ale house, and the new tenants are doing all they can to make sure it is a resounding success. All the food is freshly cooked - no chips, deep frying or anything in a basket. Clitheroe sausages - three different kinds every day - over 30 varieties of cheese, mostly English, home-made soup,

"Lancashire oven bottom muffins" baked for the pub, daily specials and a speciality night once a month. Morlands Old Speckled Hen, Fullers London Pride, Wadworths 6X and Abbot Ale.

Open: 11 - 11, (12 - 3. 7 - 10.30 Sun).
Real Ale.
Children welcome. Dogs on leads.

LITTLE LONGSTONE

Packhorse   Tel: 01629 640471

Little Longstone, Nr Bakewell, Derbys DE45 1NN (Nr Monsal Dale)
Marstons. Lynne & Mark Lythgoe, tenants

Here we have a small, two-roomed, old-fashioned 16th century pub, popular with locals and those energetic walkers on the Monsal Trail. Simply furnished, comfortable bars with a very good choice of bar food: hot beef and pork rolls, garlic and stilton mushrooms, lamb in stilton sauce, steak & kidney pies and steaks. Good puds too. Marstons Ales.

OPEN: 11 - 3; 5 - 11 (6 - 11 Sat).
Real Ale. Restaurant.
Well behaved children lunchtime and early eves.
Dogs on leads.
Live music alternate Wed eves.

MONSAL HEAD

Monsal Head Hotel   Tel: 01629 640250

Monsal Head, Bakewell, Derbyshire DE45 1NL
Free House. Nicholas Smith, licensee

There are panoramic views of the Dales from this hotel high above the valley of the River Wye. Comfortable, popular bars and a no-smoking restaurant. Reliable bar food includes home-made soups, steak & kidney pie, gammon and eggs, garlic mushrooms and also a children's menu. Ruddles Best and County, Courage Directors, Marstons Pedigree and Theakstons Old Peculiar on hand pump.

Open: 11 - 11.
Real Ale. Restaurant.
Children not after 7 in bar. Dogs on leads.

OCKBROOK

White Swan   Tel: 01332 662088

Church Street, Ockbrook, Derby
Ansells Brewery. June & Alan Newton, tenant

Set in the conservation area of a delightful Derbyshire village, the white painted 18th century White Swan - winner of Ansells Best Kept Pub Award - is a friendly mixture of young and old drinkers. It is a regular meeting place for the local car clubs. A large range of changing bar meals is offered daily, with traditional roasts on Sunday. Ansells and Marstons Pedigree Ales. There is an attractive rear garden which has won many gardening prizes over the past few years.

OPEN: 11.30 - 3; 7 - 11.
Real Ale.
Children welcome. Doubtful about dogs.

STERNDALE

The Quiet Woman   Tel: 01298 83211

Earl Sterndale, Nr Buxton, Derbyshire
Marstons. Ken & Jen Mellor, tenants

Rather a politically incorrect inn sign, but in spite of that, a wonderful example of a village local, surrounded by some of the prettiest countryside in the Peak District. Popular with walkers, there is always a warm welcome here. Sandwiches, pork pies, crusty bread and real Stilton cheese, plus good Marstons Ales. Seats outside in the large garden which has a picnic area and donkeys, geese, pigs, hens, ducks and turkeys - and no, none of them are lunch. But you can buy free range eggs. They have parking for three touring caravans, also a large park for caravettes and somewhere to pitch your tent.

OPEN: Moveable hours.
Real Ale.
Children welcome. No dogs.

WARDLOW

Three Stags Heads   Tel: 01298 872268

Wardlow Mires, Tideswell, Derbys SK17 8RW
Free House. Geoff & Pat Fuller, licensees

To sustain all those people with big boots, hairy socks and back packs, food is served all day in this charming, cottagey pub - the exception being weekdays in winter when opening time is not until 7.00. Flagstone floors allow you in with your muddy boots. Bar food ranges from home-made soups to fillet steaks with garlic butter. Home-cooked food on home-made plates - there is a pottery in the barn. The ales are selected from the smaller local breweries and could include Kelham Island Pale Rider, Springhead Bitter and Hoskins and Oldfields Navigation among others. Lots of continental and British bottled beers.

OPEN: 12 - 11 (7 - 11 weekdays winter).
Real Ale. Restaurant.
Children until 8.30. Dogs on leads.
Live music Sat eve/Sun lunch.

WHALEY BRIDGE

Shepherds Arms   Tel:01663 732384

7, Old Road, Whaley Bridge Derby/Shropshire border SK12 7HR
Marstons. Derek Abbott, tenant

Dedicated to the keen drinker - with the added attraction to us of a landlord adamant that his pub should remain music free. This town pub, dating back to the 16th century is a traditional local. Only one bar - with a flagstone floor, beams and a good fire in winter. No food - just crisps and a nut. Marstons range of ales. Seats (and children on Sundays) in the large beer garden.

OPEN: 11.30 - 3; 7 - 11 (12 - 3; 7 - 10.30 Sun).
Real Ale.
Children Sunday lunchtime in the beer garden only.
Dogs on leads.

WOOLLEY MOOR

White Horse   Tel: 01246 590319

White Horse Lane, Woolley Moor, Derbyshire DE5 6FG
Free House. Bill & Jill Taylor, licensees

There just may be classical music playing in the restaurant but there are plenty of opportunities here to get away from it if you want to. In winter you can tuck yourself into a corner of one of the bars and in summer spread yourself out in the big garden. The pub has a printed menu with the usual selection of traditional bar food and quite a number of daily blackboard specials. Much of the food is from very local sources: butcher, baker and an enthusiastic vegetable grower. In winter there are special food nights; beer festivals are held throughout the year. Draught Bass, Bass Worthington, Highgate Mild and guest beers. Excellent walks nearby.

OPEN: 11.30 - 2.30 (3 Sat); 6 - 11.
Real Ale. Restaurant. No food Sun eve.
Children in eating area or restaurant. Dogs in public bar.

DEVON

BOVEY TRACEY

Cromwell Arms Hotel
Tel: 01626 833473

Town Centre, Bovey Tracey, Devon TQ13 9AE
Free House. John & Dorothy Tribble, licensee

Pronounced "Buvvy" for those of us who are uninitiated, this delightful small town is on the edge of Dartmoor. At the centre of which you'll find the Cromwell Arms - an attractive old building, inside which are two comfortable bars and a dining room with distant views of Dartmoor. Busy and popular, they serve a traditional English menu with daily specials. Tetleys, Wadworths 6X and St Austells Hicks Special Draught. Seats on the small terrace.

OPEN: 11 - 3; 5.30 - 11.20 (12 - 3; 7 - 10.30 Sun).
Real Ale. Restaurant.
Children in restaurant only. Dogs on leads.

BRANSCOMBE

Fountains Head
Tel: 01297 680359

Branscombe, Nr Seaton, Devon EX12 3BG
Free House. Mrs Catherine Luxton, licensee

Mrs Luxton's husband runs his own brewery a mile away, so there is never any fear of this pub running dry. Two bars: both of them cosy with log fires in winter. The snug is panelled; the other used to house the village smithy. There is also a small no-smoking room for children. Fish orientated bar menu with cockles, mussels and crab sandwiches; home-made lasagne, salads, and occasionally fried sardines and salmon steaks with fresh herbs as daily specials. Fish and chip night Fridays. Speciality food nights at other times. Own brewed beers include Branoc, Jolly Geoff and Olde Stoker. Farm cider. Seats outside on the terrace.

OPEN: 11.30 - 2.30; 6.30 - 11 (11.30 - 2; 7 - 11 winter).
Real Ale.
Children in own room lunchtimes; over 10 in eating area eves.
Dogs on leads.

BRANSCOMBE

Masons Arms   Tel: 01297 680300

Branscombe, Nr Seaton, Devon EX12 3DJ
Free House. Veronique Pontoizeau, manager

What a lucky community to have two pubs offering so much. At the lower end of the village, which is scattered over the slopes of a steep green bowl, the Mason's Arms - with its thatched hats over the doors and thatched umbrellas over the tables - can't be missed. The rambling beamed bar has a roaring log fire, with a spit that is often used for roasting beef, lamb and occasionally, a whole pig. The best fresh local produce is used in the kitchens. Bar food includes soups, sandwiches, ploughmans, chicken, stilton and walnut strudel, steak & kidney pudding, grilled fish, mullet, sea bass, plaice or whatever is available. Sundays: sandwiches, ploughmans and a roast only. Part of the restaurant is no-smoking. Bass, Furgusons Dartmoor, Eldridge Pope Hardy and an occasional guest beer. Good wine list. Farm ciders.

OPEN: 11 - 3; 5.30 - 11; (11 - 2.30; 6 - 11 winter).
Real Ale. Well behaved children may be allowed, away from bar.
Dogs on leads.
Live jazz and other music Fridays.

CHURCHSTOW

Church House   Tel: 01548 852237

Churchstow, Nr Kingsbridge, Devon
Free House. Nick & Vera Nicholson, licensees

A fine 13th century village pub with a long welcoming bar, stone walls, low oak beams and a great stone fireplace complete with a bread oven. There is the usual choice of reliable bar food. The carvery Wednesday to Saturday evening and Sunday lunchtime is proving so popular you are advised to book well in advance. The restaurant is no-smoking. Bass and Furgusons Dartmoor on hand pump. There is a conservatory for days that are less than warm, and seats outside in summer.

OPEN: 11 - 2.30; 6 - 11. Closed first Mon in Feb.
Real Ale. Restaurant (not Sun eves).
Children welcome. Dogs on leads.

COLYTON

Kingfisher   Tel: 01297 552476

Dolphin Street, Colyton, Devon EX13 6NA
Free House. Graeme & Cherry Sutherland, licensees

In the 16th century Colyton was a prosperous wool town owned by the Marquis of Exeter who carelessly lost his head and his land when he had a little argument with Henry VIII. The locals clubbed together to buy the manor by a deed of Feoffment, and sixteen Feoffees direct the town to this day. The Kingfisher is a friendly pub with a comfortable bar and big open fire. It has an upstairs family and games room. Bar food and daily specials, home-made cheesecakes and fruit pies. Badger Best, Tanglefoot, Charles Wells Bombardier and several guest beers on hand pump. Farm ciders. Seats on the terrace overlooking the garden.

OPEN: 11.30 - 2.30; 6 - 11.
Real Ale. Restaurant.
Children in eating area. Dogs on leads.

DARTINGTON

Cott Inn
Tel: 01803 863777

Dartington, Nr Totnes, Devon TQ9 6HE
Free House. David & Susan Grey, licensees

Licensed since 1320, this pub is reputed to be the second oldest in the country. Plenty of beams, flagstone floors, big fireplaces and lots of room. One area is non-smoking. There is an excellent hot and cold buffet at lunchtime with a choice of salads, cold meats, Dart salmon, quiches, etc. The evening menu is more extensive and could include lamb casserole with rosemary and orange dumplings, torbay sole stuffed with crab, rib steak with mushrooms and red wine sauce and home-made puds. Bass, Fullers London Pride and Blackawton 44 Special. Farm ciders and wine by the glass. The pub has its own cricket team, so if you are feeling energetic, fixtures can be arranged. The flowery courtyard is pleasant to sit in during the summer. Dartington Hall, the largest medieval house in the west of England, is close by and worth a visit.

OPEN: 11 - 2.30; 5.30 - 11.
Restaurant.
Children in restaurant. Dogs on leads. Bedrooms.

DARTMOUTH

Cherub
Tel: 01803 832571

13 Higher Street, Dartmouth, Devon TQ6 9BB
Free House. Steven Hill, licensee

There are lots of colourful carvings in Dartmouth, inspired perhaps by the naval tradition of ornamentation. The port has been used for centuries: the Plantaganets to keep an eye on the French, later monarchs to watch the Spaniards; in 1944 to invade Europe, in 1995 to watch the Spaniards again. The lovely Cherub (with the carving) dates back to the 14th century. Heavily timbered with jettied upper floors, the pub has a comfortable beamed bar with a large fireplace. Popular with the locals, it has a tempting bar menu - soup, sandwiches, filled potatoes, ratatouille, beef in beer, seafood pasta, etc. Daily specials and home-made puddings. Flowers Original, Morlands Old Speckled Hen, Wadworths 6X and a guest beer on hand pump.

OPEN: 11 - 3; 5 - 11.
Restaurant.
Children in restaurant until 8.30. Dogs in bar only.

DODDISCOMBSLEIGH

Nobody Inn   Tel: 01647 252394

Doddiscombsleigh, Nr Exeter, Devon EX6 7PS
Free House. Nick Borst Smith, licensee

At first glance, it's more of a village house than an inn, with a proper front garden and gate. The inn sign is nearly hidden by foliage along with a notice saying "Unsuitable for Motor Vehicles". Ignore it. With map in hand, navigate the deep Devon lanes to reach the Nobody Inn with its striking beamed bar, antiques and open fires. There is a tremendous wine list, 250 different malt whiskies and varied, well thought-out bar food and changing blackboard menu. But that's not all: here you find a cheese-lover's paradise, usually about 40, many from the county. Not difficult to find a good wine to go with the cheese as between 700-800 are in the pub cellar; about 20 by the glass. Nobody's Beer (brewed by Branscombes), Branscombes Vale Branoc and Bass and other guest beers on hand pump or from the cask. Farm ciders. Seats on the terrace from where you can look at the view and appreciate the peace and quiet.

OPEN: 12 - 2.30; 6 - 11 (7 - 11 winter).
Real Ale.
Restaurant evenings only (not Sun).
No children under 14, and only in restaurant. No dogs.

DREWSTEIGNTON

Drewe Arms Tel: 01647 281224

The Square, Drewsteignton, Devon
Whitbread. Mabel Mudge, tenant

One is taking a chance including this wonderful old thatched pub, as its future is uncertain. The locals are making every effort to buy the Drewe Arms and run it as a co-operative. The social life of the village revolves around it; spiritual matters are taken care of by the church next door. Virtually unchanged since the 19th century, the ales and draught ciders are kept on racks in the tap room and regulars help themselves from the cask. Nothing fancy to eat: ham (home-cured) and cheese sandwiches. A good sandwich is very hard to beat. There is a Save the Drewe Committee - so help if you can. An unspoilt ale house should have a preservation order put on it and be supported.

OPEN: 10.30 - 2.30; 6 - 11. Real Ale. Lunchtime snacks.
Children welcome. Dogs on leads.

EAST DOWN

Pyne Arms Tel: 01271 850207

East Down, Nr Barnstaple, N Devon EX31 4LX
Free House. Jurgen & Elizabeth Kempf, licensees

It has a spacious, low-beamed bar with a wood-burning stove, horse harnesses and horse racing prints on the wall, a flagstone-floored games area with a juke box and a no-smoking gallery with tables and chairs. Good varied pub food - home-made soup, paté, ham and eggs, four different recipes for mussels, scampi provençale, etc. Selection of puddings. Courage Directors and John Smiths on hand pump. Some wines by the glass.

OPEN: 11 - 2.30; 6 - 11.
Real Ale.
No children. Dogs on leads.

EXETER

White Hart
Tel: 01392 79897

66, South Street, Exeter, Devon EX1 1EE
Davy's. Graham Stone, manager

This is an old coaching inn practically at the centre of Exeter, which you enter through a wisteria-covered loggia. The bars are abundantly beamed and filled with gleaming copper that reflects the glow of the fires in winter. Food in the Tap bar is generous traditional and includes: soups, sandwiches, filled baked potatoes, steak and oyster pie, steaks and daily specials. The wine bar - called Bottlescrue Bill's - has bare stone walls and sawdust on the floor. It serves much the same choice of food. This bar boasts its own small garden with a huge vine, colourful geraniums and lots of roses in summer. Davy's Old Wallop, special brews, Bass and John Smiths. Davy's wines, vintage port and Bucks Fizz in summer when you can also eat from a barbecue in the courtyard.

OPEN: 11.30 - 3, 5 - 11 (11.30 - 11 Sat).
Two Restaurants. No food in the two smaller bars Sun.
Real Ale.
Children welcome. No Dogs. Bedrooms.

HARBERTON

Church House Inn
Tel: 01803 863707

Harberton, Nr Totnes, Devon TQ9 7SF
Free House. Mrs Jennifer Wright, licensee

Built around 1100 AD - before the Norman conquest - this listed building is full of oak panelling and reputed to have the oldest oak screen in the country. It has a huge inglenook fireplace around which are oak pews of great antiquity. Food here is up to the mark and lunchtime specials include - fillet of plaice marinated in white wine garlic and lemon, steak & kidney pie, home-made soups, locally made sausages, curries and grills. Bass and Courage Best plus two weekly changing guest beers. Good selection of wines.

OPEN: 12 - 2.30; 6 - 11 (11.30 - 3 Sat).
Real Ale. Restaurant.
Children in family room & eating area. Dogs on leads.
Occasional jazz or folk. Morris dancers in summer.

HAYTOR VALE

Rock   Tel: 01364 661305

Haytor Vale, Nr Newton Abbot, Devon TQ13 9XP
Free House. Christopher Graves, licensee

Only 200 years old, yet this old coaching inn has gained a ghost called Belinda. Legend has it that Belinda was having an affair with the coachman and was murdered by the coachman's wife on the stairs of the pub. Some guests have seen her but not the landlord. It's a friendly local serving a small, rural community. It has two panelled rooms, both with big log fires, a no-smoking dining area and a restaurant. Good choice of bar food with all the usuals: soup, ploughmans, etc., local rabbit in mustard sauce, curries, poached Devon salmon, steaks and daily specials. Also home-made puddings and a Sunday roast. It can get very busy. Bass, Eldridge Royal and Guinness on hand pump. Malt whiskies. A pretty garden and an adjoining terrace are in high favour in summer. Being on the edge of the Dartmoor National Park there are some wonderful walks.

OPEN: 11 - 3; 6 - 11 (11 - 11 Sat).
Real Ale. (No snacks Sun or Bank Holidays.)
Children in eating area of bar. No dogs. Bedrooms.

HOLBETON

Mildmay Colours   Tel: 01752 830248

Fore Street, Holbeton, Plymouth, Devon PL8 1NA
Own Brew. Andrew Patrick, licensee

Originally the George, this friendly little pub was renamed in 1967 on the death of Lord Mildmay. The sign is painted in his racing colours. All the beers they brew here have horsey names, 50/1, Old Horsewhip, SP, and Colours Best. If there is a quiet moment, you can look over the brewery. Bar food includes ploughmans, beef in ale, Mexican dishes and daily specials. There are tables outside at the front of the pub and in the garden at the back.

OPEN: 11 - 3; 6 - 11 (occasionally all day summer).
Real Ale. Carvery Restaurant closed Mon-Thurs.
Children welcome. Dogs on leads. Bedrooms.

HOLNE

Church House   Tel: 01364 631208

Holne, Nr Ashburton, Devon TQ13 7SJ
Free House. N E & W J Bevan, lease

This pub is on the edge of Dartmoor and the place to go after walking in the beautiful National Park. It has a pine-panelled bar, a comfortable, carpeted lounge - both with big log fires in winter - and a no-smoking restaurant. Lovely views over the moors from the front of the pub. Fresh, locally produced organic vegetables, some of them home-grown; fish from Brixham; carefully chosen local meat. Lunchtime snacks could include mushrooms in garlic butter, filled baked potatoes, various ploughmans, sandwiches, omelettes and vegetarian dishes. Daily specials - perhaps grilled local sole, Dartmoor rabbit pie, casseroled Devon lamb in cider and various home-made puddings, such as fruit crumble or trifle. Furgusons Dartmoor and Palmers IPA. Guest beers vary. Farm cider and a good choice of house wines.

OPEN: 11.30 - 3; 6.30 - 11 (12 - 3, 6.30 - 10.30 winter Sun-Thurs).
Real Ale. Restaurant. No snacks evenings.
Well behaved children in eating area: none under 7 in eve.
Dogs on leads.
Bedrooms.

IDDESLEIGH

Duke of York   Tel: 01837 810253

Iddesleigh, Winkleigh, Devon EX19 8BG
Free House. Bill Pringle, licensee

Very popular village pub, full of friendly regulars, some of whom
can be found pulling their own pints when the landlord is busy
elsewhere, a tradition in this long, low 14th century thatched pub
dating back to before the arrival of the present landlord. The
customers divide themselves into categories: those who tell the
landlord later what they have had and then pay up, and those who
pull pints for themselves and anyone else and put the money
straight into the till. Too many locals around for the obvious in this
day and age - those who just serve themselves and don't pay.
Simple home-made bar food, sandwiches, soups, local sausages
and steaks. Cotleigh Tawny and Hook Norton Old Hooky from the
cask. Farm ciders and guest beers. A pretty back garden to sit in.

OPEN: 11.30 - 3; 6.30 - 11.
Real Ale. Restaurant. No food Mon in winter.
Children in eating area. Dogs on leads. Bedrooms

LITTLE HEMPSTON

Tally Ho!   Tel: 01803 862316

Little Hempston, Nr Totnes, Devon TQ9 6NF
Free House. Alan Hitchman & Dale Hitchman, licensees

Thought to be the prettiest pub in Devon, dating back to the 14th
century. It has comfortable, low beamed rooms, filled with
interesting objets d'art, fresh flowers, and pieces of antique

furniture. Wide range of bar food: home-made soups, paté, vegetarian dishes, steaks and fish fresh from Brixham. Home-made puddings. Bass, Furgusons Dartmoor and Wadworths 6X on hand pump. There is a flower-filled courtyard for sitting in during the summer.

OPEN: 12 - 2.30; 6 - 11.
Real Ale.
Children in eating area. Dogs on leads.

LUSTLEIGH

Cleave   Tel: 016477 223

Lustleigh, Nr Newton Abbot, Devon
Heavitree. A Perring, tenant

This is an attractive 15th century, thatched inn at the centre of a picturesque village nestling in the Dartmoor foothills. Lustleigh - with its thatched cottages surrounding the village green and church - is considered one of the prettiest villages in Devon. The Cleave, with its charming, low-ceilinged bar and huge inglenook fireplace, is open every day for bar meals, lunchtime and evening. Home-made soups, sandwiches, pasta dishes and their own steak & kidney pie. Home-made puddings too. Whitbread Pompey Royal, Bass, Boddingtons and Flowers Original on hand pump. Farm ciders. Morning coffee.

OPEN: 11 - 3; 6 - 11 (11 - 11 Sat).
Real Ale.
Children in no-smoking family area. Dogs on leads.

LYDFORD

Castle   Tel: 0182 282 242

Lydford, Nr Oakhampton, Devon EX20 4BH
Free House. Clive & Mo Walker, licensees

You are not far away, here, from two of the most spectacular waterfalls in Devon: the White Lady Waterfall which slides 100 ft down a rocky shute to join the River Lydd in a wooded valley below, and the Devil's Cauldron - along a twisting footpath - where the river crashes through a narrow gap, down a vertical, mossy cliff. After that excitement, back to the Castle Inn - a very pretty, pinkwashed Tudor building - for refreshment. Lots of room in the low-beamed bars which are filled with antique settles and interesting bits and pieces collected over the years, including some Lydford pennies dating back to King Ethelred the Unready. A good choice of food: home-made soups, Devon cheese platter, seafood risotto, steak & kidney or venison pies, home-made puddings. Bass, Fergusons Dartmoor, Palmers IPA, three different guest beers a week on hand pump, or from the barrel. Wines by the glass. Bucks Fizz in the summer. Seats on the terrace; also a pets corner for children. Part of the restaurant is no-smoking.

OPEN: 11.30 - 3; 6 - 11.
Real Ale. Restaurant.
Children in eating area bar (lunchtime only), Snug & Restaurant.
Dogs on leads. Bedrooms.

LYNTON

Rockford	Tel: 01598 7214

Brendon, Lynton, N Devon EX35 6PS
Free House. D W Sturmer & S J Tasker, licensees

"A pub that does food" is how the landlord describes this friendly 350 year old inn by the River Lyn. The road, one in four, gets you in training to rival a mountain goat, but the climb is worth it for the view. There is also a wonderful walk west through the valley to Castle Rockford. Before that, some honest bar food and a good pint. Home-made cottage pie, chicken and mushroom pie, smoked trout and a more elaborate menu in the evening. Courage Best, Directors and Cotleigh Tawny. Choice of wine.

OPEN: 12 - 2.30 (2 winter); 7 - 11. Closed weekday lunchtimes and two weeks Nov & Feb.
Real Ale.Children in eating area. Dogs on leads.
Folk music 3rd Sat evening in month.

MILTONCOMBE

Who'd Have Thought It   Tel: 01822 853313

Miltoncombe, Plymouth, Devon PL20 6HP
Free House. Keith Yeo & Gary Rager, licensees

Years ago this pub applied for a licence to sell spirits. Locals were generally of the opinion that the odds were not in its favour. Much to everyone's surprise the licence was granted, eliciting the reaction "Well, who'd have thought it" - and the name stuck. This also explains the celebratory inn sign of a man waving a piece of paper surrounded by a crowd of locals. There is a panelled bar in this fine old pub, with polished tables and a big fireplace: two other rooms, one no-smoking, have half barrels (with cushions) for seats. Generous helpings of bar food: home-made soups, patés, chicken or vegetable curry, grilled trout, steaks. On Sundays there is less choice but always a roast. Blackawton Headstrong, Eldridge Pope Royal Oak, Hook Nortons Best, Bass and Wadworth 6X on hand pump. Farm ciders. Tables outside on the terrace. There is also a pub ghost called Ed Bere, (how do they know his name?).

OPEN: 11.30 - 2.30 (3 Sat); 6.30 - 11.
Real Ale. Restricted food Sun lunchtime.
No children. Dogs on leads. Folk club Sun evenings.

NEWTON ST CYRES

Beer Engine   Tel: 01392 851282

Newton St Cyres, Exeter, Devon EX5 5AX
Own Brew. Peter Hawksley, licensee

Built a hundred and fifty years ago when the trains first arrived, this old station pub now brews its own beer - all of it with a railway theme: Rail Ale, Piston Bitter and Sleeper (rather strong). The landlord would rather concentrate on just the ales but realises that you have to offer good pub food to make a living. Reasonably priced bar meals include cod and parsley pie, speciality sausages, lasagne and several vegetarian dishes. Rumour has it there is a female ghost walking the pub but as the only people who have seen it are the chaps who have had quite a few beers - it could be a case of a vivid imagination! There are tables in the large sunny garden.

OPEN: 11.30 - 2.30; 6 - 11. 11.30 - 11 Sat. Cellar Bar open till midnight Fri/Sat.
Real Ale. Children in eating area. Dogs on leads.
Rock & Blues Fri/Sat eve. Folk/Jazz Sun lunch.

POUNDSGATE

Tavistock   Tel: 01364 631251

Poundsgate, Newton Abbott, Devon TQ13 7NY
Ushers. Ken & Janice Comer, lease

Legend has it that one night in 1638 the devil called at the Tavistock on his way to collect the soul of a gambler. He ordered a beer and as he drank, steam rose from his lips. He paid with a gold piece and when he'd gone the gold turned to dry leaves. Let's hope nothing so dramatic happens when you stop at this hospitable old inn for refreshment. There are big log fires and flagstone floors in the bars and a family room in what was the stables. Home-made soups - some vegetarian, ploughmans, sandwiches, curries, all day breakfasts, daily specials. Ushers Best and Founders, Courage Best. Farm cider. Mulled wine in winter. The pub has a lovely garden to sit in during the summer.

Open 11 - 3; 6 - 11.
Real Ale.
Children in family room. Dogs on leads.

RATTERY

Church House   Tel: 01364 642220

Rattery, South Brent, Devon TQ10 9LD
Free House. Mr B & Mrs J Evans, licensees

A listed building dating back to about 1028 AD, it is said to be connected to the church by a tunnel, which indicates the monks knew when they were onto a good thing. Good range of bar food, soups of course, filled rolls, home-baked ham, smoked salmon, chicken, Algerian lamb and home-made puddings. Children's menu. Furgusons Dartmoor, Dartmoor Legend and guest beer on hand pump. Range of old malt whiskies. Farm cider. Wine. Lovely views of the wooded countryside from the pub.

OPEN: 11 - 2.30; 6 - 11.
Real Ale. Children in eating areas. Dogs on leads.

SHEEPWASH

Half Moon   Tel: 01409 231376

Sheepwash, Beaworthy, N Devon EX21 5NE
Free House. Ben Inniss & Charles Inniss, licensees

Very much a fishing pub, and totally geared up for it: a rod room, somewhere to dry yourself when you fall in, and a shop where you can buy all those bits and pieces you thought you had packed. Ten miles of glorious fishing on the River Torridge and plenty of room at the bar for the "one that got away" stories. Bar snacks at lunchtime are all you could wish: home-made soup, pasties, home-cured ham, salad, ploughmans. Dinner at night includes roasts, steaks and fresh fish. Courage Best, Bass and Worthingtons Best on hand pump. Selection of malt whiskies. Impressive wine list.

OPEN: 11.30 - 2.30; 6 - 11.
Real Ale. Restaurant evenings. Snacks lunchtimes.
Children lunchtime only. Dogs on leads. Bedrooms.

SOUTHPOOL

Mill Brook   Tel: 01548 531581

Southpool, Kingsbridge, Devon TQ7 2RW
Free House. Arthur & Cindy Spedding, licensees

Very popular with yachtsmen who can virtually sail straight in and
order drinks. This tiny pub is one of a few with variable opening
times; they depend on the state of the tide in the creek, which runs
into the middle of the pretty little village. It has a charming, comfortable bar with lots of fresh flowers on the tables. Good, dependable
bar food such as soup, filled potatoes, cottage pie, smoked
mackerel, fish pie and chilli. Devon Apple Cider Cake to finish.
Ruddles Best, Bass, John Smiths on hand pump. Farm ciders.

OPEN: 11 - 3; 5.30 - 11 (summer); 11.30 - 2.30; 6.30 - 11 (winter).
May open longer in summer. Real Ale.
Children in eating room. No dogs.

STICKLEPATH

Devonshire Inn   Tel: 01837 840626

Sticklepath, Oakhampton, Devon EX20 2NW
Free House. John & Ann Verner-Jeffreys, licensees

There has been an inn here since 1640, but it is only recently that
the Devonshire reopened after being closed for some time. The
Devonshire has a low-beamed, slate-floored bar with comfortable
furnishings and a big log fire in winter. The new owners have made
a big effort to create a very welcome "new" village inn, and they are
succeeding because the food they offer - including a roast every
Sunday - is reasonably priced and freshly cooked to order; they
also cater for small dinner parties on request. Real ales include St
Austells Tinners, Bass and some guest beers. Also farm ciders.

OPEN: 11 - 3; 6.30 - 11 (11 - 11 Fri & Sat & Summer).
Real Ale.
Children welcome. Dogs on leads.

TOTNES

Kingsbridge Inn

Tel: 01803 863324

9 Leechwell Street, Totnes, Devon TQ9 5SY
Free House. Rosemary Triggs, Martyn & Jane Canevali, licensees

Situated in the oldest, highest part of this historic town, the Kingsbridge Inn dates back to the time of the Domesday Book. Pass through the low beamed rambling bar and you will find a room with an ancient spring bubbling into a stone trough. No printed menu, as everything is fresh and cooked in small quantities. The dishes are written up on a blackboard and are changed several times; the only thing not home-made is the ice cream. Food includes fish from Brixham, filled French sticks, Devon cheese platter with home-made pickle, rabbit pie, and you can always get a sandwich. There is a more elaborate evening menu. Furgusons Dartmoor, Bass, Courage Best and Theakstons Old Peculiar and a guest beer on hand pump. Farm ciders. In winter, mulled wine. The ghost here is Mary Brown, a maidservant murdered by the landlord 300 years ago and buried in one of the walls. The landlady, Mrs Triggs, and her daughter, have both seen her in daytime and at night. They both chat to her and say she is friendly but mischievous - can't say I blame her!

OPEN: 11 - 2.30; 5.30 - 11.
Real Ale.
Children in eating area. Dogs on leads.
Local groups Wed evenings.

WOODBURY SALTERTON

Diggers Rest

Tel: 01395 232375

Woodbury Salterton, Nr Exeter, Devon EX5 1PQ
Free House. Sally Pratt, licensee

Naturally, one of our antipodean cousins changed the name from the Salterton Arms to the Diggers Rest twenty-one years ago and I bet it is the only one in the country. All sounds very jolly with a summer skittle alley and a games room. It has a good-sized, comfortable, heavily beamed bar. Bar food includes filled pancakes, steak & kidney pie, liver & bacon, home-cooked gammon, curries, sandwiches and soups. There are daily specials. Always fresh vegetables and home-made puddings. No kangaroo steaks here! Furgusons Dartmoor, Tetleys and Bass on hand pump. Local farm ciders. You get some splendid views over the local countryside from the terrace of this thatched village pub.

OPEN: 11 - 2.30; 6.30 - 11.
Real Ale.
Well behaved children in family area.
Dogs on leads.

DORSET

ASKERWELL

Spyway Inn   Tel: 01308 485250

Askerwell, Nr Bridport, Dorset
Free House. Don & Jackie Roderick, licensees

Down a country lane, deep in glorious countryside near the busy market town of Dorchester - Thomas Hardy's home for many years and the setting for his novel, "The Mayor of Casterbridge" - is this rambling, beamed old pub, with scrubbed pine tables and settles, crammed with decorative rural artefacts. Familiar pub food with daily-changing specials: rabbit or steak and onion pies, mushroom leek and courgette bake, home-cooked ham, steaks and lots of salads. Ushers Best, Ruddles County and Wadworths 6X. Wines by the glass, country wines and a large selection of malt whiskies. A pretty garden to sit in and admire the view. There is a good walk to Eggardon Hill, 827 feet high, with an Iron Age hill fort and Bronze Age barrows at the summit.

OPEN: 10.30 - 2.30 (10.30 - 3.00 Sat); 6 - 11.
Real Ale.
No children. No dogs.

BOURNEMOUTH

Goat & Tricycle   Tel: 01202 314220

27-29 West Hill Road, Bournemouth, Dorset BH2 5PF
Wadworths. Mr & Mrs D Hill, managers

Close to the town centre, and without a juke box, pub games or a dart board, this well run inn is a quiet oasis in what is a bleak area for "quiet " pubs. Two bars, big winter log fires and a welcoming host. Our reporter says a keen sense of humour is essential, though it is a joy to be insulted with such abandon and good taste by the landlord! An appealing menu of home-cooked favourites: soups, prawn and cheese garlic bread, sausages and crusty bread with fried onions, cheese on toast, club sandwiches with various fillings, fish, roast, chicken curry, "all day breakfasts," daily specials and "school" puds: jam roly-poly, treacle pudding and bread & butter pudding. Wadworths ales, six guest bitters and Gales local fruit wines. Seats in an enclosed flowery courtyard.

OPEN: 12 - 3; 5.30 - 11.
Real Ale.
No dogs.

CORFE CASTLE

Fox Inn   Tel: 01929 480449

West Street, Corfe Castle, Dorset BH20 5HD
Free House. Miss A Brown & G White, licensees

Views of the castle ruins from the attractive and sheltered sunny garden, makes this old village pub particularly appealing during the summer. Cromwell destroyed the castle in 1646, and much of the stone was used to build many of the surrounding houses in the 17th century. Medieval remains have been found within the pub, and these have blended well with the changes made over the years. Traditional bar food available as well as daily specials. Gibbs Mew, Bishops Tipple, Eldridge Popes Thomas Hardy, Royal Oak, Ansells and Tetleys Bitter. Look for the old well which was found during recent restoration work inside the pub. Good walking country.

OPEN: 11 - 3; 6 - 11 (11 - 2.30; 6.30 - 11 winter).
Real Ale.
No children. Dogs on leads.

MILTON ABBAS

Hambro Arms   Tel: 01258 880233

Milton Abbas, Nr Blandford Forum, Dorset DT11 0BP
Greenalls. Ken & Brenda Baines, tenants

===

The new Milton Abbas, with its white thatched cottages, was built in the 1770s, replacing the earlier village, which was destroyed by the Earl of Dorchester as he felt it spoilt the view from his mansion. The "new" village is quite idyllic. In the summer you can sit in front of the Hambro Arms, and admire its charming 18th century buildings. In winter, tuck yourself beside the blazing log fires. Standard bar snacks, and a selection of hot dishes plus the daily specials on the blackboard. There is an evening carvery, Tuesday to Saturday, and also Sunday lunchtime. Boddingtons and Flowers Original ales. Seats outside on the terrace.

OPEN: 11 - 2.30; 6.30 - 11.
Real Ale.
No children. No dogs.

PLUSH

Brace of Pheasants   Tel: 01300 348357

Plush, Dorchester, Dorset DT2 7RQ
Free House. Jane & Geoffrey Knights, licensees

===

Over 60 years ago, an attractive group of 16th century thatched buildings were combined to create the Brace of Pheasants, which is set in a peaceful hamlet in the Piddle Valley, not far from Piddletrenthide, with its own bubbling brook. A brace of stuffed pheasants welcomes you into the pub, where their cousins feature on the menu (when in season). Inside, all is as it should be; beamed, traditionally furnished, and with big log fires in winter. Good popular bar food with imaginative "extras": hot crab savoury, patés, soft herring roes with garlic butter, steak & kidney pies and fish pies. Evening menus go up a gear. Children's menu. Both the restaurant and family room are non-smoking. Smiles Best,

Flowers Original, Wadworths 6X and between two and four guest ales always available. Seats, and a children's play area in the garden. Lovely walks.

OPEN: 11.30 - 2.30 (12 - 2.30 winter); 7 - 11.
Real Ale. Restaurant.
Children in family room. Dogs on leads.

SEMLEY

Benett Arms	Tel: 01747 830221

Semley, Shaftesbury, Dorset SP7 9AS
Gibbs Mew. Joe Duthie, tenant

You can't miss the Benett Arms when you come into Semley village on the Wiltshire/Dorset border; it's three storeys high - unusual for this part of the country - and opposite the village green. Just one bar, pleasantly furnished with a good fire in winter. Bar food includes the well tried favourites: soups, ploughmans and various sandwiches, plus omelettes, Wiltshire ham served with either salad or chips, scampi royale, trout, Greek salad, grills, occasionally bouillabaisse: also interesting daily specials from the blackboard. Home-made puddings. Gibbs Mew ales: Salisbury Best, Deacon and Bishops Tipple. Good extensive wine list. Inch's ciders. Seats in the small garden.

OPEN: 11 - 3; 6 - 11.
Real Ale.
Children in upper bar. Dogs on leads.

SHAFTESBURY

Ship Inn	Tel: 01747 853219

Bleke Street, Shaftesbury, Dorset SP7 8JZ
Badger. Steve Marshall & Pam Tait, tenants

The town of "Shaston" in Thomas Hardy's novels was modelled on the historic town of Shaftesbury. Built on the edge of a 700ft high plateau, the cottages lining the extraordinarily steep, cobbled Gold Hill, feature in many tourist brochures and advertisements. The town has some very handsome buildings, including the 17th century Ship Inn, which has an interesting, simply furnished, panelled interior reflecting its age. Bar food includes the pub stalwarts: home-made soup, sandwiches, paté, lasagne and daily specials which sometimes lean towards the continental. Badger Best and Tanglefoot ales. Farm ciders. The Ship has an indoor boules pitch and there are seats outside on the terrace.

OPEN: 11 - 3; 5 - 11 (all day Thurs - Sat).
Real Ale. Children in eating areas. Dogs on leads.

SHAVE CROSS

Shave Cross Inn   Tel: 01308 868358

Marshwood Vale, Shave Cross, Dorset DT6 6HW
Free House. Bill & Ruth Slade, licensees

A 14th century hairdresser set up here so that pilgrims wending their way to the shrine at Whitchurch could have a trim before arriving. If you feel so inclined, you can still walk the route (without the haircut). The path is opposite the pub. The pub is typical of the era, with beams, flagstoned floors, inglenook fireplaces and traditional furnishings. Bar menu varies from snacks to hot dishes. There's a children's menu and play area. Bass, Badger Best and Eldridge Pope Royal Oak. Sunny, sheltered garden.

OPEN: 12 - 2.30 (12 - 3 Sat); 7 - 11.
Real Ale. Closed Mon except Bank Holiday.
Children in lounge. Dogs in garden only.

ESSEX

BLACKMORE

Bull   Tel: 01277 821208

Church Street, Blackmore, Nr Ingatestone, Essex CM4 0RN
Pubmaster. John Faulkner, tenant

Built around 1387, this old pub has the heavily beamed bars and uneven floors so typical of a 14th century building, plus, so rumour has it, two resident ghosts. Known for its imaginative, well presented food, its blackboard menu changes weekly. You choose from either a snack menu, an à la carte or the specialist board. Fresh fish daily, home-made pies and a children's menu. Popular Sunday roasts. Greene King IPA, Tetleys, Burton Ales. Extensive wine list. There is a large garden with a children's play area.

Open: 11.30 - 2.30; 6.30 - 11.
Real Ale. Extensive wine list.
Children welcome. No dogs.

DEDHAM

Marlborough Head Hotel   Tel: 01206 323250

Mill Lane, Dedham, Essex CO7 6DH
Ind Coope (Allied). Brian & Jackie Wills, licensees

One of the finest buildings in what is an attractive and busy village. The Marlborough Head was first licensed in 1704. This large, handsome, well beamed, friendly and comfortable pub has plenty of room for diners, and anyone taking morning coffee or afternoon tea. However it can get very busy, so arrive early if you want a table for lunch. Bar food includes soup, sandwiches, baked garlic mushrooms, quiches, savoury pancakes, cold smoked duckling, half a pheasant in wine and mushroom sauce, home-made puddings. Ind Coope, Burton and Worthingtons under light blanket pressure. There is a large car park at the back of the pub. Because of the Constable connection, this village gets very crowded during the summer, and parking can be difficult. Alfred Munning's house, and a collection of his paintings can be seen at Castle House museum nearby.

Open: 10 - 11.
Real Ale.
Children in family room only. No dogs. Bedrooms.

EARLS COLNE

Bird in Hand   Tel: 078722 2557

Coggeshall Road, Earls Colne, Colchester, Essex CO6 2JX
T D Ridley & Son. Colin & Lesley Eldred, lessees

Mid-way between the villages of Earls Colne and Coggeshall, (an old wool village noted for its fine merchant's houses), and opposite the airfield used by the U.S. Air Force from 1942 to 1944 (now a Golf range - what else!), the Bird in Hand, situated as it was at the end of the runway, was regarded as a potential hazard. To lower its profile, the Americans decided to remove the pub's roof before it was inadvertently re-arranged by a low-flying aircraft. Now restored to its full height, you can see the 'before and after' photographs displayed in the saloon bar. Not a "foody" pub, it has, nevertheless, a full menu of favourite dishes - all home-made. Ridleys range of ales; draught and bottled. Seats in the large garden.

Open: 12 - 2.30; 6 - 11 (7 - 10.30 Sunday).
Real Ale.
No children under 14. Dogs perhaps.

GOSFIELD

Green Man   Tel: 01787 472746

The Street, Gosfield, Essex
Greene King. John Arnold, lease

Warm friendly service and imaginative food are the hallmarks of this pub. It has two small bars, and a no-smoking dining room. There is an exceptional lunchtime cold table, with a wonderful choice of cold meats, salmon or crab, game pies, salads, etc. The landlord is the whiz with the carving knife. Home-made soups, fresh fish, lamb chops (done pink), roast wild boar, pheasant in red wine, roast duck and home-made puddings. Good, reasonably priced wine list. Greene King IPA and Abbot on hand pump.

Open: 11 - 3; 6.30 - 11 (late supper licence).
Real Ale. Restaurant (no food and no restaurant Sun eves).
Well behaved children in eating area.
Dogs if very restrained.

HORNDEN ON THE HILL

Bell Inn   Tel: 01375 673154

High Road, Hornden on the Hill, Essex SS17 8LD
Free House. John Vereker, licensee

An attractive 15th century coaching inn with a magnificent display of hanging baskets and flowers in the summer. The Bell has been run by the same family for over 50 years; when Mr and Mrs Thompson took over the pub in November 1938 they had no electricity and the pump in the courtyard was the only source of water. Much has changed since then. Now their daughter and her husband run the pub, adding the nearby Hill House which they manage as an attractive hotel. There's only one bar in The Bell and a restaurant offering a wide choice of food and drink. Both the bar and the restaurant can be busy, so arrive early to be sure of a table. Nothing frozen here - even the vegetables are home-grown. Choice of interesting soups, such as broccoli or mussels with saffron and vegetables. Rabbit and bacon terrine, grilled salmon with mussels and chives and smoked chicken and vegetable strudel are just a few dishes from the changing menu. Home-made puddings as well. Good selection of wines, many by the glass or half bottle. The landlord has produced notes on what to drink with what, and you are also able to buy wine from him. Bass, Charrington IPA and Fullers ales on hand pump, and a weekly changing guest beer.

Open: 11 - 2.30 (3 Sat); 6 - 11.
Real Ale. Restaurant.
Children in eating area. No dogs.

INGATESTONE

| **Cricketers** | Tel: 01277 352400 |

Mill Green, Ingatestone, Essex CM4 0DS
Gray & Sons. Mrs E Marriage, tenant

An interesting old building among the mix of Tudor, Georgian and Victorian houses in this attractive village. The pub overlooks Mill Green Common, where they once played cricket, and no doubt after the match, refreshed themselves in the bar. There is talk of using the green once more for its original purpose. Two bars, one of which is used as a restaurant. Bar snacks include: jacket potatoes, filled baguettes, ploughmans, also fresh fish, steaks and daily specials. Greene King IPA and Abbot. A good choice of wines. Seats on the terrace overlooking the cricket green, and in the garden at the back of the pub.

OPEN: 12 - 3; 6 - 11.
Real Ale. No food Sun eves.
Children welcome. Dogs on leads.

LEIGH-ON-SEA

Crooked Billet   Tel: 01702 714854

51 High Street, Leigh-on-Sea, Essex SS9 2EP
Ind Coope (Allied). Andrew & Marie Heron, managers

Dating back to the 16th century, in what might be called a bracing position against the sea wall. Tudor beams and plasterwork were found when restoration work was carried out, and it is thought the pub was originally a farmhouse. From the lounge bar you can sit and look out to sea, warmed by a solid fuel stove. During the winter there is a choice of over 12 different beers from the barrel, reducing to six in the summer. Bar food consists of filled rolls, ploughmans and a good selection of fish dishes. There is a big terrace where pretty hanging baskets and window boxes are a feature during the summer, and from where you have a view of the working harbour.

Open: 11 - 11. Lunchtime meal snacks only.
Real Ale. No food Sun lunchtime.
No children. Dogs on leads in evening.

MILL GREEN

Viper   Tel: 01277 352010

Mill Green, Nr Ingatestone, Essex CM4 0PS
Free House. Fred Beard, licensee

If you address a postcard quite simply to "The Viper Inn, England," you can ignore the town, county and postcode - it will reach its destination. The Viper is quite unique, probably named when there was an abundance of vipers (adders) on the local common land. A 14th century listed building, in an enchanting wooded setting, with a pretty flowery garden. It has four bars, two with carpets, two parquet (for those still in their walking boots). The food is simple bar food of the fill-a-gap variety, not sit down meals. There is a monthly changing choice of three ales from the smaller, less well known breweries. Seats outside in the attractive garden.

Open: 11 - 2.30 (3 Sat); 6 - 11.
Real Ale. Lunchtime snacks.
Dogs on leads.

NORTH FAMBRIDGE

Ferry Boat   Tel: 01621 740208

North Fambridge, Essex CM3 6LR
Free House. William Boyce & Roy Maltwood, licensees

A very traditional, timber-clad, 500 year old Essex pub, situated by the River Crouch - a favoured sailing river, muddy but popular if you are inclined towards this damp energetic sport. Appealing interior with settles and benches on a tiled floor and nautical mementos hanging about. There is a dining conservatory for families. A varied selection of food: a lot of fish, sandwiches, soups, ham and eggs - all the vegetables are fresh. Roasts on Sundays. Flowers IPA and two guests on hand pump. Wine by the glass.

Open: 11 - 3; 6 - 11 (7 - 11 Winter).
Real Ale. Restaurant.
Children in Conservatory. Dogs on leads.

PELDON

The Peldon Rose   Tel: 01206 735248

Mersea Road, Colchester, Essex CO5 7QJ
Free House. Alan & Ariette Everett, licensees

Aptly named with its rose-pink walls, this mainly 14th century rambling country pub has two heavily beamed bars, and a big no-smoking dining conservatory which is only opened at the weekend. Lots of tables in the bars, but the pub can get very busy. Seats in the garden during the summer. Sandwiches, salads, lasagne, boeuf bourgignon, Sunday roasts and fish when available. Daily cream teas in the summer, and at weekends during the winter. Boddingtons, Flowers Original and IPA, perhaps one guest on hand pump. Choice of wines.

Open: 11 - 2.30; 5.30 - 11.
Real Ale. Restaurant only Fri & Sat eves.
Children welcome away from bar. Dogs on leads.

PLESHEY

White Horse   Tel: 01245 237281

Pleshey, Chelmsford, Essex CM3 1HA
Free House. John & Helen Thorburn, licensees

A mile long rampart, built in Norman times, encircles the village of Pleshey, protecting it from the marauding natives. The pub itself dates back to the late 15th century; original timbers and floors can still be seen in the present bar. Plenty of room to spread out, and seats on the terrace and in the garden during the summer. Extensive bar food and a full à la carte menu is provided in the restaurant. The pub also holds speciality months - during which they will offer varying menus from different countries. You will need to telephone for details. A range of beers is available, selected from the best of British brewing. Boddingtons, Jennings, Nethergate Best and Tolly Original on hand pump. There is an extensive wine list from various parts of the world. Also a pub ghost, a lady in blue with her cat. The cat you see in daylight is real, and belongs to the pub.

Open: 11 - 3; 7 - 11.
Real Ale. Restaurant.
Children welcome. No dogs.

SAFFRON WALDEN

Kings Arms   Tel: 01799 522768

Market Hill, Saffron Walden, Essex
Free House. Brian Banks, manager

The street plan of Saffron Walden, with its wonderful 15th and 16th timber-framed houses, dates back to the 12th century when the original market was established under the castle walls. Originally Chipping (Market) Walden, it was renamed Saffron Walden after the discovery that the profitable saffron crocus grew well in the local soil. It's a lovely old town with a market place and tree-lined High Street. Not far from the market you'll find this comfortable, friendly pub serving traditional home-cooked lunches, ploughmans, sandwiches, sausages, etc. Greene King IPA ale, Carlsberg and Kronenbourg on cask. Farm cider. Seats in the garden.

Open: 11 - 3; 5 - 11 (11 - 11 Sat).
Real Ale.
No food Sunday. Dogs on leads.

STOCK

Hoop   Tel: 01277 841137

21 High Street, Ingatestone, Essex
Free House. Albert Kitchin, licensee

Food is available all day in this 450 year old pub and they offer, on average, 500 different ales over the year: some on hand pump, some straight from the cask. They provide a good selection of dishes, with the emphasis on fish: grilled monkfish or skate, swordfish, trout florentine with dill sauce, paella. The all day menu is simpler: soups, omelettes, hotpot. The range of ales, including some from the tiny independent breweries, is so extensive it is best to go and see what's on offer. There is a beer festival on May 1st each year at which you have a choice of 150 ales. Farm cider, wines by the glass, mulled wine in winter. Seats outside in the pretty garden.

Open: 11 - 11.
Real Ale. Meals & snacks all day.
Children in eating area. Dogs on leads.

TILLINGHAM

Cap & Feathers   Tel: 01621 779212

8 South Street, Tillingham, Nr Southminster, Essex CM0 7TH
Crouch Vale. John Moore, tenant

A traditional, old-fashioned 15th century pub. Clapboard and tiles - so familiar in the eastern counties of England. Cosy, low-beamed timber rooms have a timeless quality which encourages you to linger and appreciate all that's on offer. There is a no-smoking family room, and an area with an old bar billiards table that takes one old shilling to operate (we remember those well). Bar food changes daily. The pub smokes its own food so there could be smoked beef or trout, also beef and venison pies, soups, lasagne and home-made puddings. Crouch Vale Woodham IPA, Best Bitter, SAS, Willie Warmer in winter and a guest beer. Farm cider and English wines.

Open: 11.30 - 3; 6 - 11.
Real Ale.
Children in No-Smoking family room.
Dogs on leads. Bedrooms.

WIDDINGTON

Fleur de Lys   Tel: 01799 540659

High Street, Widdington, Saffron Walden, Essex CB11 3SG
Free House. Richard Alder, licensee

Percy the Peacock has given this pub his vote of approval. A resident of the local wildfowl park, he decided that village life was more congenial. A born escapee, he has been returned several times but prefers the village to wander in for the odd snack, and the pub tree as his des.res. Only one bar in the pub and a no-smoking family room. The emphasis here is on the food, but there is always a good choice of beer on offer. Generous sandwiches, home-made soups, garlic mushrooms. Curries are a favourite. Choice of fish, venison and local game, vegetarian dishes and home-made puds. On Sunday there is always a roast and occasionally fresh fish. Adnams, Bass, Courage Directors, Timothy Taylors, Wadworths IPA and Whitbread Castle Eden ales. There are seats on a lawn at the side of the pub.

Open: 12 - 3; 6 - 11.
Real Ale. Restaurant, not Sun evening.
Children in Restaurant & No-smoking family room.
Dogs on leads.
Folk music Fri evening.

WOODFORD GREEN

Travellers Friend   Tel: 0181 5042435

496/498 High Road, Woodford Green, Essex IG8 0PN
Free House. M J Morris, licensee

Just by looking at the address you can surmise that two houses have been made one, presumably when first licensed in 1832. If you happen to go upstairs you can see the join. An interesting feature of the partially panelled, main bar are its interesting "snob screens" - opaque glass screens, a foot square, which rotate to form a solid barrier for customers who want to conduct private business with each other without being overheard or their lips being read by anyone else. Traditional English lunchtime menu. A choice of sandwiches, lasagne, chicken curry, a roast and various salads. Ridleys IPA, Courage Directors and Best. Westons draught cider and two guest beers.

OPEN: 11 - 11 Mon - Sat. (12 - 3; 7 - 10.30) Sun.
Real Ale. No food evenings or Sunday.
Children welcome. Dogs on leads.
Al Fresco Jazz band twice yearly.

GLOUCESTERSHIRE

ALDERTON

Gardeners Arms   Tel: 01242 620257

Alderton, Tewkesbury, Glos
Free House. J Terry, licensee

Six miles east of Tewkesbury, in a village well off the beaten track, you'll find this 16th century, black and white thatched pub to whose door someone has clearly beaten a path, as it is consistently fully booked for lunch on Sundays. This isn't surprising as it is renowned for its imaginative, well chosen food and well kept ales. Recently enlarged and refurbished, the Gardeners Arms is as relaxed and welcoming as ever. Bar food is served at lunchtime only: soup, ploughmans, paté - always a wide choice of dishes - all of generous proportions. Juicy home-cooked ham seems to be popular; also the blackcurrant sorbet with brandy snaps. In the evening there is an à la carte restaurant, when you'll find the menu shifts up a gear. Set roast on Sunday, usually two sittings - book well in advance. Theakstons, McEwans and Wadworths 6X. Seats in the small garden.

OPEN: Mon - Thu: 11 - 2; 6.30 - 11. Fri - Sat: 11 - 2.30; 6.30 - 11.
Sun: 12 - 3; 7 - 10.30.
Real Ale. Only a roast lunch Sun.
Children welcome. Dogs in bar lunchtime only.

AMBERLEY

Black Horse
Tel: 01453 872556

Littleworth, Amberley, Stroud, GL5 5AL
Free House. Patrick O'Flynn, licensee

Facing West with wonderful views of the surrounding countryside, including Minchinhampton Common which is owned and managed by The National Trust, the Black Horse is a friendly local pub - local in the true sense of the word as it is communally owned. One bar, one no-smoking family room and a new conservatory. Familiar satisfying pub food: soup, ploughmans, sandwiches, steak and kidney pie, chicken dishes and salads. Archers Best, Tetleys, Fullers London Pride and other guest beers. Seating on the terrace and in the pretty garden.

OPEN: 12 - 3; 6 - 11.
Real Ale.
Children welcome. Dogs on leads.

APPERLEY

Coalhouse Inn
Tel: 01452 780211

Apperley, Glos GL19 4DN
Free House. Mr & Mrs McDonald, licensees

The Coalhouse is situated amid green fields at Coalhouse Wharf, on an isolated stretch of the River Severn between Tewkesbury and Gloucester. In summer you can sit out on the grassy bank by the river. In winter, when the Coalhouse is cut off by floods, you hail a passing boat - in some winters the river overflows into the bar! Informal, welcoming, with a buzz of conversation, it offers a traditional pub menu of well cooked and well presented food. The local Floodwater Bitter is a favourite, other ales include Eldridge Popes Royal Oak Strong Ale, Wadworths 6X, Guinness and various draught lagers. Draught cider.

OPEN: 12 - 2.30; 7 - 11 (6 - 11 summer).
Real Ale. Children welcome. Dogs on leads.

ASHLEWORTH QUAY

Boat Inn   Tel: 01452 700272

Ashleworth Quay, Glos GL19 4HZ
Free House. Irene Jelf & Jaqui Nicholls, licensees

Run by the Jelf family for hundreds of years, this small 15th century pub on the banks of the river Severn offers the sort of welcome you would expect from a pub with centuries of experience serving the traveller. It has two, timeless, simply furnished rooms and a small back tap room with a couple of settles and the casks of ales. Filled rolls and ploughmans for lunch served with home-made chutney. Beers include Exmoor Gold, Arkell BBB Oakhill Bitter and a guest ale. Westons Farm cider. Seats in the flowery sunny courtyard.

OPEN: 11 - 3; 6 - 11 (11 - 2.30; 7 - 11 winter).
Real Ale. Lunchtime snacks.
Children welcome. Dogs on leads.

BISLEY

Bear Inn   Tel: 01452 770265

George Street, Bisley, Glos GL6 7BD
Pubmaster. N S Evans, tenant

An extra accolade here, as the licensees have ripped out the piped music - so all is as it should be in this lovely 16th century inn. Architecturally it is very attractive, with a colonnaded front supporting the upper storey, under which is a small flagstoned sitting area; it also has seats in the garden. Tremendous efforts are being made on the food front. Using fresh local produce, the menus change daily: perhaps asparagus, mussels and prawn parcels, marinated cod, fried potatoes with garlic and herb butter and vegetable pasties. Bubble and Squeak is served with the Roast on Monday (very Mrs Beaton). Home-made puds. Bass, Flowers Original and Tetleys on hand pump.

OPEN: 11 - 3; 6 - 11.
Real Ale. No food Sun or Mon eves.
Children in own room. Dogs on leads.

BRIMPSFIELD

Golden Heart   Tel: 01242 870261

Nettleton Bottom, Birdlip, Glos GL4 8LA
Free House. Catherine Stevens, licensee

There are four small bars in this well-beamed 16th century country pub; two of the three are no-smoking and the other is a children's room. Each of the four bars has a blackboard menu - dishes vary from well-filled sandwiches, stuffed pancakes, fresh fish, steak & kidney pie to a variety of salads. Outside there are seats on a sunny terrace, where the local hens and geese will gather up the crumbs - and no, they are not on tomorrow's menu! Hook Norton, Ruddles and Worthington permanently on hand pump. Guest barrels behind the bar are changing all the time. Scrumpy and wine by the glass.

OPEN: 12 - 2.30; 6 - 11.
Real Ale.
Children welcome. Dogs on leads.

BROAD CAMPDEN

Bakers Arms   Tel: 01386 840515

Broad Campden, Nr Chipping Campden, Glos GL55 6UR
Free House. Carolyn Perry, licensee

Popular with walkers following the Heart of England Way. It has big log fires in the beamed bar during the winter, seats outside on the terrace in summer. Reasonably priced bar food: soups, smoked haddock bake, ploughmans, a very popular pork chops in cider and a meat loaf are among the dishes on the menu. Fruit crumbles, steamed puddings and other favourites for afters. Ales change all the time, but five usually on hand pump, mainly from small independent breweries such as: Stanway, Morlands, Hook Norton and lots more. Folk music nights the 3rd Tuesday of every month. And there are occasional hot-air balloon meetings at the pub.

OPEN: 12 - 3; 7 - 10.30.
Real Ale.
Children welcome. No dogs.
Folk night 3rd Tues in month.

BROCKWEIR

Brockweir Inn   Tel: 01291 689548

Nr Chepstow, Gwent NP6 7NG
Free House. George & Elizabeth Jones, licensees

This pub is close to the Welsh border and is a favourite with energetic people tramping the path by Offa's Dyke. The Dyke runs from Prestatyn at its north end, to Chepstow in the south, and this defensive earthwork is thought to have been constructed by the Mercian King Offa in the 8th century. The 16th century Brockweir offers a welcome respite from the onward march. Traditional bar snacks and more substantial dishes always available. Freeminer Bitter, brewed not far away in the Forest of Dean (Freeminer supply the House of Commons), Hook Norton Best and a changing guest on hand pump. The ales are beautifully kept; Mr Jones, a retired chemist, is very proud of his beers.

OPEN: 12 - 2.30 (3 Sat); 6 - 11.
Real Ale.
Children in family room.
Dogs on leads. Bedrooms.

CHEDWORTH

Seven Tuns
Tel: 01285 720242

Chedworth, Cheltenham, Glos GL54 4AE
Free House. Barbara & Brian Eacott, licensees

Nearer to Cirencester and North Leach than Cheltenham, this is a typically attractive 17th century Cotswold pub, very popular during the summer in the walking season. In winter there will be a big log fire in the lounge bar, where you can sit and relax. All the noisy fruit machines, video games, pool table, etc are in a separate room beyond the public bar. In the evening there is a full à la carte menu in the lounge bar; a bar menu popular with walkers (and many others) is available the rest of the time. George's Traditional Bristol Bitter and Old Ambrose Bitter are brewed especially for the Seven Tuns by a small Bristol Brewery; John Smiths and Courage Best are on draught. Plenty of tables outside.

OPEN: 12 - 2.30; 6.30 - 11. (Sats: 11.30 - 3; 6.30 - 11.) Closed Mon lunchtimes.
Real Ale.
Children & Dogs in bottom bar only.

CHIPPING CAMPDEN

Kings Arms Hotel
Tel: 01386 840256

High Street, Chipping Campden, Glos GL55 6AW
Free House. Stan Earnshaw, licensee

You are not far away from the theatrical delights at Stratford-on-Avon in this charming, small, 16th century hotel overlooking the market square of this attractive Cotswold Village. The Kings Arms, with its log fires, fresh flowers and candlelit dining room, caters for those who want to dine either before or after a performance. Very popular bar food is available in the Saddle Room at lunchtime: soups, vegetarian dishes, country paté, hot game pie and various salads are among the dishes on offer. No real ales, but a very good wine list; over 10 by the glass. Seats outside in the extremely pretty garden. Near Stratford-on-Avon, and the gardens at Hidcote and Kiftsgate.

OPEN: 11 - 11. (Food served 12 - 3; 6 - 9.30; all day summer.)
Restaurant.
Children welcome. Dogs on leads. Water for the dog.
14 bedrooms.

CLEARWELL

Wyndham Arms   Tel: 01594 833666

Clearwell, Nr Coleford, Glos GL16 8JT
Free House. John & Rosemary Stanford, licensees

In the centre of the village of Clearwell, in a valley on the edge of the Forest of Dean, the 600 year old Wyndham Arms continues to do what it has been doing for centuries: looking after the traveller in the best way possible. In the comfortable beamed bar there is an excellent choice of food: mussels crustade, chicken liver paté, open sandwiches, chef's specials, hot seafood platter, beef mignon, pork tenderloin "cordon bleu"; most of the vegetables, fruit and herbs home-grown. The 18 dish hors d'oeuvre trolley is very popular. All food is cooked to order, so expect a little delay. Seats outside on the terrace during the summer. If you are lucky enough to be staying here, and off exploring the countryside, the Wyndham Arms can provide you with a well packed hamper. Bass and Hook Norton on hand pump. Excellent choice of malt whiskies and a good wine list. Some wines by the glass.

OPEN: 11 - 11.
Real Ale. Restaurant.
Children welcome. Dogs on leads. Bedrooms.

COLN ST ALDWYNS

New Inn   Tel: 01285 750651

Coln St Aldwyns, Nr Cirencester, Glos GL7 5AN
Free House. Brian Evans, licensee

Flower baskets and ivy covered walls make this 16th century
Cotswold village pub look very attractive. It has a classy
restaurant with a chef to match who's aiming high. Menus thought
out daily could include: pheasant and lentil terrine, steak & kidney
in ale, braised oxtail served with red cabbage. Bar food is of the
sandwiches, ploughmans and filled baguettes variety, and there is
a selection of puddings. In the evening there is the choice of
either a table d'hôte or an à la carte menu. Hook Norton and
Wadworths 6X ales and other guest beers on hand pump. Seats
outside in the garden. Summer barbecues.

OPEN: 11 - 2.30; 5.30 - 11 (11 - 11 Summer Sats).
Real Ale. Restaurant.
Children in eating area. Dogs on leads.
Bedrooms.

CORSE LAWN

Corse Lawn Hotel   Tel: 01452 780479

Corse Lawn, Glos GL19 4LZ (nr Tewkesbury & in fact in Worcs!)
Free House. Denis Hein, licensee

As the name implies, this is not a pub but the bar of an utterly
relaxed and welcoming hotel. Corse Lawn House, now an elegant
country house hotel, was originally a Tudor inn which burnt down
early in the 18th century and was rebuilt in 1745 in the Queen Ann
style as a coaching inn. An interesting feature is the old "coach
wash" at the front of the hotel which has been retained as an
unusual ornamental pond. The proprietor is French, the staff
English, and the atmosphere Franglais. Food from the bar/bistro
could include: sandwiches, omelettes, Mediterranean fish soup,

gallantine of duckling with orange chutney, cassoulet with chicken breasts, garlic sausage and haricot beans, shoulder of lamb provençal, jugged venison with port and mixed herbs and good puddings. Flowers Ale and John Smiths Yorkshire Bitter. Hein cognac and over 300 wines. Monsieur Hein is somewhat larger than life and when consulted about his inclusion in THE QUIET PINT said "No, it is not quiet here because of the noisy proprietor." Corse Lawn is off the beaten track and takes its name from the wide mile-long green either side of the road.

OPEN: 11 - 3; 6 - 11.
Real Ale.
Children welcome. Dogs on leads.
Bedrooms.

DURSLEY

Old Spot Inn   Tel: 01453 542870

Hill Road, Dursley, Glos
Free House. Ric Sainty, licensee

When Ric and El (short for Elena) Sainty took over The Old Spot - built in 1776 and a school throughout the last century - they were urged by some patrons "to give them a bit of music". The furthest they ever got was an occasional evening of live folk music. "Now," says El, "we're hallowed ground!" Such a very friendly welcoming pub makes The Old Spot a compulsory stop on any journey through Dursley. Don't expect gourmet food, though. All you will get are sandwiches of rare beef and home-cooked ham. Well kept local Uley brewery ales, including Old Ric - named after the landlord - are made with Uley's own spring water. Other beers include Hog's Head Bitter, Old Spot Prize Ale, Pig's Ear Strong Beer and Pigor Mortice, which they brew for Christmas. Guest ales too. The pub has its own boules pitch, and a small garden.

OPEN: 11 - 11. Sun: 12 - 3; 7 - 10.30.
Real Ale.
Children at landlord's discretion. Dogs on leads.

EBRINGTON

Ebrington Arms   Tel: 01386 593223

Ebrington, Nr Chipping Campden, Glos GL55 6NH
Free House. Gareth Richards & Andrew Geddes, licensees

Obviously no music, but no machines either. Only the TV goes on
for the Five Nations Rugby Match. There is also an enthusiasm
for dominoes. The local since 1764, it has one beamed,
flagstoned bar with an inglenook fireplace and an adjoining dining
room. The menu is written on the beams of the bar and it can take
you some time to read it all. Traditional bar food: sandwiches,
sirloin steak baguette, eggs and chips, omelettes, steak & kidney
pies and steaks. Hook Norton Best, Donnington SBA and guest
beers on hand pump. Farm cider. Seats outside on the sheltered
terrace.

OPEN: 11 - 2.30; 5.30 - 11 (11 - 11 summer Sats).
Real Ale. Restaurant.
Children in eating area. No dogs.

GUITING POWER

Ye Olde Inne   Tel: 01451 850392

Winchcombe Road, Guiting Power, Nr Stow-on-the-Wold, Glos
GL54 5UY
Free House. Bill & Julia Tu, licensees

At the far end of the village, Ye Olde Inne has been freshened up
with a facelift by its licensees. It's a 17th century stone building
with three small beamed rooms. The main bar has a big log fire,
the public bar has the darts board and there's a dining room -
although you can eat anywhere you can find a table. Usual bar
food: soups, chilli, steak & kidney pies, also pigeons in red wine,
curried nut roast and some exciting Burmese and Thai dishes,
introduced by the landlord. Seats in the garden with views over

the surrounding countryside. Hook Norton and Theakstons Best, plus guest beers on hand pump. Several malt whiskies.

OPEN: 11.30 - 3; 5.30 - 11 (11.30 - 2.30; 6 - 11 winter).
Real Ale. Restaurant.
Children in eating area and restaurant.
Dogs in public bar only.

KINGSCOTE

Hunters Hall   Tel: 01453 860393

Kingscote, Tetbury, Glos GL8 8XZ
Free House. David Barnett-Roberts, licensee

First licensed in the 14th century, this eye-catching, creeper covered inn, is a popular local. It has a back room with pool, darts and a jukebox; also a no-smoking family gallery above the bars. The garden is planned for children. Bar food changes daily; there will be a cold buffet in the dining room at lunchtime and other dishes which range from lamb casserole with red wine, trout with almonds, sweet and sour pork to home-made puds. A restaurant menu features in the evening. Bass, Hook Norton, Wadworths 6X and Uley Old Spot on hand pump. Wines by the glass, and a selection of malt whiskies.

OPEN: 11 - 3.30; 6 - 11.
Real Ale. Restaurant (No Sandwiches Sun).
Children welcome. Dogs on leads.

LECHLADE

Trout Inn   Tel: 01367 252313

Lechlade on Thames, Glos GL7 3HA
Courage. Bob & Penny Warren, lease

A lovely place to stop if you are walking the Thames Footpath. Lechlade is an attractive village with a number of handsome

Georgian buildings, and it is where the Leach and Coln rivers join the young Thames. The Trout, which dates back to the 13th century, has been considerably re-built since then, but inside there are pleasant, low-beamed bars, one of which is over 350 years old, and the other a mere stripling of 100, and usually, there is an outside bar functioning during the summer. In the restaurant the menu is dependable - as dependable as the popular bar food: home-made soups, paté, salmon, steaks and locally produced sausages, daily specials and home-made puds. The pub does get very busy. There is a no-smoking area in the restaurant. Wadworths 6X, John Smiths Yorkshire and Courage Best ales. They have their own boules pitch. On a warm day you can either sit in the big garden, or by the side of the river, to watch the water flow by.

OPEN: 10 - 3; 6 - 11 (all day Sats summer).
Real Ale. Restaurant.
Children in eating area of bar.
Dogs on lead (not in dining or children's room).
Live Jazz Tues & Sun eves.

LOWER ODDINGTON

Fox Inn   Tel: 01451 870888

Lower Oddington, Nr Stow-on-the-Wold, Glos
Free House. Nick & Victoria Elliot, licensees

Lower Oddington is a rather grand village, with more houses of manor-house size than usual, although the modest frontage of The Fox does not bring it into that category. When redecorated a few years ago, any "popular modern" features were eliminated. The main area has flagstone floors, big wooden tables and a large open fireplace; plenty of room for all the dogs, children and clients. Other rooms sort of ramble off. Specials are on the blackboard, otherwise there is a good selection of well-chosen bar food with bistro leanings from the handwritten menu: French bread sandwiches, Arbroath Smokies gratinée, egg mayonnaise and anchovies, timbal of smoked salmon, roast rack of lamb with caper sauce, chicken breast wrapped in bacon with garlic cream sauce, boeuf bourgignon and dauphinoise potatoes. The Fox's banana ice cream and toffee sauce or "chocolate challenge" to finish. There are roasts on Sundays. Hook Norton, Shepherd Neames Spitfire and Marstons Pedigree on hand pump. As the proprietor is a wine merchant, wines are interesting, reasonably priced and extensive - some by the glass. Wonderful large walled garden. There is a 12th century church in the village with some interesting wall paintings - well worth a visit.

OPEN: 12 - 3; 6 - 11.
Real Ale.
Children in eating area. Dogs on leads.

NAILSWORTH

Weighbridge Inn   Tel: 01453 832520

The Longfords, Nailsworth, Minchinghamton GL6 9AL
Free House. Janina Kulesza, licensee

The building dates back to 1220 but they have had the builders in since then, so that there are now three, traditionally furnished rooms housing an interesting collection of country artefacts. No restaurant food, just good pub grub. Two-in-one pie is a speciality of the house: half steak and mushroom and half cauliflower cheese with a short pastry crust; also steak & mushroom pie, Turkish sweetcorn and pepper pie, vegetable and lentil crumble, pizzas and puddings. The ales change frequently but there could be Marstons Pedigree, John Smiths and Courage Best. Other guest beers too. A good number of wines by the glass or bottle. Seats outside in the sheltered garden.

OPEN: 11 - 2.30; 7 - 11 (6.30 - 11 Sat).
Real Ale.
Children in rooms away from bar. Dogs on leads.

NEWLAND

Ostrich
Tel: 01594 833260

Newland, Nr Coleford, Glos GL16 8NP
Free House. Richard & Veronica Dewe, licensees

Charming, 16th century pub in a little village between the Wye Valley and the Forest of Dean. One low-beamed bar with big winter log fires. Popular with walkers, but very muddy boots off at the door. Bar menu at lunchtime only - all home-cooked, ranging from wild boar, venison, pheasant, moules marinière, lovely soups and home-baked bread. In the evening there are over 25 dishes to choose from. Usually eight different ales on hand pump. There is also a German keg lager and farm ciders.

OPEN: 12 - 2.30 (3 Sat); 6.30 - 11.
Real Ale.
Children in dining room only. Dogs on leads. Bedrooms.

OAKRIDGE LYNCH

Butchers Arms
Tel: 01285 760371

Oakridge Lynch, Nr Stroud, Glos GL6 7NZ
Free House. Peter & Brian Coupe, licensees

East of Stroud on the Eastcombe Bisley road, along high-sided lush Gloucestershire lanes, it is well worth hunting out the Butchers Arms so you can enjoy the varied choice from both the bar menu and the barrels of beer. Traditional choice of lunchtime food: sandwiches, ploughmans, plus cauliflower cheese, beef and ale pie and omelettes. During the evening meals are served in the restaurant only. Archers Best, Butcombe Bitter and Ruddles County are among the ales kept. Plenty of room to park and there are seats in the garden from where you can enjoy views over the village to the valley below.

OPEN: 12 - 3; 6 - 11.
Real Ale. Restaurant Wed - Sat eves, Sun lunch.
Children in anteroom only. Dogs on leads.

REDBROOK

Boat Inn   Tel: 01600 712615

Lone Lane, Penalt, Monmouth, Gwent, S Wales
Free House. Steffan & Dawn Rowlands, licensees

Worth searching out for its amazing situation, perched on the
bank of the River Wye; clinging on would be more to the point.
Strictly speaking the Boat is in Wales - via a footbridge across the
Wye from its Gloucestershire car park. It is very popular with our
energetic friends, so walking boots and hairy socks are the norm.
You will find a genial bar, good, familiar bar food including the
house dish of Panhaggerty (cheese, potato, onion and garlic)
which they have been serving for years. There is a garden, (and
from what I remember, parts of that are perpendicular), from
where you can watch the river. Up to ten ales from casks behind
the counter: Bass, Boddingtons, Fullers London Pride,
Theakstons Old Peculiar among them, but they change all the
time.

OPEN: 11 - 3; 6 - 11 (11 - 11 Sat).
Real Ale.
Children welcome. Dogs on leads.
Folk music Tues eve. Jazz Thurs eve.

SAPPERTON

Bell Inn   Tel: 01285 7602998

Sapperton, Cirencester, Glos GL7 6LE
Free House. Gordon & Violet Wells, licensees

On the side of a ridge facing the beech woods along the Frome
River valley, Sapperton is popular with both walkers and canal

enthusiasts. The two-and-a-half-mile Sapperton Tunnel was cut through the hill in 1789 to link the Thames and the Severn rivers. The eastern entrance is now restored and is well worth a visit. After the walk or the sightseeing, head for the bars of the Bell Inn. Good value bar food: soups, sandwiches, local Gloucester sausages, and grilled gammon steaks. Tables at the front of the pub. Flowers and Whitbreads West Country PA ales and others, all on hand pump.

OPEN: 11 - 2.30; 6 - 11.
Real Ale.
Children in eating area. Dogs on leads.

SAPPERTON

Daneway Inn   Tel: 01285 760297

Sapperton, Cirencester, Glos GL7 6LN
Free House. Liz & Richard Goodfellow, licensees

At the end of the now abandoned Sapperton tunnel, the Daneway was originally built in 1794 to accommodate the canal workers. Inside the lounge bar, do look at the wonderfully grand Dutch fireplace which came out of the long-since-demolished Amberley House. Lunchtime bar food varies from filled rolls, baked potatoes and ploughmans to lasagne and beef and ale pie. There are additions to the menu in the evening. Bass, Wadworths 6X, Archers Best and Daneway Bitter, which is brewed locally, plus guest beers. Farm cider. Tables in the pretty garden overlook the Canal and the river valley.

OPEN: 11 - 2.30 (3 Sat); 6.30 - 11.
Real Ale.
Children in no-smoking family room. No dogs.

SHEEPSCOMBE

Butchers Arms
Tel: 01452 812113

Sheepscombe, Nr Painswick, Glos GL6 7RH
Free House. Johnny & Hilary Johnston, licensees

Dating back to 1670, the Butchers Arms is very much the village local. Facing due south with wonderful views, it is so sheltered you can sit outside in comfort in the early spring. Very traditional, with a timeless atmosphere, huge log fires, walls covered with old pictures and prints, no fruit machines or juke box, just lots of chat. Good, varied bar menu and evening specials, such as poached salmon with prawn sauce, half roast duck with Grand Marnier and orange sauce, steaks, mixed grills and home-made puds. Bass, Hook Norton Best, Old Hooky and Boddingtons Ales. Farm ciders and a good wine list. Local singing groups visit on special occasions.

OPEN: 11 - 11 (11 - 2.30; 6 - 11 winter).
Real Ale. Restaurant.
Children in eating areas. No dogs.
Live music on special occasions.

STOW-ON-THE-WOLD

Coach & Horses
Tel: 01451 830208

Longborough, Nr Stow-on-the-Wold, Glos
Donnington. Andy Morris, tenant

This is a family orientated pub. The adjoining field is a site for caravan club members in which there is a play area with swings and slides for children. If you are only here for the beer, Donningtons Ales are on hand pump. As you are near the brewery, you can be assured they are all in tip-top condition. Familiar bar food of sandwiches, ploughmans, toasties, home-made soup, steak and kidney pie and grilled Donnington trout; the dining area is no-smoking. Seats outside on the terrace and the small lawn.

OPEN: 11 - 3; 6 - 11.
Real Ale.
Children in eating area. Dogs on leads.
Occasional live Jazz.

STOW-ON-THE-WOLD

Queens Head
Tel: 01451 830563

Market Square, Stow-on-the-Wold, Glos GL54 1AB
Donnington. Timothy Eager, tenant

Among the fine stone buildings in the Market Square you will easily find the Old Queens Head, pretty as a picture with its climbing roses and hanging baskets. Inside there are two bars: the lounge bar at the front, and a family room at the back where the landlord has put the games and fruit machine and - with a macabre sense of humour - his coffin (made of yew, by the way - very grand), which is listed as pub furniture on the tax return. The bar menu offers soups, ploughmans, sandwiches, savoury flans, cottage pie, cheese and potato pie, seasonal specials and good home-made puds. There are seats outside in the courtyard, and at the front of the pub. Donningtons ales, and mulled wine in winter.

OPEN: 11 - 2.30; 6 (6.30 Sat) - 11.
Real Ale.
Children in back bar. Dogs on leads.
Occasional Jazz Sun.

TODENHAM

Farriers Arms
Tel: 01608 650901

Todenham, Moreton-in-the-Marsh, Glos GL56 9PF
Free House. Mrs Sylvia Rickards, licensee

In unspoilt countryside, Todenham is a quiet village a mile off the Stratford/Oxford road and 2½ miles south of Shipston-on-Stour. There's a beamed and comfortable bar in the 18th century

Farriers Arms, which is well frequented by local farmers and walkers. The landlady does all the cooking, so booking for Sunday lunch is a must. Traditional bar snacks available every day, but Tuesday and Sunday it's roast beef for lunch. Hook Norton and Tetleys on hand pump and Farriers house wine.

OPEN: 12 - 2.30; 7 - 11.
Real Ale. No food Tues. Roast Sunday lunches.
Children in eating area. Dogs on leads. Bedroom.

UPPER ODDINGTON

Horse & Groom   Tel: 01451 830584

Upper Oddington, Moreton-in-the-Marsh, Glos GL5 60XH
Free House. Graham & Phillicity Collins, licensees

In the heart of the Cotswolds, this 16th century stone-built inn has flagstoned floors, heavily beamed rooms with big log-filled inglenook fireplaces, and a large, colourful garden with a stream, pond and play area. Good, popular bar menu using the best fresh local produce, all home-made: well known for fresh fish bought daily and a selection of home-made puddings. Wadworths 6X, Hook Norton Best and guest beers.

OPEN: 11 - 2.30; 6 - 11 (6.30 - 11 winter).
Real Ale. Restaurant.
Children welcome. Dogs on leads. Bedrooms.

WOODCHESTER

Ram Inn   Tel: 01453 873329

Station Road, South Woodchester, Nr Stroud, Glos
Free House. Michael & Eileen McAsey, licensees

Gloucestershire does have the most wonderful scenery and from the Ram Inn the views are spectacular. Traditionally furnished, the beamed bar has no less than three log fires during winter. A changing menu includes the usual sandwiches and ploughmans, various stews, venison pie, lasagne; always fresh vegetables. The ales change frequently but there are usually eight or nine on hand pump. Serious beer drinkers flock here.

OPEN: 11 - 3; 5.30 - 11 (11 - 11 Sat).
Real Ale. Restaurant not Sun eves.
Children welcome.
Dogs on leads.

HAMPSHIRE

BENTWORTH

Sun Inn   Tel: 01420 562338

Bentworth, Nr Alton, Hants GU34 5JT (at Sun Hill off A339 from Alton)
Free House. Richard & Jan Beaumont, licensees

Originally two cottages, this fine old 17th century pub is tucked away down a country lane at the edge of the village. Two connecting, beamed, comfortable bars, with big log fires make it especially appealing during the winter. A newly built extension allows more people to enjoy the praiseworthy catering. Daily specials on the blackboard, otherwise dishes range from soups, sandwiches, ploughmans, filled baked potatoes to steak & kidney pies, salmon fishcakes, ham and eggs, salads and home-made puddings. Ruddles Best, Bass, Wadworths 6X, Marstons Pedigree and Gales country wines. Tables outside amongst the flowering tubs.

OPEN: 12 - 3; 6 - 11.
Real Ale. No food Sun evening Nov - Feb.
Children in garden room. Dogs on leads.
Occasional Morris Dancers.

AUGMENTING THE DIRECTORY

We know there are more pubs and wine bars eligible for inclusion in THE QUIET PINT than are listed here. Please help us to find them for our next edition by completing the nomination forms at the end of this Book.

BOLDRE

Red Lion
Tel: 01590 673177

Ropehill, Boldre, Nr Lymington, Hants
Eldridge Pope. John & Jenny Bicknell, lease

On the edge of the New Forest, not far from Lymington, this 17th century, flower-festooned pub has all those artefacts you associate with past country life - including mantraps and chamber pots! - displayed around its four well-beamed rooms. Usual range of reliable bar food, plus meals in a basket, and quite a choice of ice creams to follow. Eldridge Pope ales plus guest beers. Wines by the glass. Seats in the attractive garden.

OPEN: 11 - 3; 6 - 11.
Real Ale. Restaurant.
No children under 14 inside pub. No dogs.

BURITON

Five Bells
Tel: 01730 263584

(off A3, S of Petersfield)
Free House. John Ligertwood, licensee

N.B: One bar has music, one without.
Close to the South Downs Way, the Five Bells offers a welcome haven to walkers and locals alike. Low-beamed bars, log fires, good ales and an inventive menu. Substantial snacks: various curries, vegetarian dishes, choice of fish, dressed local crab, game in season and casseroles. A three course menu is available in the dining room and there are also Sunday lunches. Ballards Best, Adnams Best, Ind Coope Burton, Ringwood Old Thumper and a guest beer. Seats on the terrace and in the sheltered garden.

OPEN: 11 - 2.30 (11 - 3 Fri & Sat); 5.30 - 11.
Real Ale. Restaurant not Sun eve.
Children in restaurant & snug. Dogs in public bar.
Jazz last Mon, Folk or Blues each Wed in month.

CHERITON

Flower Pots
Tel: 01962 771318

Cheriton, Alresford, Hants SO24 0QQ
Own Brew. Paul Tickner, Joanna Bartlett, Patricia Bartlett, licensees

Built in the early 19th century by the retired head gardener from Abingdon Park (worth a visit), the pub, with its past horticultural leanings, is aptly named. Popular locally, it even has its own brewery - The Cheriton Brewhouse - providing several reasonably priced ales to go with the good value bar food. You will find well-filled jacket potatoes, sandwiches, stews and curries, plus daily specials. Their own beer includes Cheriton Best, Diggers Gold and Pots' Ale. Seats outside at the front and the rear.

OPEN: 11.30 - 2.30; 6 - 11.
Real Ale. No food Sun eves in winter.
Children in family room. Dogs on leads. Bedrooms.

DROXFORD

White Horse Inn

South Hill, Droxford, Hants SO32 3PB
Free House. Sidney Higgins, licensee

Not far from Soberton - a peaceful Meon-valley village with a flint church tower, reputedly built in the 16th century by a butler and dairymaid - is the contemporaneous White Horse, an old coaching Inn, with a quiet, beamed lounge bar, no-smoking restaurant, and a public bar with the games and juke box. They serve a good selection of bar food which could include: soup, sandwiches, plain or toasted, gammon steak, salads, vegetarian dishes, daily specials and frequently a choice of fish. Burts Nipper Bitter, (from the Isle of Wight), Morlands Old Speckled Hen, Wadworths 6X and a guest beer. Tables in the sheltered, flowery courtyard.

OPEN: 11 - 3; 6 - 11 (Back bar all day Sat).
Real Ale. Restaurant, no-smoking, closed Sun eves.
Children in family room and restaurant. Dogs under control.
Live bands most Tues eves.

IBSLEY

Old Beams Inn   Tel: 01425 473387

Ibsley, Nr Ringwood, Hants
Free House. R Major & C Newall, licensees

An attractive, half-timbered, 600 year old thatched pub, looking as pretty as a picture when the cherry trees are out in the spring. Inside is one large open space and a newly built conservatory extension. There is always a good choice of well-cooked meals with lots of daily specials. The impressive cold buffet - cold meats, seafood and lots of salads is very popular - quiche, pork in cream and mustard sauce, grilled fish, lasagne, chillies, and not forgetting ploughmans and sandwiches. Quite a range of ales: Gibbs Mew, Bishops Tipple, Ringwoods Best, Old Thumper, Gales HSB and Bass. Imported bottled beers and wines by the glass. Seats in the garden among the trees.

OPEN: 10.30 - 2.30; 6 - 11 (10.30 winter).
Real Ale. Restaurant (not Sun eve).
Children in eating areas and family room.
Small dogs only.

LANGSTONE

Royal Oak   Tel: 01705 483125

19 High Street, Langstone, Havant, Hants PO9 1RY
Whitbread. Mr Warren, manager

A 16th century pub on the edge of a natural harbour - an extra high tide and the local swans join you for a drink, as the water nearly reaches the front door. Comfortable in winter with its open fires, it is appealing in all seasons. Traditional range of bar food: home-made soups, well filled French bread, a vegetarian dish, local fish and a roast of the day. Flowers Original, Gales HSB, Boddingtons, Morlands Old Speckled Hen and Wadworths 6X on hand pump. Seats at the front of the pub or in the garden behind, where there is a children's corner with goats, rabbits and a pot-bellied pig.

OPEN: 11 - 11.
Real Ale.
Children in eating area.
Dogs on leads in part of pub.

OVINGTON

Bush Inn   Tel: 01962 732764

Ovington, Nr Alresford, Hants SO24 0RE
Free House. Geoff & Sue Draper, licensees

To appreciate this pretty cottagey pub fully, try coming during the week, or out of season, when it is a little quieter. In an idyllic position on the fast-flowing River Ichen, it is popular not only for its excellent trout stream, but for its riverside paths where you can either work up an appetite, or walk off the meal you have just enjoyed. Inside the pub there are three comfortable bars, each with roaring log fires in winter. The usual traditional bar meals are readily available. There are daily specials on the blackboard which lists a short and more adventurous choice of dishes. Gales HSB, Flowers Original, Badger Tanglefoot, Wadworths 6X and usually a guest beer. Various country wines. Seats overlooking the river and, naturally enough, lovely walks.

OPEN: 11 - 2.30; 6 - 11.
Real Ale. Evening restaurant (not Sun).
Children in eating area lunchtimes & restaurant evenings.
Dogs on leads.

PRIORS DEAN

White Horse Inn   Tel: 0142 0588387

Priors Dean, Nr Petersfield, Hants GU32 1DA
(Clutching a good map, you go up a track past E Tilstead/Privett
crossroads, between Petersfield & Winchester)
Free House. Jack Eddleston, licensee

When locals tell you about a pub they have known all their lives,
you assume it is fairly easy to find. This one is not. If there were a
"hunt the pub" game, this one would be starred as "very difficult".
High on the Downs, with views on either side, this 17th century
farmhouse has no pub sign. Simple and traditional, think of a
country pub 20 or so years ago, and you will know what to expect.
In those days you were lucky if you could get a nut from the
cardboard stand on the counter, or a packet of crisps, (with blue
salt twist), from a tin marked Smiths. Limited choice there may be
here, but you can get sandwiches, soup (in winter made on the
Aga), and ploughmans, plus daily specials. Ballards Best,
Courage Best and Directors, No Name Bitter, John Smiths and
Theakstons Old Peculiar are among the ales on offer.
Considerable number of country wines, including wine from a
local vineyard. Seats in the garden.

OPEN: 11 - 2.30 (11 - 3 Sat); 6 - 11.
Real Ale. No meals or snacks Sun lunchtimes.
Children not allowed in.
Well behaved dogs on leads.

ROTHERWICK

Coach & Horses   Tel: 01256 762542

The Street, Rotherwick, Nr Basingstoke, Hants RG27 9BG
Badger. Sean McAusland, manager

Here you can be sure of a bowl of soup and a sandwich any time
during the day, and when you are travelling by car across country

you really appreciate pubs like this. It's 16th century, covered in creeper and surrounded by flowers; and inside there are attractive, small, beamed rooms, one of which is no-smoking. About five different varieties of sausage are on the menu, steak & kidney and other pies, stews, steaks and Sunday roast. Children's dishes. Well-kept beers: Gribble Black Adder, Badger Best, Hard Tackle and Tanglefoot, Charles Wells Eagle and Wadworths 6X. Seats outside amongst the flowers.

OPEN: 11 - 11.
Real Ale. Restaurant.
Children in eating area. Dogs on leads.

STEEP

Harrow Inn   Tel: 01730 262685

Steep, Petersfield, Hants GU32 2DA
Free House. Edward C McCutcheon, licensee

Another pub that is difficult to find, but here all you do is locate Sheet Church and turn left, follow the sign to Steep - over the motorway bridge and hey presto! (This isn't a typographical error, Sheet and Steep are two different places.) The Harrow Inn, probably 15th century, is beamed, hung with hops and dried flowers, with old oak benches in the public bar which has a big inglenook fireplace. Beer is served through a hatch from the barrels behind. Unchanging, wonderfully traditional - to be treasured. Home-cooked hams, scotch eggs, soups and salads. Flowers, Boddingtons and Whitbread beers. Country wines. Tables in the wild garden.
OPEN: 11 - 2.30 (11 - 3 Sat); 6 - 11.
Real Ale.
Children in garden only. Dogs on leads.

TICHBORNE

Tichborne Arms   Tel: 01962 733760

Tichborne, Nr Alresford, Hants SO24 0NA
Free House. Christine & Peter Byron, licensees

A village which takes its name from the Tichborne family who lived here from 1135. The Tichborne Dole ceremony, was started in 1150 by Richard de Tichborne. It is celebrated on March 25th each year, when flour is distributed to the villagers. Thatched, as are many buildings in the Itchen Valley, the Tichborne Arms is very much the centre of village life. Very popular, it can get busy - the home-cooked bar food being a particular attraction. Using fresh local produce, there is usually a soup, sandwiches, ploughmans, well filled baked potatoes and salads plus daily specials. Wadworths 6X, Boddingtons, Flowers IPA and Original from the cask. Tables in the garden.

OPEN: 11.30 - 2.30; 6 - 11.
Real Ale.
No children under 14. Dogs on leads.

UPHAM

Brushmakers Arms   Tel: 01489 860231

Upham, Nr Bishops Waltham, Hants (village signposted from Winchester)
Free House. Sue & Andy Cobb, licensees

Brushes for every occasion. Not quite, but there is quite a collection hanging around the pub. It has a comfortable, good-sized bar divided by a wood-burning stove in a central fireplace. Better than average choice of bar food and a Sunday roast. Bass and Ringwood Best on hand pump plus two guest beers. A choice of malt whiskies and country wines. Seats outside on the terrace and the lawn.

OPEN: 11 - 2.30; 6 - 11 (11 - 11 Sat).
Real Ale.
Children welcome away from bar.
Dogs on leads.

VERNHAM DEAN

George Inn   Tel: 01264 737279

Vernham Dean, Andover, Hants SP11 0JY
Marstons. Candy Lacy-Smith, Derek Pollard, tenants

A rambling, friendly, popular, attractive old village pub in a pretty garden with its own vegetable patch - so you will know most of the vegetables accompanying the home-cooked food will be produced "in-house" so to speak. Soups, toasted sandwiches, selection of ploughmans, interesting savoury pies and game in season. Marstons Pedigree and Best on hand pump. Seats and tables in the lovely garden.

OPEN: 11 - 2.30 (11 - 3 Sat); 6 - 11.
Real Ale. No meals/snacks Mon or Wed eves.
Children in family room. Dogs on leads.

WELL

Chequers Inn   Tel: 01256 862605

Well, Odiham, Hants RG25 1TL
Free House. Christopher Phillips, Rupert Fowler, licensees

Deep in the lovely Hampshire countryside, at its best on a glorious early summer's day, you will find the 17th century Chequers: beamed and panelled, with shelves of books to read if you are waiting for someone, or just want a book with your beer. Home-cooked food. The menu which is chalked on the blackboard in the bar changes daily, and is quite enterprising. There could be pasta, coronation chicken, seafood vol au vents, smoked salmon and scrambled eggs and other dishes. Fremlins, Flowers Original and Boddingtons ales. Good range of wine. Tables in the garden.

OPEN: 11 - 3; 5.30 - 11.
Real Ale. Restaurant (not Sun).
Children welcome. Dogs on leads.

WINCHESTER

Wykeham Arms   Tel: 01962 853834

75 Kingsgate Street, Winchester, SO23 9PE
Eldridge Pope. Mr & Mrs Graeme Jameson, lease

South of the Cathedral Close you'll find one of the best pubs in town. Six rooms radiate from a central bar (where the serious drinking goes on), so there is plenty of room for you to sample the extremely popular bar food. The lunchtime menu changes daily so either book a table, or get there early to avoid disappointment as all Winchester seems to beat a path to the door. If you have to wait, make your way to the room at the back where you will find a set of Ronald Searle's 'Winespeak' prints: they are quite hilarious and put any wine-pseud in his place. Several no-smoking areas. Eldridge Pope Dorchester, Hardy and Royal Oak ales. Seats on the terrace and small lawn.

OPEN: 11 - 11. No meals/snacks Sun.
Real Ale. Evening restaurant (not Sun).
No children. Dogs on leads. Bedrooms.

HEREFORD, SHROPSHIRE & WORCESTERSHIRE

ASTON ON CLUN

Kangaroo Inn   Tel: 01588 660263

Clun Road, Aston on Clun, Shropshire SY7 ATW
Free House. Pam Wright, licensee

It has been called the Kangaroo - no one knows why - since 1820 - and like Johnny Walker whisky, "it's still going strong". It is located in an area that has deep-rooted connections with the novelist Mary Webb and the poet A E Houseman, who called this part of the country "the quietest under the sun". From the top of nearby Hopesay Hill you get marvellous views of the Long Mynd to the north and the Welsh hills to the west. If you don't make it to the top of Hopesay, you can still appreciate the splendid views of the Clun Valley from the pub garden. The Kangaroo has a juke box, but it's rarely played except in the late evening, presumably to help clear the pub. There are, however, plenty of quiet areas, including the dining room. It is famous for its home-made pies - steak & kidney, game, venison in season, vegetarian, roo burgers, alligator and kangaroo pies - steaks too (beef). Bass, Worthingtons, Highgate Mild and one guest beer.

OPEN: 12 - 3; 7 - 11 (12 - 3; 7 - 10.30 Sun).
Real Ale.
Children in family room.
Dogs on leads.

BEWDLEY

Little Pack Horse
Tel: 01299 403762

31 High Street, Bewdley, Worcs DY12 2DH
Free House. Peter & Sue D'Amery, licensees

Busy, cheerful and slightly eccentric, this 16th century town pub has tremendous appeal, full of fascinating objects, including an incendiary bomb (dud, I hope). Reasonably priced traditional bar food of the home-made variety: soups, filled baked potatoes, chilli, lasagne, salads and steaks. Beers do change but you could find Ind Coope Burton, Marstons, Holt Plant and Deakins Entire, also Lumphammer Ale which is brewed for the "Little Chain" of pubs to which the Little Pack Horse belongs. Note: there is no nearby parking.

OPEN: 11 - 3; 6 - 11 (all day summer Sats).
Real Ale.
Children in back bar or stable room. No dogs.

BIRTSMORTON

Farmers Arms
Tel: 01684 833308

Birts Street, Nr Malvern, Worcs WR13 6AP
Free House. Colin Moore, licensee

Situated in a country lane, this black and white timbered pub with its low-beamed, convivial, rambling interior, offers a good range of bar food. This includes sandwiches, ploughmans, salads, steak & kidney pie, trout and almonds, steaks and good puddings. Ruddles Best, Courage Best, Hook Norton Old Hooky and John Smiths on hand pump. Seats in the garden during summer. Good walking country.

OPEN: 11 - 2.30 (3 Sat); 6 - 11.
Real Ale.
Children welcome. Dogs on leads.
Self-catering cottage available.

BISHOPS CASTLE

Three Tuns   Tel: 01588 638797

Salop Street, Bishops Castle, Shropshire SY9 5BW
Own Brew. Dominic Wood, licensee

Pubs that have been brewing their own beers for several centuries are now few and far between. The Three Tuns is a fine example of one that has been brewing for the last 300 years. The brewery, now a listed building, was rebuilt in Victorian times, but was first mentioned in 1642. The inn and a black and white barn next to it probably date from that time. Inside, the pub retains many original features, including heavy oak beams and a good Jacobean staircase. The bar menu includes a number of fish and vegetarian dishes, a selection of Indian curries, steaks and pub specials. From the brewery comes XXX Bitter, Mild, a stout called Jim Wood's and the winter ale is Old Scrooge. Halls and Westons ciders. Interesting small wine list. Seats on the terrace and in the sheltered summery garden. The pub has its own garden centre, open from Easter to October. Lovely walking country.

OPEN: 11.30 - 3; 6.30 - 11 (perhaps longer in summer).
Real Ale. Restaurant.
Children welcome if well behaved. Dogs in bar & snug.

BRETFORTON

Fleece   Tel: 01386 831173

The Cross, Bretforton, Nr Evesham, Worcs
Free House. N J Griffiths, licensee

On the edge of the Cotswold hills, the village of Bretforton dates back to a Saxon deed of 714 AD and The Fleece is one of the gems of the village. Originally a medieval farmhouse, it became an inn during the 19th century. During its lifetime it has been added to and extended and these alterations can be seen by the changes in the timber framing at the front of the pub. Once completely thatched, the roof is now a mixture of thatch and stone. Beer was brewed in the back kitchen, continuing well into this century. The same family had lived here for over 500 years and when Miss Taplin died in 1977, she left The Fleece and all its wonderful contents to the National Trust who run it as an unspoilt country pub. Inside remains much as it was throughout the 19th century; the family collection of furniture, pewter, china and other ornaments and artefacts are still in their place. An unique interior which must be seen to be appreciated (don't miss the witch's marks still on the flagstones in front of the fire). It seems a bit mundane to talk about food and beer, but special as this place is, it is still the village local and as such provides good ales and an equally good choice of generous, varying bar food. Uley Old Spot and Pig's Ear, M and B Brew X1 and Hook Norton Best. Country wines and farm ciders.

OPEN: 11 - 2.30; 6 - 11 (no food Mon eve, or Sun eve Jan & Feb).
Real Ale.
Children welcome. No dogs.
Occasional live entertainment.

BRIDGES

Horseshoe Inn   Tel: 01588 650260

Bridges, Nr Ratlinghope, Shrewsbury, Shropshire SY5 0ST
Free House. John & Brenda Muller, licensees

The 16th century Horseshoe is under the westerly side of the Long Mynd, a ridge of hills rising to 1700 ft, from where you can get commanding views of the beautiful Shropshire countryside. From the seats in front of the Inn you can overlook the little river Onny. A short bar menu is served at lunchtime only: sandwiches, ploughmans and a few hot dishes - enough to give the walkers among you the energy to continue. Adnams Bitter and Extra, Shepherd Neame Spitfire and two guest beers. Westons farm cider. On a fine summer day the sky will be filled with the gliders from the Long Mynd Gliding Club taking advantage of the standing wave the ridge is famous for.

OPEN: 11 - 3; 6 - 11.
Real Ale.
Children in own room. Dogs on leads.

BRIMFIELD

Roebuck   Tel: 01584 711230

Poppies Restaurant, Brimfield, Nr Ludlow, Shropshire SY8 4NE
Free House. Carole Evans, licensee

If you want to do some serious eating, this is really a restaurant
with a pub attached; but it is still a pub - with a restaurant; very
much the village local, so if you want a pint and above average
bar food, this is the place to come. The choice is considerable: hot
crab pot with toast, warm salad of smoked chicken with sun-dried
tomatoes, crispy bacon and tomato croutons, fish cakes with
parsley sauce, smoked haddock and tarragon tart with leek
sauce, old fashioned steak & kidney pie and a fantastic choice of
puddings. Fifteen different English farmhouse cheeses. There is
an even more extensive menu in the restaurant, where they also
do set three-course lunches. Woods and Hobsons ales. Half
bottles of wine from a good wine list.

OPEN: 12 - 2.30; 7 - 11 (closed Sun & Mon & 2 weeks in Feb).
Real Ale. Restaurant.
Children welcome.
Dogs in the snugbar.
Bedrooms.

BROADWAY

Crown & Trumpet   Tel: 01386 853202

Church Street, Broadway, Worcs WR12 7AE
Whitbreads. Andrew Scott, lease

Situated next to the church in this picturesque village, which is regarded as the gateway to the Cotswolds, the honey-coloured stone 17th century Crown & Trumpet Inn is very much the village local. The bar is attractively beamed, with log fires in winter. There is an extensive menu with many seasonal and local dishes, most of which are home-made. Sunday lunches and a range of real ales: Flowers IPA and Original, Morlands Old Speckled Hen, Wadworths 6X and a guest beer which could come from the local brewery. Seats outside on the terrace amid the flower-filled tubs.

OPEN: 11 - 3 (2.30 winter); 5 - 11.
Real Ale.
Children in eating area. Doubtful about dogs. Bedrooms.
N.B: Sat Sing-alongs! Radio played.

CARDINGTON

Royal Oak   Tel: 01694 771266

Cardington, Nr Church Stretton, Shropshire SY6 7JZ
Free House. John Seymour, licensee

You will find the creeper-covered, 15th century Royal Oak behind the church in the small village of Cardington. In lovely countryside, not far from the Stretton hills from the top of which you have the most wonderful views over a picturesque valley. Inside the pub there is a rambling, well beamed bar with a big inglenook fireplace with good log fires during the winter. Varied, reliable bar food at lunchtime includes the traditional ploughmans, soups and sandwiches, plus a selection of hot dishes. There is a separate evening menu. Bass and a couple of guest ales. Tables on the terrace at the front of the pub with views over the undulating countryside.

OPEN: 12 - 2.30; 7 - 11.
Real Ale. No food Sun evening.
Children at lunchtime only.
Dogs on leads.
One double bedroom.

CORFTON

Sun Inn   Tel: 01584 861239

Corfton, Nr Craven Arms, Shropshire SY7 9DF
Free House. Teresa & Norman Pearce, licensee

They say it's the oldest licensed premises in Corvedale - between Ludlow and Much Wenlock. An expert looking at the original timbers - that you can still see inside - would date it as 17th century. The lounge bar has a dining area where you have a choice of an à la carte menu or bar snacks, and a children's menu. There is a varied selection of dishes: lamb and leek casserole, liver and bacon, lamb Shrewsbury, gammon and various steaks; quite often the blackboard lists a considerable number of fish, and several vegetarian dishes. Flowers IPA and Boddingtons Mild are the permanent ales but approximately 120 guest ales are brought in over the year. Seats in the garden.

OPEN: 11 - 2.30; 6 - 11 (12 - 3; 7 - 10.30 Sun).
Real Ale.
Children welcome. Dogs on leads.

DEFFORD

Monkey House   Tel: 01386 750234

Woodmancote, Hereford
(No pub sign. The last cottage after Oak Public House)
Free House. Graham Collins, licensee

An experience not to be missed. Simple and unspoilt, there are only a few of these unique places left in the country - what you might call a dying breed, to be preserved at all costs. This black and white cottage without any inn sign is a traditional cider house. Cider is served from a barrel into a jug, through a hatch, into a mug. Beer available in cans (very 20th century), nuts and crisps.

You can also bring your own picnic to enjoy with the cider. (No hamper charge!)

OPEN: 11 - 2.30; 6 - 10.30 (11 Fri & Sat).
Closed Mon eves & all day Tues.
Cider. No food.
No dogs.

FOWNHOPE

Green Man   Tel: 01432 860243

Fownhope, Nr Hereford HR1 4PE
Free House. Arthur & Margaret Williams, licensees

Close to the meandering River Wye in the lovely Herefordshire countryside, this black and white timbered 15th century inn has a fascinating history. It had Civil War connections; it was then an 18th century petty sessions court, after that a coaching inn and now it's an hotel where everyone is welcome. Comfortable, with big log fires, it has a no-smoking dining room and a residents' lounge. Good value bar food, roasts on Sundays, also children's meals. Well kept ales: Hook Norton Best, Courage Directors, Marstons Pedigree, Boddingtons and Sam Smiths OB on hand pump. Farm ciders. Overlooking the river, the attractive garden has lots of room for drinks and afternoon tea. A unique sign, which was commissioned decades ago, hangs over the entrance to the coachhouse yard and reads in part: "You travel far, You travel near, it's here you find the best of Beer, You pass the East, You pass the West, if you pass this, you pass the Best."

OPEN: 11 - 3; 6 - 11.
Real Ale.
Two Restaurants.
Children welcome. Dogs on leads.

HANLEY CASTLE

Three Kings   Tel: 01684 592686

Hanley Castle, Worcester WR8 0BL (N of Upton upon Severn off B4211)
Free House. Mrs Sheila Roberts, licensee

Run by the same family for eighty years, it is a wonderfully unspoilt pub without even a cigarette machine. Lots of small rooms, each with their own atmosphere, in this attractively timbered 15th century building. A good choice of bar snacks, ranging from soups, sandwiches, ploughmans to omelettes. Specials, which can take half an hour to prepare include: Beef Wellington, Venison in Red Wine Sauce, Salmon en croûte with Broccoli and Cream Sauce, grilled trout and steaks. And a selection of puddings. Beer is served through a hatch and includes Thwaites and Butcombe Bitter plus a couple of guest beers. Range of malt whiskies and farm ciders. Seats on the terrace overlooking the village green.

OPEN: 11 - 3; 7 - 11.
Real Ale. No food Sun eves.
Children in family room. No dogs. Bedrooms.
Live music Sun & alternate Sat eve. Folk alternate Thurs.

HOPESGATE

Stables Inn   Tel: 01743 891344

Drury Lane, Hopesgate, Nr Minsterley, Shropshire SY5 0EY
Free House. Denis & Debbie Harding, licensees

In what is only a small hamlet of eight houses, this pub was built in 1680 to sustain the drovers travelling between Montgomery and Shrewsbury markets, on what was then a busy thoroughfare. Now it's a quiet country lane. Small, with a beamed bar and big log fire, the Stables has a daily changing blackboard menu listing the home-made, lunchtime bar food: potted shrimps with toast and salad, local sausages, creamy stilton and mushroom hotpot, pasta carbonara and then treacle tart or bread & butter pudding. There is a table d'hôte menu in the small evening dining room using the best local produce: game in season, Welsh spring lamb, fresh seafood and properly cooked vegetables. Woods Special, Tetleys Bitter and two guests on hand pump. A choice of farm ciders and an interesting wine list. From the pub there are spectacular views over the Stiperstones and Long Mountain, one of the most beautiful areas of south Shropshire.

OPEN: 11.30 - 2.30; 7 - 11 (12 - 2; 7 - 11 winter). Closed Mon.
Real Ale. Restaurant (not Sun eve).
Children in eating area. No dogs.

KEMPSEY

Walter de Cantelupe Inn   Tel: 01905 820572

Main Road, Kempsey, Worcs WR5 3NA
Free House. Martin Lloyd Morris, manager/owner

Not far outside Worcester, this was originally just a cider house, but since being taken over in 1991 by the present owner, the inn has been gaining an enviable reputation for its food. When possible, locally produced vegetables, meat and cheese are used to create a reasonably priced, well chosen menu. Quality wines by the glass. Regular free tasting sessions. The radio is on at lunchtime in two of the eight corners of the pub, in order for you to catch up with world events, but definitely no music - conversation is all the rage here. Marstons Bitter, Pedigree and Wadworths 6X. Timothy Taylors Landlord may take over from Pedigree - the customers are voting with their beer glasses. Two guest ales a week from the smaller breweries: Barnsley Bitter, or Felinfoel Double Dragon amongst others. Seats in the flowery hidden garden.

OPEN: 12 - 2.30; 5.30 - 11 (12 - 3; 7 - 10.30 Sun).
Real Ale. (Closed lunch Mon except mid-Summer).
Children lunchtime & early evening. No dogs.

KNIGHTWICK

Talbot Hotel   Tel: 01886 821235

Knightwick, Nr Worcester WR6 5PH
(At Knightsford Bridge off A44 Worcester-Bromyard)
Free House. Anne & Wiz Clift, licensees

Set in a lovely part of Worcestershire and on the banks of the River Teme, the Talbot, parts of which date back to the 14th century, continues to provide hospitality as it has been doing for the past 500 years. Beamed, comfortable bars, panelled dining room, imaginative, well cooked food, well-kept ales and good wines. A daily changing menu for both the bar and restaurant: salmon quiche, king prawns and garlic noodles, game casseroles in season, several fish dishes and good home-made puds to follow. Hobsons Bitter, Worthingtons and Bass on hand pump. Wines by the glass. Seats outside and opposite the pub. Lots of walks nearby.

OPEN: 11 - 11.
Real Ale. Restaurant.
Children in eating area until 7.30. Dogs on leads.
Bedrooms.
Folk Night alternate Fri. Morris Dances winter Wed.

LEDBURY

Feathers Hotel   Tel: 01531 635266

High Street, Ledbury, Herefordshire HR8 1DS
Free House. D M Elliston, licensee

Situated in the main street of this unspoilt market town, The Feathers, three storeys high, is a dazzling example of timber-framed building at its best. Architecturally a jewel. Inside there is a big, well-beamed, very attractive bar and an elegant restaurant. Good lunchtime snacks: home-made soups, fresh salmon with green peppercorns, fillet of trout with dill cream on a base of pumpernickel, venison sausages and imaginative puddings. Three course Sunday lunch. Courage Directors, Crown Buckley Reverend James, Worthington BB and Bass on hand pump plus a guest beer. Large wine list and choice of malt whiskies and farm ciders.

OPEN: 11 - 11.
Real Ale. Restaurant (not Sun eves).
Children in eating area. Dogs on leads.
Bedrooms.
Live music Thurs and alternate Tues.

LEOMINSTER

Grape Vaults   Tel: 01568 611404

Broad Street, Leominster, Herefordshire HR6 8BS
Free House. Mrs Pauline Greenwood, licensee

One of the nicest small 17th century pubs: lately very well restored, it has all the advantages of an English country inn, but in town. No fruit machines, computer games or juke box. Just the hum of conversation and the chink of glasses. Wide ranging bar menu of home-cooked food: soups, deep-fried brie in ale batter, steak & kidney pie, cottage pie, ham and leak pie with potato topping, ham on the bone and fresh cod in their own beer batter - using Marstons Best! Ales could be Banks Mild, Marstons Bitter, Merry Monk and Pedigree - these do change - 28 different guests made an appearance last year.

OPEN: 11 - 3; 5 - 11. (12 - 3; 7 - 10.30 Sun).
Real Ale.
No children. Dogs on leads.

LUGWARDINE

Crown & Anchor   Tel: 01432 851303

Cotts Lane, Hereford. Off A438 E of Hereford
Free House. Nick & Julie Squires, licensees

In what is virtually a dormitory village for Hereford, the old timbered Crown and Anchor was closed for some time but has now been brought back into the fold. It has comfortable, friendly bars plus one room especially for families. They offer a good variety of traditional bar food and well kept ales. Eel pie is one of the specialities of the house, the eels caught in the nearby River Lug. Worthington BB, M&B Mild, Hook Norton, Best Bass and a weekly changing guest beer all on hand pump. A range of wines.

OPEN: 11.30 - 11.
Real Ale.
Children welcome. Dogs on leads.

OMBERSLEY

Crown & Sandys Arms   Tel: 01905 620252

Ombersley, Droitwich, Worcs WR9 0EW
Turn left at roundabout in village
Free House. R E Ransome, licensee

Considerably older than it looks, the original timber-framed inn was remodelled in the early 19th century and is enclosed in the Dutch gabled shell you see today. Situated at the south end of the attractive village of Ombersley, it has comfortable, beamed and timbered bars with huge inglenook fireplaces. There is an interesting, imaginative choice of home-cooked food, bar meals and daily specials using local game, wild boar, venison cooked in various ways and an à la carte menu in the restaurant. They also have a fine wine list. Traditional draught ales - Hook Nortons Best, Old Hooky and about four varying guest ales on hand pump. Tables in the garden during the summer.

OPEN: 11 - 2.30; 5.30 -11.
Real Ale. Restaurant.
Children if well behaved. Not babies.
No dogs.

OMBERSLEY

Kings Arms   Tel: 01905 620315

Ombersley, Droitwich, Worcs WR9 0EW
Free House. Chris & Judy Blundell, licensees

The old timbered pub has been rearranged inside to give more space for diners, but it still has rambling, beamed rooms with good log fires in the inglenook fireplaces. Plenty of choice from the changing menu, including tried and tested pub fare with specials such as grilled mussels, seafood pasta, deep-fried camembert, steaks, vegetarian dishes and a selection of home-made puddings. Boddingtons, Bass, Flowers Original and a range of malt whiskies. Tables in the courtyard amongst the summer flowers.

OPEN: 11 - 2.45; 5.30 - 11 (12 - 10.30 Sat).
Real Ale. Food all day Sunday.
Children in eating area till 8.30. No dogs.

PEMBRIDGE

New Inn   Tel: 01544 388427

Market Square, Pembridge, Hereford HR6 9DZ
Free House. Jane Melvin, licensee

In the small, medieval village surrounded by meadows and orchards, the New Inn was 'new' in the 14th century, very much the same date as St Mary's Church. A charming, traditional pub with two beamed bars and not a right angle between them. Well chosen home-cooked food: soups, paté, casseroles and interesting puddings. Ruddles Best and County plus one guest beer a month. New world wines and a considerable range of malt whiskies. Tables outside with views of the church, whose separate bell tower was used as a refuge during the Welsh Border wars.

OPEN: 11 - 3; 6 - 11 (6.30 - 11 winter).
Real Ale. Restaurant (no Sun evening).
Children in eating area until 9pm. No dogs.
Bedrooms.

PULVER BATCH

White Horse   Tel: 01743 718247

Pulver Batch, Nr Shrewsbury, Shropshire SY5 8DS
Whitbreads. James Macgregor, lease

Everywhere you go in Shropshire seems to unveil another vantage point from where you can see another aspect of this glorious county; the White Horse is no exception. It is at the end of the village from where there are magnificent views. Dating from the 13th century, it has rambling, beamed, traditionally furnished rooms, well decorated with blue and white plates, mugs, copper kettles, pictures and other interesting objects. Sturdy bar food: soups, ploughmans, lasagne, casseroles, trout and steaks. A longer, more sophisticated menu is a feature during the evening. Wadworths 6X, Flowers Best Bitter and Boddingtons are the regular ales. Lots of malt whiskies, and wine by the glass. No garden but there is a big car park.

OPEN: 11.30 - 3; 7 - 11.
Real Ale.
Children welcome. Dogs on leads.

WENLOCK EDGE

Wenlock Edge Inn   Tel: 01746 785403

Hilltop, Wenlock Edge, Shropshire TF13 6DJ
Free House. Stephen Waring, licensee

Wenlock Edge is a 400 million year old coral reef. The inn, by comparison, is a mere stripling, dating back to the 17th century. In fact, it was only licensed as a pub in 1925. Run by the Waring family, it has a reputation for creating a very friendly, welcoming atmosphere, and for serving English cooking at its best. Good stews, garlic mushrooms in cream and sherry, honey baked ham with either salad or hot vegetables, venison casserole, and steaks in the evening and very more-ish puds. Websters Yorkshire Bitter and two locally brewed ales: Hobsons Best and Town Crier. Selection of malt whiskies and wines by the glass. There are Monday storytelling evenings when a local group swops stories from "the Edge". Ask about Ippikin, a thief who lived in a cave near Lilleshall Quarry.

OPEN: 11.30 - 2.30; 6 - 11 (6.30 - 11 winter). Closed Mon lunch.
Real Ale. Restaurant. (No meals Mon except Bank Hols.)
Children in restaurant (not under 10 after 8pm).
Dogs on leads.
Bedrooms

WEOBLEY

Ye Olde Salutation   Tel: 01544 318443

Market Pitch, Weobley, Hereford HR4 8SJ
Free House. Chris & Francis Anthony, licensees

Still the village local, where you can meet for a drink and a chat, even though this old pub has gained a reputation for its imaginative food. Lambs' kidneys in red wine sauce, steak & Guinness pie, salmon and broccoli gratin, hot filled rolls (home-baked bread), and vegetarian dishes. There is an à la carte menu in the no-smoking restaurant and a very popular three-course lunch on Sundays. Boddingtons, Bass, Hook Nortons Best and Westons cider. A selection of wines and malt whiskies. Seats on the terrace at the back of the pub.

OPEN: 11 - 3; 7 - 11.
Real Ale. Restaurant (not Sun evening).
Children in eating areas.
No dogs.

WISTANSTOW

Plough Inn   Tel: 01588 673251

Wistanstow, Craven Arms, Shropshire SY7 8DG
Woods. Colin James, manager/licensee

The chief distinction of this Plough Inn is its high reputation for good beer - which isn't surprising as it's tied to the highly-rated Wood Brewery next-door. The full product range can be sampled at the bar, and if you want to see how it's made, a tour of the brewery can be arranged. It has also acquired a reputation for the quality of its restaurant food and its bar specials. Woods Parish, Special and Wonderful are regularly on tap. The choice is expanded in Spring with Shropshire Lad, in Autumn with Woodcutter, and at Christmas with Christmas Cracker - what else! Seats outside, overlooking the south Shropshire hills and Wenlock Edge, the tree-covered limestone escarpment that stretches over 16 straight, north-easterly miles.

OPEN: 12 - 3; 7 - 11.
Real Ale. Restaurant.
Children in family room.
Dogs on leads in bar only.

HERTFORDSHIRE

ALDBURY

Valiant Trooper
Tel: 0144 2851203

Trooper Road, Aldbury, Nr Tring, Herts HP23 5RW
Free House. Dorothy O'Gorman, licensee

Here's another pub that's ideally situated for the country walker and anyone looking for a good pint and bar food in the lovely, wooded Chiltern hills, not far from the Ridgeway Path. Short, familiar bar menu plus blackboard specials: cottage pie, mixed grill, liver and bacon casserole or fish pie; all home-cooked using fresh ingredients - no chips. Bass, Greene King Abbot, Fullers London Pride and John Smiths Bitter plus a weekly changing guest beer. Farm ciders. Charming, cottagey garden to sit in. (Recognised as one of the best value pubs in Hertfordshire.)

OPEN: 11 - 11 (12 - 2.30; 7 - 10.30 Sun).
Real Ale.
Restaurant (not Sun eve); No meals/snacks Sun or Mon eve.
Children in one room lunchtime. Dogs on leads.

AYOT ST LAWRENCE

Brocket Arms
Tel: 01438 820250

Ayot St Lawrence, Herts AL6 9BT
Free House. Toby Wingfield Digby, lease

George Bernard Shaw made his home in this peaceful village from 1906 until his death in 1950. His house, Shaws Corner is a late Victorian Gentleman's residence, which has hardly altered since his death; his typewriter is still in the study and his hats are hanging in the hall. Among the timber framed village cottages, the 14th century Brocket Arms is also largely unaltered. The interior is full of beams, big inglenook fireplaces and rustic furniture. A popular bar menu includes summer salads, home-made hot dishes and a daily changing blackboard menu. Theakstons Best, Greene King IPA, Wadworths 6X, Marstons Pedigree and two weekly changing guests which could include Bishops Tipple and Old Peculiar. Farm cider. A suntrap of a garden has seats and a children's play area. There is also a house ghost (a monk).

OPEN: 11 - 2.30; 7 - 10.30 (11 - 11 summer).
Real Ale. Restaurant (not Sun or Mon eve).
Children Sat & Sun only away from bar. Dogs on leads.
Bedrooms.

BARLEY

Fox & Hounds   Tel: 01763 848459

High Street, Barley, Nr Royston, Herts SG8 8HU
Own Brew. Rita Nicholson, licensee

This is a rambling, beamed 15th century village local that brews its own beer. The selection is not limited to what is brewed in-house, however: there are usually between eight and ten other ales on offer, with many more during the real ale festivals licensee Rita Nicholson organises from time to time. There is an extensive choice of bar food. A huge blackboard menu virtually covers one wall. The licensee's son is the cook, and all the food is home-made. Lots of pies, casseroles, curries, steaks and seafood. Lighter bar snacks available at lunchtime, as well as a selection of vegetarian dishes, a children's menu, and a carvery on Sundays. Half the dining area is non-smoking. The Fox and Hounds' own three ales are: Nathaniel's Special (mild), Old Dragon (strong), and Flame Thrower (very strong). Ciders, wines by the glass and a selection of malt whiskies. There is a barbecue in the garden; they also have their own skittle alley.

OPEN: 12 - 2.30; 6 - 11 (12 - 11 summer Sats).
Real Ale. Evening restaurant.
Children in family room & restaurant. Dogs on leads.

CHENIES

Red Lion
Tel: 01923 282722

Chenies Village, Rickmansworth, Hertfordshire WD3 6ED
Free House, Heather & Mike Norris, licensees

A four-square, white painted old pub, hung about, if that is the right word to use, with a wonderful display of hanging baskets. Inside, there is a large main bar and a small dining area in what was the original 17th century cottage. A varied selection of very popular, home-cooked bar food could include: soup, salmon and tarragon paté, pasta with mushrooms in a garlic sauce, several different "special" pies and spicy prawns and scallops on a bed of herby rice. All dishes are served with fresh vegetables, but NO CHIPS. Also filled French sticks, baps and jacket potatoes. Daily specials from the blackboard. Wadworths 6X, Adnams Bitter, Benskins Best and two local ales - Marlow Rebellion and Tring Ridgeway. They have a short wine list, and house wines by the glass. If you want a little "culture," Chenies Manor House - a Tudor Manor built by the Earl of Bedford in 1526 and still with its original Tudor garden - is not far away.

OPEN: 11 - 2.30, 5.30 - 11.
Real Ale. No children. Dogs on leads.

FLAUNDEN

Bricklayers Arms
Tel: 01442 833322

Hogpits Bottom, Flaunden, Herts HP3 0PH
Free House. R Mitchell & Stuart Lawson, licensees

This small, popular, low-built, creeper-covered pub has an appealing, rambling, beamed interior. It is so popular, in fact, that it is filled to the gunnels at weekends. During summer weekends they cope by overflowing into the attractive garden. In winter, though, it's first come, first served to a place by the fire. Well chosen, imaginative food is one of the attractions, along with the well kept ales and friendly atmosphere. Good generous bar food is served at lunchtime and ranges from the familiar soups and filled baked potatoes, ploughmans and sandwiches, to cottage pie, vegetable bake, curried chicken, fish pie, steak in ale pie, steaks and daily specials. An à la carte menu is served in the dining room during the evening. Adnams Pedigree and Chiltern Beechwood ales. Shepherd Neame Spitfire is a popular guest beer, Flowers Original, IPA and others. Seats in the lovely cottagey garden. Good walks nearby.

OPEN: 11 - 2.30 (11 - 3 Sat); 6 - 11.
Real Ale. Restaurant.
Children in restaurant. Dogs on leads.

NORTH MYMMS

Woodman   Tel: 01707 650502

Warrengate Road, North Mymms, Herts AL9 7TT
Free House. John Stewart, manager

A nice old pub, built in 1732, serving interesting food and good ale. Very popular with the students from the local veterinary college. Traditional bar food, but the emphasis is on offering restaurant food at pub prices. Mr Stewart, the manager, is from Inverness and frequently goes to Scotland to bring back supplies, so you will find salmon, pheasant and grouse in season and other game dishes featuring on the menu. Courage Directors, Best, Bitter, Wadworths 6X and Marstons Pedigree. Large garden at the front, and a beer garden at the back that overlooks the surrounding countryside.

OPEN: 11 - 3; 5.30 - 11.
Real Ale. No food Sun.
No children. No dogs.

SAWBRIDGEWORTH

King William IV   Tel: 01279 722322

Vantorts Road, Sawbridgeworth, Herts
Courage. Derek Tunmore, tenant

A fine old pub on a quiet lane, with an affable host and clientele. Some years ago it was voted "Friendly Pub of the Year". Beer is well kept, all the food is locally supplied, freshly cooked and good value. The special "Willie's Sausages" are made by the local butcher, 100 yards or so from the pub. No juke box, just a TV in the snug off the main saloon and normally switched on only for major sporting events. Courage beers, Beamish stout and a guest. No garden, but there are seats outside the front of the pub, so you can watch the world go by.

OPEN: 11 - 11.
Real Ale. No food Sunday.
Children welcome. Dogs on leads.
Occasional live music.

ST ALBANS

Rose & Crown   Tel: 01727 51903

10 St Michael Street, St Albans, Herts AL3 4S6
Greenalls. Neil Dekker, tenant

The town was named after the Christian martyr, St Alban, beheaded on the hill on which the cathedral now stands. The 300 year old Rose and Crown, in the shadow of the 9th century Abbey, was built alongside the original Watling Street, and opposite the remains of the Roman town of Verulamium. Inside, the old pub is well beamed, with a big inglenook fireplace - without a single right-angle to be seen. The landlord specialises in American style sandwiches with names like: Clark Gable, Lauren Bacall, Betty Boo and others. Many-layered, try these and you know you have had a sandwich. "Serf's" sandwiches available too, (roast beef, paté, ham or cheese) plus hot pub dishes. Greenalls ales, farm ciders and choice of malt whiskies. Plenty of tables outside in the garden among the flowers.

OPEN: 11 - 3; 5.30 - 11 (6 - 11 Sat).
Real Ale. No food Sunday.
Children in eating area. Dogs on leads.
Live music Thurs & Sun eves.

THUNDRIDGE (Nr Wadesmill)

Sow & Pigs   Tel: 01920 463281

Thundridge, Nr Ware, Herts SG12 0ST
Greenalls. Chris Severn, tenant

A comfortable, friendly village local. It has a small, panelled central bar, with rooms off, one of which is the dining room. With a name like this you are not surprised when bacon or ham feature in the menus, but that is not the only dish offered here. Usual variety of bar food, with daily specials: steaks, chicken dishes, sausage and onions and their own "very special" fish and chips. Adnams, Theakstons Old Peculiar and 6X plus guest beers. Picnic tables on the sheltered area by the car park.

OPEN: 11 - 3; 6.30 - 11 (6 - 11 Sat).
Real Ale. Restaurant.
Children in eating area. No dogs.

WATTON AT STONE

George & Dragon   Tel: 01920 830285

High Street, Watton at Stone, Herts SG14 3TA
Greene King. Kevin Dinnin, lease

Pink-washed and on the main road - you can't really miss it, nor should you. If you want a relaxed, civilised pub, complete with daily newspaper, proper napkins, interesting pieces of furniture, plus a reputation for good imaginative food, this is the place to be. Carbonnade of Beef, Darne of Salmon in whisky and lemon juice, lamb's liver in cream and brandy and black pepper sauce, chicken breast in light pastry with bacon and onion in white wine sauce plus light snacks such as: cornets of smoked salmon filled with avocado mousse, filleted smoked eel and bacon served on a bed of dressed mixed leaves, millionaire's bun which is fillet steak and a bread roll, or billionaire's bun which has twice as much steak! And if you really must, sandwiches, ploughmans and home-made puddings too. Very popular with everyone from near and far. Greene King ales, short wine list and choice of malt whiskies. Some tables in the restaurant are non-smoking. Seats in the attractive garden.

OPEN: 11 - 2.30; 6 - 11 (11 - 11 Sat).
Real Ale. Restaurant (not Sun eve).
Children in family room & restaurant. No dogs.
Occasional live entertainment.

KENT

BIDDENDEN

Three Chimneys
Tel: 01580 291472

Biddenden, Nr Ashford, Kent TN27 8HA (1 mile W of village on A262)
Free House. C F Sayers & G A Sheepwash, licensees

Set in the Kentish Weald, famous for its hops and cherries, a mile and a half west of the attractive village of Biddenden, you'll find this black and white 15th century country pub. Sitting slightly below the level of the main road, it is easy to miss, so you have to watch out for the inn sign depicting a man and a three-armed signpost. Friendly, busy, with rambling low-beamed bars and log fires in winter. Good imaginative food on offer: home-made soups - curried parsnip, tomato and celeriac, hot crab starter, kipper paté, ham and parmesan pancakes, beef and tomato casserole are just a few examples. Four puddings which change daily. There is a family garden room and tables in the pretty garden filled with shrubs, roses and nut trees - Kent cobs I hope. Range of eight or more ales tapped from behind the bar could include: Marstons Pedigree, Morlands Old Speckled Hen, Brakspears, Fremlins, Adnams Best. A strong local cider, local wines and a varied wine list. Wines by the glass and half bottles available.

OPEN: 11 - 2.30; 6 - 11.
Real Ale. Restaurant.
Children in restaurant.
Dogs on leads.
Occasional live entertainment.

BROMLEY

Bird in Hand
Tel: 0181 462 1083

62 Gravel Road, Bromley, Kent BR2 8PF
Courage. John & June Moyce, licensees
Richard & Jo Bradley, managers

Built in 1830 in what was then open countryside, the Bird in Hand is now surrounded by suburban Bromley and deserves wide support because there are plans to rip out its rarely used wiring for piped music. Manager Richard Bradley told QUIET PINT that the atmosphere in the pub is so good, he didn't feel it needed piped music. All he needs is a bit of encouragement to make the final rip. A feature of this small, immaculately kept establishment, is the wonderful beer garden - the licensees' pride and joy. They are keen gardeners and keep everything as it should be. Hanging baskets outside too, so when you see the floral display, you know you have come to the right place. Just one bar serving food at lunchtime only. There is a roast every day; ham egg and chips, gammon steaks, sandwiches and ploughmans - good basic, hearty English food - all home-cooked. Courage ales, Best and Directors.

Open 11 - 3; 5.30 - 11 (12 - 3; 7 - 10.30 Sun).
Real Ale.
Children in the garden only, with the dogs.

CHIDDINGSTONE

Castle
Tel: 01892 876247

Chiddingstone, Nr Edenbridge, Kent TN8 7AH
Free House. Nigel Lucas, licensee

Tucked in the lea of Chiddingstone Castle - whose mock 19th century medieval façade conceals a 17th century interior - the Castle Inn dates back to 1420. Originally Watership House, the building was first licensed and renamed in 1730. Still the centre of village life, it is part of an unspoilt Tudor village which was bought by the National Trust in 1939 for £25,000, and is considered to have one of the finest village streets in Kent. The Castle's heavily beamed saloon and public bar can get very crowded in summer, so arrive early to be sure of room to eat. An extensive bar menu is available: home-made soup, home-made paté, king prawns in garlic butter with French bread, a daily pasta, lots of different salads, sandwiches and of course daily specials. Some very interesting French ice cream to follow plus other puddings. More elaborate, two or three-course meals available in the saloon bar or restaurant. The ales are Larkins Traditional and Sovereign, also Harveys Sussex. There is a very pretty courtyard with tables.

OPEN: 11 - 3; 6 - 11 (all day Sat).
Real Ale. Restaurant.
Children welcome. Dogs on leads.

CHILLENDEN

Griffins Head   Tel: 01304 840325

Chillenden, Nr Canterbury, Kent CT3 1PS (off Eastry/Nonington road)
Shepherd Neame. Mark J Copestack, tenant

A typical country pub where you may meet the local farmer, half the cricket team, vintage car enthusiasts or just people dropping in. Dating back to 1286, the Griffins Head is heavily beamed and rambling, with two big inglenook fireplaces. The rooms are decorated with old photographs, a collection of oil pressure lamps and heaters, a formidable number of unusual beer bottles and artefacts relating to the brewing trade. Only one bar serving three different areas, and a dining room. Shepherd Neame ales: Spitfire, Master Brew, Best Bitter and Bishops Finger. Lots of picnic tables in the large garden; a barbecue in the middle of the car park, lit at weekends during the summer. On the 1st Sunday of every month the local vintage car enthusiasts meet and admire each others' vehicles - the landlord is a car enthusiast, not only of vintage, but of racing cars too. The Griffin has its own cricket pitch, cricket eleven, and keen followers.

OPEN: 11 - 11.
Real Ale. No food Sun eves.
No children. Dogs on leads.
Annual Jazz Festival.

CHISLEHURST

Ramblers Rest   Tel: 0181 467 1734

Mill Place, Chislehurst, Kent BR7 5ND
Courage. Peter Grierson, tenant

Situated on a large wooded common, close to Chislehurst cricket ground and golf club, access to the pub is along a driveway off the Chislehurst/Bromley road (A 222). The Ramblers Rest is just what you would expect of a 17th century Kent building - painted clap-board under a Kent peg-tiled roof. Bedecked with flowers during the summer, its inside is a wealth of beams and a warm welcome. Familiar, well tried bar food served at lunchtime only: steak and kidney pie, spaghetti bolognese, chilli, fisherman's pie, toasties, sandwiches, salads and ploughmans. Courage ales plus guest beers. Seats in the secluded garden.

OPEN: 11 - 3; 5.30 - 11.
Bar menu. No food evenings or Sunday.
Children in eating area. Dogs on leads.

COBHAM

Darnley Arms   Tel: 01474 814218

The Street, Cobham, Kent DA12 3BZ
Free House. Trevor & Beryl Howard, licensees

Cobham village, written about in Charles Dickens' *Pickwick Papers,* stands at the gates of Cobham Hall, the former residence of the Earls of Darnley, now a school. The present Darnley Arms is a mere stripling, dating back only to the 18th century, but there has been an inn on this site for over 600 years. Rumour has it that there is a tunnel connecting the pub to the nearby church - quite a way to go for the communion wine! Good range of bar food: sandwiches, ploughmans, home-made pies, egg mayonnaise, tiger prawns, various fish dishes and grills. Steamed pudding or ice cream for afters. Courage ales on hand pump and a selection of wines and liqueurs.

OPEN: 11 - 3; 6 - 11.
Real Ale. No food Sun eves.
Children if well behaved. No dogs.

CONYER QUAY

Ship   Tel: 01795 521404

Teynham, Nr Sittingbourne, Kent ME9 9HR
Free House. Alec Heard, licensee

There is the most extraordinary number and variety of drinks on offer in this old smugglers' inn. The cellars must be huge, and the behind-bar capacity equally so to accommodate so many. Standing room only, I should think, on tasting nights. Propping up, more like. For you afficionados, here is the list: 60 bottled beers from 30 countries, 5 hand pumps with constantly changing ales (over 250 different beers last year), local farm cider and country wines. 300 wines from many parts of the world. 175 malt whiskies, 75 blended whiskies, Irish whiskies, 150 different liqueurs, 50 rums, 25 ports, 50 cognacs, armagnacs and brandies. After all that you will appreciate the good variety of bar food which includes local oysters and other fish-orientated dishes, as well as more traditional fare. Situated only yards away from the river, you can arrive by boat and row yourself home.

OPEN: 11 - 3; 6 - 11. Midnight supper licence.
Real Ale. Restaurant.
Children in restaurant but telephone first.
Dogs on leads.
Occasional live entertainment.

ELHAM

The Kings Arms
Tel: 01303 840242

The Square, Elham, Nr Canterbury, Kent CT4 6TJ
Whitbread. Edward Walsh, licensee

The Church and some attractive Georgian and earlier houses form The Square in this very attractive village, set in a valley of chalk hills on the road from Canterbury to Folkestone (the scenic route). The main door of the Kings Arms opens into the fairly small bar, behind which is a spacious dining room. A favourite with locals having a pre-prandial drink, it is also a very popular place to have lunch. Jolly, friendly, blissfully quiet except for contented chat and the thump of darts. A fairly extensive menu: sandwiches, filled potatoes, salads, beef stroganoff, whole trout, chicken Kiev, chicken tagliatelle with garlic bread, vegetarian dishes and many more. Whitbreads, Fremlins Bitter, Flowers Original and Murphys. Choice of wines. Seats in the garden and a couple of tables at the front of the pub overlooking the square. Parking is hit and miss. One of the locals turns up in a pony and trap and ties up in the old stable yard! Probably the best way to arrive.

OPEN: 11 - 3; 6 - 11 (12 - 3; 7 - 10.30 Sun).
Real Ale, Restaurant.
No children in bar. Dogs on leads.

FAIRSEAT

Vigo Inn
Tel: 01732 822547

Fairseat, Nr Wrotham, Sevenoaks, Kent TN15 7JL
Free House. Mrs P J Ashwell, licensee

On top of the North Downs, the North Downs Way passes the pub en route to Trosley Country Park. Originally an old drovers' inn, the paddock next to it will probably still accommodate your cattle or horses. When you have settled your livestock, and got your drink in hand, you can join in a game of 'Dadlums' - an old table skittles game that is so unusual, it is listed in the Guinness Book of Pub Games. Currently, food is limited to filled rolls, but there are plans to change this and offer a fuller menu. Quite a selection of well kept ales: Youngs Bitter, Special and Oatmeal Stout, Harveys XX Mild and Best Bitter. Kilkenny Irish Beer, Liefmans Kriek, Belgian Cherry Beer and lots of local fruit juices plus wine by the glass and farm cider.

OPEN: 12 - 3 Tues - Sun; 6 - 11 Mon - Sat; 7 - 10.30 Sun.
Real Ale. No food Sunday.
Children. Dogs on leads.

FOLKESTONE

The British Lion   Tel: 01303 251472

10 The Bayle, Folkestone, Kent CT20 1SQ
Pubmaster. Brian Matthews, tenant

Before the meddling Victorians got their hands on Folkestone, it was a charming old town built on the top and up the sides of a 500ft cliff. The Bayle, on the eastern side of the Parish Church of St Mary & St Eanswythe, is one of the few relatively unspoilt areas left. It is a charming enclave of mostly Georgian houses (with one or two horrendous blots), and the even older, timbered, British Lion. The pub is extremely attractive visually, and one of a very few in the whole of Folkestone worth a second glance. Externally 16th century and looking very smart and newly painted, the British Lion is quite plain inside, with one small bar and a room to one side. Straightforward bar food: filled rolls, sandwiches - toasted and plain, filled baked potatoes, seafood platter, omelettes, salads and steaks. Boddingtons, Flowers Original, Castle Eden and Bass ales. A selection of malt whiskies. Picnic tables in the small courtyard.

OPEN: 11 - 3; 6 - 11.
Real Ale.
No children. Dogs on leads.

GROOMBRIDGE

Crown   Tel: 01892 864742

10 The Walks, Groombridge, Kent
Free House. Bill & Vivienne Rhodes, licensees

Together with a charming terrace of tile hung 18th century cottages, this Tudor pub is in an enviable position, situated on the edge of the sloping village green, with views over the green towards the village below. Inside the Crown there are lots of beams, ancient timbers, and an inglenook fireplace. A good varied menu - lots of salads, steak & mushroom pie, home-cooked ham, properly cooked vegetables, sandwiches and Sunday roasts. Harveys IPA, Courage Directors and Ruddles Best, local farm cider, house wines by the glass. Groombridge Place is very near and well worth a visit.

OPEN: 11 - 2.30 (3 Sat); 6 - 11 (11 - 11 Summer Sats).
Real Ale. Restaurant (evenings). No food Sun eves.
Children in restaurant.
Dogs on leads.
Occasional Morris dancers.
Bedrooms.

HADLOW

Artichoke Inn   Tel: 01732 810763

Park Road, Hamptons, Hadlow, Kent TN11 9SR
(off Hadlow/Plaxtol road)
Free House. Terence & Barbara Simmonds, licensees

This remote little pub is in an area noted for its hop gardens and orchards. As there are only two small beamed rooms, it can be quite a squeeze if it's busy. During the summer you can spread out on the terrace, enjoy your drink and admire the surrounding countryside. Good reliable home-made bar food - casseroles, vegetable pies, steak & kidney pies, king prawns, steaks and lasagne plus the usual ploughmans and sandwiches. Greene King Abbot, Youngs Special and Fullers London Pride on hand pump.

OPEN: 11.30 - 2.30; 6.30 - 11 (closed Sun eves in winter).
Real Ale. Restaurant (not Sun eve).
Children in eating area.
No dogs.

KINGSDOWN

Zetland Arms   Tel: 01304 364888

Wellington Parade, Kingsdown, Deal, Kent CT14 8AF
(pub on the beach at the end of South & North roads)
Newcastle & Scottish. T J Cobbet, tenant

Nothing much to look at but in a wonderful position to take full advantage of those glorious summer days. You collect your pint and sandwich, sit on the sea-wall and gaze out to sea. When a North easterly gale is blowing you can watch the waves crashing against the sea defences from the safety of the bar. Just one bar, always very popular, with helpful, friendly staff. Food is fairly traditional with dishes such as quiche, fish and chips, a pint of prawns and crab or prawn sandwiches. Shepherd Neame Master Brew, Ruddles County, Websters Yorkshire Bitter and Guinness on hand pump. Carlsberg and Holstein lagers also on draft. Water for the dog.

OPEN: 11 - 3; 6 - 11 (12 - 3; 7 - 10.30 Sun); 11 - 11 Summer.
Real Ale.
Children welcome.
Dogs on leads.

LUDDESDOWNE

Cock Inn   Tel: 01474 814208

Henley Street, Luddesdowne, Kent DA13 0XB (nr Meopham)
Free House. Andrew Turner, licensee

Luddesdowne is a remote village at the junction of four valleys between Gravesend and Meopham. Luddesdowne Court, near the church, thought to date from 1100 AD, is reputed to be one of the oldest inhabited houses in the country. In Meopham itself, Meopham Green will be of interest to all cricket enthusiasts; tradition has it that it was the site of the first cricket match in 1778 between the local team and a team from Chatham. The Cock Inn, set in pleasant countryside has been a public house since the early 1700's; before that it was probably a farmhouse. Evidence of its age can still be seen as some of the old supporting timbers are still in place. Open log fires in the bars whose walls are decorated with an interesting collection of old posters and rural artefacts. There is a short, well chosen menu: toasted sandwiches, filled jacket potatoes, pint of prawns, dressed crab, a selection of pies - steak pie and venison pie - and a rack of pork ribs. A range of cask conditioned ales is kept. Adnams is the main beer, another eight or more are changed regularly. Two farm ciders and some lagers. Seats in the large garden during the summer.

OPEN: Mon - Fri: 12 - 2.30; 5 - 11.
(Sat: 12 - 11. Sun: 12 - 3;7 - 10.30).
Real Ale. Lunchtime meals & snacks. No food Sundays.
Children's room, no children in the bar.
Dogs on leads.

MARSHSIDE

Gate Inn   Tel: 01227 860498

Boyden Gate, Nr Marshside, Canterbury, Kent CT3 4EB
(off A28 Canterbury/Margate road nr Upstreet)
Shepherd Neame. Christopher Smith, tenant

Down a lane off the Canterbury to Margate road, this friendly, busy, unspoilt country pub has just two connecting rooms warmed by a central fireplace. Offering a well cooked, simple menu, the pub has a thriving trade. Fresh local produce is used whenever possible - sandwiches, lots of home-made pickles, spicy sausage hotpot, home-made flans and puddings. At lunchtime the dining area is no-smoking. Shepherd Neame ales are tapped from the cask. In summer you can sit outside by the stream and feed the assortment of ducks and geese that have made their home there. (No duck à l'orange here!)

OPEN: 11 - 2.30 (3 Sat); 6 - 11.
Real Ale.
Children in eating area and family room. Dogs on leads.
Piano Sun eve. Jazz Tues. Folk Fri.

PLUCKLEY

Dering Arms   Tel: 01233 840371

Pluckley, Ashford, Kent TN27 0RR (nr station)
Free House. James Buss, licensee

All H E Bates' fans know Pluckley - home of Pop Larkins. They made very good bricks in Pluckley too. It also has the reputation of being the most haunted village in England. Originally a hunting lodge for the Dering family, the Dering Arms has the distinctive arched "Dering" windows which can be found on all the estate houses. The same windows, thought to bring good luck, are seen even further afield in houses nearer Canterbury. Imposing in its architecture, the main beamed bar has high ceilings, stone floors and a huge fireplace. There is also a small intimate restaurant. The pub provides a good, varied menu, using the finest local ingredients. Many fish dishes: potted crab, fillet of halibut and local trout, home-baked pies, steaks, selected cuts of port and lamb. Every meal is prepared to order. They offer an extensive bar menu. Gourmet evenings are held several times a year. Ales include specially brewed Dering ale and Goachers Maidstone ale. Good range of wines and local farm cider. Garden parties and musical evenings are held in the large garden. Telephone for details.

OPEN: 11 - 3; 6 - 11.
Real Ale. Restaurant (closed Sun evening).
Children in restaurant and eating area.
Dogs on leads.
Folk music every 3rd Sunday.
Bedrooms.

SNARGATE

Red Lion   Tel: 01797 344648

Snargate, Kent, B2080 Brenzett-Appledore road
Free House. Doris Jemison, licensee

In an area filled with Red Lions, this one is in open country between Snargate and Appledore. The pub has somewhat flexible opening times, so don't expect the door to be unlocked on the dot. When the door is open you walk straight into the bar, large enough to accommodate at least six people sitting down, and only a few more than that standing. This bar is also the passageway to the other two, equally small, totally unspoilt rooms. Timeless is the word you would use; beers from the barrel, crisps from the box, maybe a nut! - and coal fires in winter. The gas light fittings are still there, although electricity has crept in as there is a spotlight over the dartboard. You come here for the experience, the good ale, not the comfort. Ales are Batemans XB Bitter, Rother Valley Level Best, (brewed at Northiam) and Orkney Skullsplitter.

OPEN: 11 - 3; 7 - 11. (12 - 4, 7 - 10.30. Sun).
Real Ale.
No children.
No dogs inside.

SOLE STREET

Compasses Inn   Tel: 01227 700300

Sole Street, Crundale, Canterbury, Kent CT4 7ES
(country lane between Godmersham and Petham)
Free House. John & Sheila Bennett

Off the beaten track along a quiet lane between Godmersham and
Petham. Two rooms front and back in this 15th century pub.
Polished flagstone floors and a restored bread oven in one,
polished boards, beams and log fire in the other. Varied bar food -
soups, filled rolls, ploughmans, steak & kidney pie, salmon cod &
mushroom pie and puff pastry parcels with various fillings. The
blackboard specials change several times a week. There is a
large garden with an aviary, goats, sheep, and a climbing frame
which is presumably for the children, not the goats. Fullers
London Pride and ESB, Boddingtons, local cider and fruit wines.
Lots of interesting walks nearby.

OPEN: 11 - 3; 6.30 - 11.
Real Ale.
Children in garden room. No dogs.

SUTTON VALENCE

Swan Inn   Tel: 01622 843212

Broad Street, Sutton Valence, Maidstone, Kent
Whitbread. Tom & Jill Peters, licensees

The village of Sutton Valance is built on the slope of a steep hill
six miles south of Maidstone. Famous for its public school which
was founded in 1576, the village has a number of notable

buildings, one of which is the Swan Inn. Built in 1467, well before the public school was thought of, the Swan is a comfortable, well beamed, friendly, old pub with two bars, public and saloon, and a separate restaurant. No foreign food in the restaurant, just good wholesome familiar English fare: Steaks, gammon, chops, Dover sole, King prawns. Bar snacks range from scampi to egg and chips, sausage and chips. Not a big menu, but what they do they try to do well. Ales are Fremlins, Flowers Original and Wadsworths 6X. Guinness and several lagers. A favourite with the labbies of the shooting set, the landlord knows them all by name. Water available, and dog biscuits kept under the counter.

OPEN: 11- 3; 6 - 11.
Real Ale.
Children welcome. Dogs on leads.

TOYS HILL Nr WESTERHAM

Fox & Hounds   Tel: 01732 750328

Toys Hill, Nr Westerham, Kent
Greene King. Hazel Pelling, licensee

Several years ago this fine old establishment with not a juke box to be seen, let alone piped music, won a fight with Allied Lyons to retain the look and feel of a pub. The Brewery had plans for modernising it with restaurants, fun areas and music. But the locals rebelled; and after several months of wrangling, Allied Lyons gave in. "We're having a party next year to celebrate winning that battle ten years ago," Hazel Pelling told THE QUIET PINT, "we don't like anything that destroys the harmony of the place - and that includes mobile phones, which are disruptive and noisy. Anyone thinking of making a call is hurled straight into the gents' lavatory or the car park." Food is limited to lunchtime snacks - ploughmans, caulifower cheese, etc. Sundays and Bank Holidays filled rolls only. Greene King IPA, Abbot Ale, Guinness on hand pump. Cider and Harp lager. Let the correspondent who told us about this pub have the last word. She said, "The Fox is rather like a front room; furnished with somewhat battered sofas and chairs. In winter there are two log fires, which add to the cosy atmosphere. And there's NO POP MUSIC, which is heaven!" Shows what you can do if you try.

OPEN: 11.30 - 2.30; 6 - 11 Mon - Fri; 11.30 - 3. 6 - 11 Sat.
11.30 - 3; 7 - 11.30 Sun.
Real Ale.
Children with parents in special area, lunchtimes only.
Dogs on leads.

LANCASHIRE WITH GREATER MANCHESTER, MERSEYSIDE & CHESHIRE

BALDERSTONE

Myerscough Hotel   Tel: 01254 812222

Whalley Road, Balderstone, Blackburn, Lancs BB2 7LE (on A59)
Robinsons. John Peddar, tenant

Very much a favourite meeting place for lunch during the week,
this friendly country pub is popular with businessmen and families
from the nearby British Aerospace plant. You really can't miss it,
as a Canberra bomber and Lightning fighter are parked on the
other side of the road. Plenty of room in the beamed, comfortable
bars where they serve good, traditional bar food. Robinsons ales
and Hartleys XB plus a good selection of malt whiskies.

OPEN: 11.30 - 3; 5.30 - 11.
Real Ale.
Children in front room till 8.30. No dogs except guide dogs.
Wednesday Quiz night.
Bedrooms.

BARTHOMLEY

White Lion   Tel: 01270 882242

Barthomley, Nr Crewe, Cheshire CW2 5PG
Burtonwood. Terence Cartwright, proprietor

The White Lion is an extremely attractive, thatched, timber-framed, early 17th Century inn. Opposite, is a 15th Century church where Robert Corke, who was landlord at the time of the Civil War, must have watched what has come to be recorded in history books as the Barthomley Massacre. According to the present landlord - Terry Cartwright, who is the 19th since the pub was first licensed in 1614 - recently discovered evidence shows that the incident was blown up out of all proportion. The "massacre" was used for propaganda purposes preparatory to the trial of Charles I. The men smoked out of the bell-tower and severely beaten up were actually a bunch of contemporary "Skinheads" - rather than "Roundheads" - who had been hurling drunken abuse at a King's Troop. The White Lion's three beamed rooms, some with panelling and one with a bar, have not changed much in appearance over the centuries. The fare they offer today is undoubtedly as popular as it ever was. They serve very reasonably priced lunchtime food, including soups, filled French sticks, hot beef sandwiches and home-made hotpot. Saturday & Sunday: only pies and rolls available. The pub gets very busy over weekends, but they can always find you a pie and a pint. Burtonwood Mild, Bitter, Forshaws and Top Hat on hand pump.

OPEN: 11.30 - 11. Closed Thurs lunchtime.
Real Ale. Lunchtime meals & snacks.
No children in main bar. Must be gone by 8.30.
Dogs on leads. Bedrooms.

BLACKSTONE EDGE

White House   Tel: 01706 378456

Blackstone Edge, Little Borough, Rochdale, OL15 0LG
Free House. Neville Marney, licensee

A great favourite with walkers on the Pennine Way, which crosses the road outside this windswept old pub high on the moors. There is a warm welcome in the main bar with its glowing coal fire. From another room you have a view over the moors: you can see either where you came from or where you are going. Alternatively, if it all looks too tiring: book a taxi home. Daily specials as well as the usual bar food: home-made soups, sandwiches, quiche, steak &

kidney pies, garlic mushrooms, salads and steaks. Children's portions. Marstons Pedigree, Moorhouse Pendle Witches' Brew, Theakstons Best and Black Sheep Bitter. Farm ciders and several malt whiskies. Remove the muddy boots and leave them in the porch. Only clean shoes or socks inside the bars.

OPEN: 11.30 - 3; 7 - 11.
Real Ale. Restaurant.
Children welcome. No dogs.

BRINDLE

Cavendish Arms   Tel: 0125 4852912

Sandy Lane, Brindle, Nr Chorley, Lancs
Burtonwood. Peter Bowling, tenant

A cheerful village pub with lots of comfortable seating inside and outside on the terrace and small lawn. In the bar there are interesting stained-glass partitions depicting a skirmish near the river estuary between the Vikings and Anglo-Saxons. There are also a number of Devonshire family heraldic emblems on display - hardly surprising as they bought the village in the 16th century. Good familiar bar food: home-made pies, lasagne, crispy cod, roast beef and Yorkshire pudding and daily changing specials. Burtonwood ales and a range of malt whiskies.

OPEN: 12 - 3; 5.30 - 11.
Real Ale. Restaurant (no meals or snacks Sun eve).
Children in eating areas. No dogs.

CROSBY, LIVERPOOL

Crows Nest   Tel: 0151 9313081

63 Victoria Road, Crosby, Liverpool, Merseyside
Boddingtons. Norman Thomas, licensee

You know just where you are when you read the sign outside this pub. "No music, no pool, no fruit machines, no footballers and no food." It is just serious drinking here. Good traditional beer and conversation. Frequented largely by professionals - teachers, barristers and the like. A few years ago the brewery proposed installing a juke box but a petition forestalled that for a couple of years. Then one did suddenly appear, but customers were "persuaded" not to use it and it soon vanished. A popular local with bar, snug and lounge. Cains Mild, Boddingtons and various lagers, stouts and cider. No garden, but one is being laid out.

OPEN: 11.30 - 11.
Real Ale.
Children allowed if well behaved.
No dogs.

DELAMERE

Fishpool Inn   Tel: 01606 883277

Fishpool Road, Delamere, Nr Northwich, Cheshire CW8 2HP
Greenalls. Michael & Kathleen Melia, tenants

The name Delamere. is taken from the Norman forest which used to cover much of Cheshire. The present forest is largely coniferous and man-made but very popular, as it has many marked paths for walkers. The fish pool is still there in the form of a pike-filled lake, which centuries ago was fished by the monks from the local abbey. This rambling, beamed old pub has probably been a centre of great activity for all its 300 years. Good wholesome bar food available: sandwiches, pies, Cumberland sausages, fresh salmon steaks, etc. Greenalls Bitter, Mild and Original on hand pump. Choice of wines.

OPEN: 11 - 3; 6 - 11.
Real Ale.
Children in eating area.
No dogs.
Bedrooms.

GARSTANG

Th'Owd Tithe Barn
Tel: 01995 604486

Church Street, Garstang, Lancs PR3 1PA
Free House. Kerry & Eunice Matthews, licensees

A converted farm barn by the Lancaster Canal, four miles from Beacon Fell Park, with its coniferous forest, moorland and views to the Welsh mountains and Lakeland hills. Low-beamed, flagstoned bar and dining area, well polished pews and tables, an old kitchen range and collection of antique farm tools take you back a century or two, which the licensees encourage by dressing the serving wenches in period costume. The choice of food ranges from the usual bar snacks to a selection of roasts, pies, salads and plain ham and eggs. Children are catered for and the ice cream menu has to be seen to be believed. Mitchells Bitter and Lancaster Bomber. Tetley Mild, Murphys and Carlsberg lager. The speciality of the house are its fruit wines: 21 different flavours brought in by the barrel - they sell more of this than they do beer. Seats on the terrace from where you can watch the boats and ducks on the canal.

Open 11 - 3; 7 - 11 (6 - 11 Sat) Closed Mon. Open Bank Holidays.
Real Ale. Restaurant.
Children till 6 pm. No dogs.

GEE CROSS

Grapes Hotel
Tel: 0161 3682614

Stockport Road, Gee Cross, Hyde, Ches SK14 5RU
Robinsons. Brian Samuels, tenant

On the bend of the steep hill in the old village of Gee Cross, opposite an imposing Victorian-Gothic (dissenting) church, the pub, a large, gabled and bay-windowed building in the "Stockport" style of architecture, has leaded lights and engraved Edwardian windows. It has four large carpeted rooms with red ceilings, brass light fittings, and tiles from bar top to floor. Cheerful and friendly staff and customers. Robinsons traditional ales stocked, including Bitter and Best Mild. A bowling green is attached to the pub so you can while away the time encouraging the experts.

OPEN: 12 - 3; 5 - 11.
Real Ale.
No children. No dogs.

GOOSNARGH

Bushells Arms   Tel: 01772 865235

Church Lane, Goosnargh, Preston, Lancs PR3 2BH
Whitbreads. David & Glynis Best, tenants

An extremely popular pub, not far from the M6 (exit 32). The home-cooked food here - based on fresh local produce - leans imaginatively towards the Mediterranean and especially Greece, although Lancashire hotpot, Cumberland sausage casserole and the like are not forgotten. Daily specials are listed on the blackboard and two of the eating areas are non-smoking. Tetleys and Boddingtons ales. A good wine list features a monthly special choice. There are seats outside in the garden.

OPEN: 12 - 3; 6 - 11. Closed some Mondays.
Real Ale.
Well behaved children in eating area until 9 pm.
No dogs.

HESWALL

Black Horse   Tel: 0151 342 2254

Village Road, Lower Heswall, Merseyside P60 0DP
Bass Taverns. Kevin McCardle, manager

Over a hundred years old, the Black Horse, once a hotel, is well known as somewhere to come and have a chat. It has the equipment to play the dreaded wallpaper music, but Kevin McCardle, who took over the pub earlier this year, won't use it. "Mine's a talking pub at our clients request," he says. Whatever music they do play is live - an Irish night for example, or a pianist dropping in and playing for a pint. Inside there is a big lounge and a conservatory. Standard English fare: sandwiches, jacket potatoes, crusty rolls with hot fillings, sizzling steaks, and mixed grills - all served with chips. Daily specials, vegetarian dishes - good filling pub food. Bass Mild XXXX, special draught and varying guest ales. No garden and a very small car park.

OPEN: 11.30 - 11.
Real Ale. No food Sundays.
No children admitted at the moment.
No dogs.

LYTHAM

The Taps   Tel: 01253 736226

Henry Street, Lytham, Lancs FY8 5LE
Whitbreads. Ian Rigg, manager

===

This one's really for the true beer enthusiast. It is not far from the beach, so there's a seashore theme running through the pub (fish, boats and things) - but the real interest here is in the beer. In one year a thousand different varieties of ales were available - not all at once! No doubt all the others being brewed will be tasted by the Taps' patrons in due course - at that rate you take pot luck (if that's the expression with beer), as who knows what's on offer. Traditional bar food with home-made daily specials.

Open 11 - 11.
Real Ale. Lunchtime meals & snacks, not Sunday.
Children in eating area at mealtimes.
Dogs on lead.

MANCHESTER

Royal Oak   Tel: 0161 445 3152

729 Wilmslow Road, Didsbury, Manchester 20 RO
Marstons. Arthur Gosling, tenant

What a wonderful choice. Cheese and ale, sherry and port. For more than 30 years the landlord has been tracking down cheeses from all sorts of places - a truly knowledgeable cheese enthusiast who has created a sort of Paxton and Whitfield in Manchester. A choice of two cheeses - and this is no mean sliver, more a hunk - with a chunk of bread and salad for £2.80. You should get yourself over there rapidly. If you're not into cheese you can usually get soup and country paté. Marstons, Burton and Pedigree, Bateman Mild and a guest beer plus sherries and port from the barrel. Delicious with cheese.

Open 11 - 11.
Real Ale. Lunchtime snacks, not weekends or Bank Holidays.
No children. No dogs.

MELLOR

Devonshire Arms   Tel: 01614 272563

Longhurst Lane, Mellor, Nr Marplebridge, Stockport SK6 5PP
Robinsons. Brian Harrison, tenant

A cheerful, friendly pub with a reputation for good imaginative home-made food. It has a constantly changing menu but there is a leaning towards curries and spicy dishes. Varied soups, steamed fresh mussels, chicken and peppers in spicy sauce, smoked sausage, vegetarian dishes, steaks and home-made puds. Robinsons ales, lots of malt whiskies and a good selection of wine.

OPEN: 11 - 3; 5.30 - 11.
Real Ale. Meals & snacks lunchtime & Mon evening.
Well behaved children in eating area.
No dogs. Trad Jazz Thurs eve.

SMALLWOOD

Blue Bell Inn
Tel: 01477 500262

Smallwood, Nr Congleton, Cheshire
Greenalls. Robert Slack, tenant

Off the beaten track and in lovely countryside you'll find the black & white 16th century Bluebell Inn. Open log fires in the beamed bar and lounge, a room for children, and a very attractive garden. Bar food is limited, but there is always soup and a sandwich or two. Greenalls Ales and a selection of malt whiskies.

OPEN: 11 - 11. Pub closed Mon lunchtime.
Real Ale.
Children welcome.
No dogs.

SUTTON

Ryles Arms
Tel: 01260 252244

Hollin Lane, Higher Sutton, Nr Macclesfield, Ches SK11 0NN
Free House. Frank Campbell, licensee

The landlord tells us that he threw out piped music many years ago and certainly nobody has missed it since. Food is important here; though as the local hunt was turning up when we first talked to the landlord, I don't think it was the luncheon menu they were going to be asking for. Traditional bar food: soups, ploughmans, quiches, curry, roast and steak & kidney pie. Part of the dining area is non-smoking and there is also a no-smoking family room. Ruddles Best, County and Marstons Pedigree on hand pump, plus a guest beer.

OPEN: 11.30 - 3; 7 - 11.
Real Ale.
Children in family room until 8.
No dogs.

UPPERMILL

Cross Keys   Tel: 01457 874626

Off Church Road, Uppermill, Saddleworth, Nr Oldham OL3 6LW
Lees. Philip Kay, tenant

This isn't just a pub at the centre of the local community: it is the meeting place for every interest group in the vicinity. Monday night clog dancing, gun club every other Sunday, bridge school Monday and Friday evening, also Saturday lunchtime. It is also the headquarters of the local mountain rescue team. Last but not least, the Cross Keys sponsor the Road Running and Fell Races in August. After all that, you need the good, hearty varied bar food, Lees range of ales and a choice of malt whiskies. Seats outside on the terrace among the flowers. If anyone has the time to look, there is a lovely view and - if you have the energy - good walks.

OPEN: 11 - 11 (11 - 4; 6.30 - 11 winter). All day Sat & Bank Holidays.
Real Ale.
Children in side rooms. Dogs in Butler's Room!
Clog Dancing Mon & Folk Wed evenings.

WALLASEY

Magazine Hotel   Tel: 0151 639 3381

7 Magazine Brow, Wallasey, Merseyside LA5 1MP
Bass Taverns. Martin Venables, manager

Built on the banks of the river, this 18th century black and white pub dates back to the days when the sailing ships had to unload their gunpowder before being allowed to dock. The gunpowder was put into the magazine, 50 yards away - which is why the pub is so called. It was originally an hotel, but when the unloading of gunpowder ceased and the hotel trade died out, it survived by becoming a simple pub. It has one main bar and lots of small rooms full of beams and shiny brass. Lunchtime food only: soups, steak and kidney pies, lasagne, mixed grills and daily specials. Evenings are devoted to the serious drinker. Bass draught is the only ale.

OPEN: 11 - 11 (12 - 3; 7 - 10 Sun).
Real Ale. No food Sat & Sun.
Children allowed. Dogs in garden.

WHARLES

Eagle & Child   Tel: 01772 690312

Church Road, Wharles, Kirkham, Preston PR4 3SJ
Free House. Brian & Angel Tatham, licensees

There's no food here and it is open only on weekday evenings. Strictly a drinking pub. No doubt there's a crisp or a nut to be found somewhere as in days of old, but really it's just a sensible, attractive, thatched country pub with interesting low beamed cosy bars, old furniture and warming fires in winter. Boddingtons ales and three changing guest beers. Some seats outside.

OPEN: 7 - 11 (12 - 3; 7 - 11 Sat & Sun).
Real Ale. No food.
No children. No dogs.

WHITEWELL

Inn at Whitewell   Tel: 01200 448222

Forest of Bowland, Clitheroe, Lancs BB7 3AT
Free House. Richard Bowman, licensee

Owned by the Queen, deep in the lovely rolling English countryside of the Forest of Bowland, next to the village church and overlooking the River Hodder, this 14th century building is an inn of many parts. As well as an hotel and pub it's a wine merchant; pictures are for sale in the picture gallery, cashmere sweaters and hunting gear on sale in the shop. Bored with all that? Lots of magazines and guide books to read and a piano to play. Traditional, well cooked bar food and a more adventurous restaurant menu are available. Interesting soups, game casseroles, and lots of fish. Marstons Pedigree and Boddingtons ales. Extensive, interesting wine list. View of the river from the restaurant and the seats in the garden.

OPEN: 11 - 3; 6 - 11.
Real Ale. Restaurant (not Sun lunchtime).
Children welcome. Dogs on leads.
Pianist Fri evening.

WINCLE

Ship   Tel: 01260 227217

Wincle, Nr Macclesfield, Cheshire SK11 0QE
Free House. Andrew Harmer & Penelope Hinchcliffe, licensees

Thought to be one of the oldest pubs in Cheshire, The Ship was renamed in 1911 after Shackleton's Antarctic Expedition. His ship -Nimrod - is depicted in the pub sign. Deep in the lovely Cheshire countryside, this comfortable old pub offers a good range of bar food: from soup, sandwiches, home-made steak & kidney pie, grilled trout, steaks to Venison casserole. Brown bread & butter ice cream. The house speciality is fondue bourgignon. Boddingtons Bitter and a changing guest beer on hand pump. Selection of wines. Good walking country.

OPEN: 12 - 3; 7 - 11. Closed Mon Nov - March.
Real Ale.
Well behaved children in family room.
Dogs on leads.

LEICESTERSHIRE WITH LINCOLNSHIRE, NOTTINGHAMSHIRE & HUMBERSIDE

BEVERLEY

White Horse Inn
Tel: 01482 861973

22 Hengate, Beverley, Humberside
Sam Smiths. John Southern, lease

There are many fine old Georgian buildings in Beverley and the White Horse is among them. Known as Nellie's - after a redoubtable landlady - the pub has a timeless quality which is much appreciated in these days of "themed" and "restored" pubs (the gas lighting here is original). Just traditional bar food plus a roast on Sundays. There is a no-smoking room behind the bar. Sam Smiths ales, no guest beer.

OPEN: 11 - 11.
Real Ale. Lunchtime meals & snacks.
Children welcome (not in main bar).
Dogs on leads.

BURROUGH ON THE HILL

Stag & Hounds
Tel: 01664 454375

Burrough on the Hill, Leicestershire
Free House. Craig Pinnick, licensee

Half an hour's walk from the Stag and Hounds - five minutes by car - is Little Dalby and Little Dalby Hall, the traditional birthplace in 1720 of Stilton cheese. The same distance away to the north is Melton Mowbray, home of the famous pie. With such a natural affinity to the good things in life, it isn't surprising they are keeping up the momentum at this interesting old coaching inn. Recently taken over by Mr Pinnick, who used to run a French restaurant, the pub is now gaining a reputation for serving excellent French style restaurant food at pub prices. All the food is freshly cooked; all the herbs home grown. Five ales constantly available: Batemans, Ruddles County, Marstons Pedigree and Burrough Hill Bitter. Excellent choice of wines.

OPEN: 11 - 2, 6 - 11; (11 - 3 Sat).
Real Ale.
Restaurant.
Children in the beer garden.
No Dogs.

COLEBY

Bell	Tel: 01522 810240

Far Lane, Coleby, Lincs LN5 0AH
Pubmaster. Robert Pickles & Sara Roe, tenants

This friendly, busy village pub has a comfortable main bar with big log fires at either end, a restaurant and, nicely separated from them, a room with all the noisy bits, including satellite TV. Reasonably priced snacks of the sausage/burger variety are served in the bar and pool room. The restaurant menu is more extravagant: garlic mushrooms in basil and tomato sauce, plaice stuffed with prawns and mushrooms, chicken en croûte and daily specials. Wednesday night is fish night and there are also speciality nights. Marstons Pedigree, Bass and Tetleys ales. Range of malt whiskies. Seats in the garden.

OPEN: 11 - 3; 7 - 11 (6 - 11 summer Sats).
Real Ale. Restaurant.
Children welcome.
Dogs on leads.
Jazz every Friday.

COLSTON BASETT

Martins Arms   Tel: 01949 81361

School Lane, Colston Bassett, Notts NG12 3FD
Free House
Lynne Strafford Bryan & Salvatore Inguanta, licensees

First licensed 300 years ago, it was the squire's residence before that. A touch of bygone formality remains in the smart interiors and uniformed staff, but it is still a welcoming pub. The above average bar menu includes Melton Mowbray pork pies and local Stilton. You won't get a slice of processed ham or tired tomatoes in your sandwiches here - we are into the off-beat and the different: chicken sausages with leek salad, stuffed filo parcels, fish hotpot, pork fillets in ginger sauce, and some original puds. Adnams, Bass, Fullers London Pride and Batemans XB are among the ales they keep. Interesting wine list. Tables outside in the large garden with views over National Trust parkland.

OPEN: 12 - 2.30; 6 - 11.
Real Ale.
Restaurant (no food Sun eve; no snacks/bar food Mon eve).
Children in garden.
No dogs.

GLOOSTON

Old Barn   Tel: 01858 545215

Glooston, Nr Market Harborough, Leics NE16 7XT
Free House. Charles Edmondson-Jones & Stewart Sturge, licensees

Situated on an old Roman road in the small hamlet of Glooston, this 16th century Old Barn Inn is hard to miss at the height of summer. Behind the hanging baskets even the windows are fringed with flowers. The main bar is located behind the restaurant. There is also a smaller bar at the front of the pub, and at the back, up steps, is a no-smoking snug. A blackboard menu shows daily specials. Bar food ranges from home-made soups to hot beef sandwiches and seafood lasagne. There is also a separate evening menu. Theakstons Best Bitter and three other hand pumps for the landlord's choice which could be: Boddingtons, Abbots, Robinsons or Fullers; also, several European bottled beers and a choice of wines. Seats at the front of the pub and in the garden behind.

OPEN: 12 - 2; 7 - 11 (closed Sun eve & Mon lunchtime).
Real Ale. Restaurant (not Sun eve).
Children if well behaved.
Dogs on leads.
Bedrooms.

GRANTHAM

Beehive   Tel: 01476 67794

Castle Gate, Grantham, Lincs
Free House. John Bull & S J Parkes, licensees

Aptly named, as it has its own hive of bees. It's high enough up a lime tree next to the pub to be of no concern and is reputed to be one of the oldest colonies of bees in the country. One hopes honey glazed ham features occasionally. Traditional bar food: ploughmans, soup, fresh sandwiches, daily specials and home-made puddings. Boddingtons, Adnams and a guest beer on hand pump. And is there honey still for tea?

OPEN: 11 - 3; 5 - 11 (7 - 11 Sat). Closed lunch Sun & Bank Hols.
Real Ale. Lunchtime food daily.
Children in eating area lunchtime.
Dogs on leads.

HECKINGTON

Nags Head   Tel: 01529 460218

34 High Street, Heckington, Lincs NG34 9QZ
Wards. Bruce & Gina Pickworth, lease

For some reason the Nags Head is a popular name in these parts; there are several in the vicinity. But don't be waylaid - this is the one you want. It's a 17th century coaching inn with the emphasis on food. It has a comfortable, two roomed bar with a coal fire, friendly landlord, and well presented bar food, sandwiches, vegetarian dishes, daily specials and a Sunday roast. Wards Sheffield Best, Kirby Strong and Vaux Samson ales. Wines by the glass. Tables in the garden. Heckington has a very attractive 14th century church, and an interesting eight-sailed windmill, circa 1830 - the last in the country.

OPEN: 11 - 3; 5 - 11.
Real Ale.
Children welcome.
No dogs.
Quiz night Sun. Bedrooms.

HOSE

Rose & Crown   Tel: 01949 60424

Bolton Lane, Hose, Leics
Free House. Carl & Carmel Routh, licensees

One of the reasons you would beat a path to the door of the Rose & Crown is to sample the tremendous range of beers kept there - many from small breweries in the west and north of the country. Notice of the glories to come is given well in advance, but there have been beers from: Ashvine Brewery in Somerset, Hanbys in Shropshire, Hadrians of Newcastle-on-Tyne and Harviestoun. After all that you would want a roll or two (filled), or a choice of home-made pies, steaks, salads, vegetarian dishes and daily specials. There is a non-smoking restaurant. Tables on the terrace at the back of the pub.

OPEN: 12 - 2.30; 7 - 11.
Real Ale. Restaurant.
Children in bar & eating area until 9 pm.
No Dogs in lounge or restaurant.

HULL

Ye Olde White Harte   Tel: 01482 26363

25 Silver Street, Hull HU1 1JG
Scottish & Newcastle. Brian & Jenny Cottingham, managers

The property of kings and the home of governors, this was an important private residence and it was not until the 18th century that the building became licensed. Aptly named, and not to be confused with the modern White Hart which is not too far away. This one really is old, with the beams, panelling, two huge sit-in fireplaces and all the architectural features you would expect of a building dating back to the 16th century. Here the decision was made by the Governor of Hull to lock the gates of the City against Charles I. Not that it did him much good, as he was beheaded by the Parliamentarians soon after. Almost destroyed by fire in the 19th century, this exceptional old building has outlived the owner of the mysterious skull it houses and which has been passed down through the generations. Very busy during weekday lunchtimes. The bar food includes: sandwiches, paté, pies, salads, changing specials and Ye Olde White Hart's special mixed grill, which should set you up for the day. The dining area is up the fine old staircase. Youngers and Theakstons ales plus a weekly changing guest beer. (An interesting note: women weren't admitted to the pub until 1969.)

OPEN: 11 - 11.
Real Ale. Lunchtime Restaurant.
Children in room upstairs to eat (not in bar). No dogs.

LAXTON

Dovecote Inn   Tel: 01777 871586

Moor House Road, Laxton, Newark NG22 0NU
Free House. Stephen & Betty Shepherd, licensees

Probably the only village retaining medieval strip cultivation: rotating the crops to keep soil fertility - three cropped - one fallow. If only the EEC farming policy were so simple. Lots of different areas in the Dovecote, all the noisy bits in the pool room, the rest blissfully quiet. Home-cooked bar food: soup, sandwiches, ploughmans, a selection of vegetarian dishes, choice of salads, steak and kidney pie and interesting daily specials. Bass, Mansfield ales and Worthingtons. Tables on the small terrace. The village has a fine restored 12th century church.

OPEN: 12 - 3; 6.30 - 11 (12 - 3; 6.30 - 10.30 Sun).
Real Ale.
Children in eating area.
Dogs on leads.

LEICESTER

Welford Place   Tel: 01533 470758

9 Welford Place, Leicester LE1 6ZH
Sam Smiths, Miss Sara Hope, general manager

Lucky Leicester, to be favoured by the inspiration behind Welford Place. Somewhere to meet your friends from 8 in the morning until 12 at night 365 days of the year. In the city centre, adjacent to the New Walk Centre and Phoenix Arts, Welford Place is a delightful Victorian building constructed in 1877. From breakfast to your post-theatre brandy, you will find a welcoming, friendly environment. As with its associated premises, the Wig & Mitre in

Lincoln, there are menus for all times of the day from a leisurely lunch to a quick snack before an evening's entertainment. Draught beers, a comprehensive wine list and an extensive selection of spirits, brandies and liqueurs served from 10.30 to 12 midnight. Room for everything - a cup of coffee or a function for 200 guests.

OPEN: 8 - 12 midnight, 365 days of the year.
Real Ale. Restaurant.
Children in eating area and restaurant.
Dogs on leads.

LINCOLN

Wig & Mitre   Tel: 01522 535190

29 Steep Hill, Lincoln, LN2 1LU
Sam Smiths. Toby & Michael Hope, licensees

More like a club than a pub, though still a pub, the Wig & Mitre has evolved into a meeting place, reading room, restaurant and, as they say themselves, "a haven of peace". Situated on the Pilgrim's Way just below the Cathedral, this inn dates back to the 14th century. Many of the original timbers were reused when the old building was restored 20 years ago. "Food is in perpetual motion" throughout the day from an early breakfast to a sandwich and an à la carte menu; tea too, even breakfast in the afternoon if you so wish. Nothing is too much trouble. Wines (nearly 100 and many by the glass), ales and spirits are available from 11 in the morning until midnight. Sam Smiths ales on hand pump, and as you would expect, freshly squeezed orange juice (remember all those breakfasts) and coffee.

OPEN: 8 - 11.
Real Ale. Restaurant.
Children in eating area & restaurant.
Dogs on leads.

LOUGHBOROUGH

Swan in the Rushes
Tel: 01509 217014

21 The Rushes, Loughborough, Leics
Free House. Andrew Hambleton, licensee

A solid, Victorian town pub with an excellent reputation for good quality, home-cooked bar food which complements its extensive range of European bottled beers and the six or more beers on hand pump. These could include: Theakstons Old Peculiar, Archers Golden, Batemans XXB, Fullers London Pride and a couple of guests. There is also a selection of farm ciders which change periodically. With all this on offer, it is not surprising the pub is very popular and can get crowded. Service does, nevertheless, remain friendly and efficient.

OPEN: 11 - 2.30; 5 - 11 (11 - 11 Fri & Sat).
Real Ale. No food Sat - Mon eves.
Children in dining room. Dogs on leads.
Live music Sat.

NOTTINGHAM

Ye Olde Trip to Jerusalem
Tel: 0115 9473171

Brewhouse Yard, Castle Road, Nottingham NE1 6AD
Hardys & Hansons. Patrick Dare, manager

Reputed to be the oldest pub in England - although others do claim a similar distinction, Ye Olde Trip does, nevertheless, have a lot more to interest historians than its age. It was built into the rock below the castle and was, at one time, its brewhouse. The present building was probably rebuilt on the site of the original inn during the 17th century. Previously named "The Pilgrim," it was the meeting point for crusaders before they sailed to deal with the heathen hordes. Architecturally of interest, the panelled rooms have alcoves cut into the rock, and the cellars are in rock caves. An impressive part-panelled, part rockface, high-ceilinged bar upstairs is open only during very busy periods, and is worth seeing if at all possible. Traditional, sustaining bar food, daily specials plus a few vegetarian dishes. Hardy and Hansons ales and Marstons Pedigree. Seats outside in the courtyard.

OPEN: 11 - 11; (12 - 2.30; 7 - 10.30 Sun).
Real Ale. Lunchtime meals & snacks.
No children.
No dogs.

OLD DALBY

Crown   Tel: 01664 823134

Debdale Hill, Old Dalby, Nr Melton Mowbray, Leics LE14 3LF
Free House. Lynne Strafford, Bryan & Jack Inguanta, licensees

A converted farmhouse, still with its charming, rambling rooms, the Crown is now the focus for those discerning people who want to combine good food with the relaxed ambience to be found in a friendly country pub. The food here has the reputation of being really home-made. You can, if you're lucky, follow the herbs in from the garden. Even the bread is kneaded "in-house", so you know you are in the company of people who really care about their food. A wide range of ales is on offer, amongst which could be Kimberly Bitter, Woodfordes Wherry and Timothy Taylors Landlord. Choice of malt whiskies and a good wine list. Tables on the terrace overlooking the large garden.

OPEN: 12 - 2.30; 6 - 11.
Real Ale. Restaurant (not Sun eve).
Children welcome away from bar.
No dogs.

STAMFORD

George of Stamford
Tel: 01780 55171

71 High Street, St Martins, Stamford, Lincs PE9 2LB
Free House. Ivo Vanocci & Chris Pitman, licensees

Undeniably handsome, the George, with its fine Georgian façade, belies its great age. There are parts of a Norman hospice incorporated in the fabric of this famous old coaching inn, which was built by Lord Birley in the 16th century. On the York to London road, the London and York bars - which face each other just inside the George - were the waiting rooms for the up and down coaches that stopped here each day. It is still a focal point for the local community, whether dining, or enjoying a glass of wine or pint of ale in the comfortable bar. There is a lunchtime buffet in the garden room; also an extensive menu of excellent bar food. Adnams ales, a considerable wine list and all the other niceties you associate with a well run establishment - freshly squeezed orange juice, good coffee and afternoon teas. There is a very attractive cobbled courtyard at the rear of the creeper-covered George, filled with tables and chairs amid flowering tubs and hanging baskets.

OPEN: 11 - 11.
Real Ale. Restaurant (two).
Children welcome.
No dogs.
Bedrooms.

STRETTON

Ram Jam Inn
Tel: 01780 418776

Great North Road, Oakham, Rutland LE15 7QX
Free House. Tim Hart, licensee

They admit that this is more a restaurant than a pub, although from the outside it looks very much like an old coaching inn. Food is served all day from an interesting varied bar menu. Fresh fish daily (not Mondays) and a roast every Sunday. Only one bar, but a comfortable lounge for lounging and a no-smoking restaurant. Ruddles County and Best plus a variety of bottled beers. Good wines. There are seats on the terrace behind the pub.

OPEN: 11 - 11.
Real Ale. Restaurant.
Children welcome.
No dogs.

UFFORD

Olde White Hart   Tel: 01780 740250

Main Street, Ufford, Lincolnshire PE9 3BH
Youngers. Chris & Sally Hodton, tenants

This is a pretty 17th century pub in a large attractive garden, so there's plenty of space to wander in, and to camp if you have brought your tent. There is also a terrace on which you can sit in summer. Popular with walkers and cyclists. The pub has two comfortable bars and a recently refurbished snug. Lunchtime snacks include a variety of exotic dishes which change from week to week. The usual sandwiches, maybe stuffed pancakes or rump steak in garlic sauce, daily specials, and on Sunday there is a roast lunch and hot beef rolls. Theakstons Best, XB and Old Peculiar. Guest beers and lots of imported bottled beers. Wines by the glass and farm cider.

OPEN: 11 - 2.30 (3 Sat) 6 - 11.
No food Sun eve or Mon.
Real Ale.
Children in eating areas.
Dogs on leads.
Live music Sun evenings.

WEST LEAKE

Star Inn
Tel: 01509 852233

Melton Lane, West Leake, Nr Loughborough, Leicestershire
Gibbs Mew. Linda Collin, licensee

There are fine views across beautiful countryside from this lovely old coaching inn. Inside the beamed bars are comfortably furnished and in winter they have open log fires. A happy mix of drinkers and diners make it lively, cheerful and friendly. Food is home-cooked and the menu changes daily. There could be soup, mushrooms in cream and garlic sauce, paté, roast leg of pork, chicken chasseur and a choice of puddings. Bass and Theakstons ales. Over a dozen malt whiskies. Seats and tables outside during the summer.

OPEN: 11 - 3; 6 - 11.
Real Ale.
Children in family room.
Dogs on leads.

MIDLANDS

BRIERLEY HILL

Vine
Tel: 01384 78293

10 Delph Road, Brierley Hill, W Midlands DY5 2TN
Bathams. Melvin Wood, manager

Also known locally as The Bull and Bladder from the stained glass Bull's Head and the freely interpreted bunch of grapes which decorates the front window. Plenty of room in this bustling pub. Not quite a permanent beer line to the brewery, but as it is next door there could well be! Popular, well made and reasonably priced lunchtime snacks, sandwiches and lots of salads. Bathams Bitter and Mild on hand pump, also Delf Strong Ale in winter.

OPEN: 12 - 11.
Real Ale. Lunchtime snacks (not Sun).
Children in own room. Dogs on leads.
Live music Sun & Mon: Blues/Jazz/Folk.

CRICK

Red Lion
Tel: 01788 822342

52 Main Road, Crick, Northants NN6 7TX
Free House. Tom & Mary Marks, lease

Always useful to know of a stopping place if you have to travel on motorways (M1 junction 18). In winter this comfortable thatched pub has log fires in the low ceilinged bar, and in summer, you can relax on the terrace at the back of the pub and admire the floral display. Reasonably priced lunchtime snacks - the usual filled rolls, ploughmans, steak & kidney pie, gammon and a chicken dish. Steaks and fish available on the evening menu. John Smiths, Websters Yorkshire, Hook Norton Best and Courage Directors.

OPEN: 11.30 - 2.30; 6.30 - 11.
Real Ale. No food Sun eves.
Children in family room lunchtime only. Dogs on leads.

EARLSDON

Royal Oak   Tel: 01203 674140

Earlsdon Street, Earlsdon, Coventry CV5 6EJ
Free House. Ray Evitts, licensee

Having taken over this pub about two years ago, the landlord has made it immensely popular with those who appreciate good beer served in pleasing, unfussy, friendly surroundings. Large wooden communal tables and comfortable chairs. Waiter service in the rear bar. House rules are rigorously applied - no dogs, no music, no noisy, rowdy behaviour and no food! Ansells ales, Bass, Tetley, draught Guinness and guest beers.

OPEN: 5 - 11; Mon - Sat: 12 - 2.30; 7 - 10.30 Sun.
Real Ale. No food.
No dogs.

FIVEWAYS

Case is Altered   Tel: 01926 484206

Case Lane, Fiveways, Hatton, Nr Warwick CV35 7JD (N of Warwick)
Free House. Mrs Gwen Jones, licensee

Down a country lane about three miles from Warwick, this is a basic, old-fashioned pub in the best possible sense. The bar is beamed, has a red tiled floor, old wooden tables and chairs and log fires during the winter. Popular with locals, and at weekends with walkers and cyclists. No food, but sandwiches can be ordered. Ansells Ales, Sam Smiths and Flowers Original.

OPEN: 11.30 - 2.30; 6 - 11.
Real Ale. No food.
No dogs.

FOTHERINGHAY

Falcon Inn   Tel: 01832 6254

Fotheringhay, Nr Oundle, Northants PE8 5HZ
Free House. Alan Stewart, licensee

A busy, lively, friendly, informal village pub with a reputation for good value, imaginative food, both at lunchtime and in the evening. All the dishes are home-made so they are restricted in number. It is advisable to book to ensure that the particular dish you have chosen hasn't run out. Usual bar staples, ranging from sandwiches, ploughmans to salmon fish cakes. Specials could include roast duckling with apple and rosemary stuffing, coq au vin and venison cutlets. Greene King, Adnams, Elgoods Cambridge, Nethergate and Ruddles County. Tables in the garden. Fotheringhay Castle is not too far away and is well worth a visit.

OPEN: 10 - 3; 6 - 11 (7 - 11 Mon winter).
Real Ale. Restaurant (not Mon).
Children in eating area and restaurant.
Dogs in tap room.

KENILWORTH

Virgins & Castle   Tel: 01926 53737

7 High Street, Kenilworth, Warwicks CV8 1LY
Davenports (Greenalls). Alan & Sue Gregory, managers

The ruins of Kenilworth Castle, which dates back to Norman times, dominate this attractive town in the heart of England, through which the River Avon meanders. There are four rooms in this old town pub, all beamed, all different, and all with their own character. Good bar food includes soup, sandwiches and ploughmans plus a choice of vegetarian dishes and daily changing casseroles, steak & kidney pies, etc. Davenports Ales, Wadworths 6X, Greenalls Original and a guest beer. Seats outside in the walled garden.

OPEN: 11 - 3; 5 - 11 (all day Sat).
Real Ale. Restaurant.
Children in rooms without bar.
Dogs on leads.
Trad Jazz Summer Sundays. Folk Tues.

LAPWORTH

Navigation Inn   Tel: 01564 783337

Old Warwick Road, Lapworth, Warwicks
M & B (Bass). Andrew Kimber, lease

A busy, friendly canalside pub which, though popular all year, comes into its own during warm summer days when you can sit out on the lawn and watch the water flow by. Appetising bar food: filled rolls, lasagne, beef guinness and mushroom pie, steaks, curries, etc. Anything can be going on in the garden, from a barbecue to visiting Morris dancers, or a theatre company. Draught Bass, M&B Mild Brew X1 and changing guest beer. Farm ciders during the summer. There are tables on the lawn which runs down to the water's edge.

OPEN: 11 - 2.30; 5.30 - 11 (11 - 3; 6 - 11 winter). Sat all day summer.
Real Ale. No food Sun & Mon eves winter.
Children in eating area before 9 pm. Dogs on leads.
Occasional Morris Dancing/folk music.

NEWBOLD ON STOUR

White Hart Inn   Tel: 01789 450205

Stratford Road, Nr Stratford on Avon
M & B (Bass). Mr & Mrs J Cruttwell, lease

There is a juke box in the public bar but if you chat a lot in the main bar you may not hear it. A popular local, offering a good selection of reasonably priced food. It gets very busy on Friday and Saturday evenings. You should book if you want to have a Sunday lunch. Home-made soups, ploughmans, braised lamb in wine and herbs, poached salmon in cream herb sauce and paella. Bass and Worthingtons Best on hand pump. Seats outside at the front of the pub amid the flowers.

OPEN: 11 - 2.30 (3 Sat); 6 - 11.
Real Ale. Restaurant (no food Sun eve).
Children welcome. Dogs on leads.

ORLINGBURY

Queens Arms   Tel: 01933 678258

11 Isham Road, Orlingbury, Kettering, Northants NN14 1JD
Free House. Paul Stanbrook, licensee

Bought by the landlord from Grand Met in 1992, this fine 18th century listed building has been turned into a gimmick-free pub, regularly serving at least nine real ales. Friendly, welcoming with a large L-shaped bar and smaller lounge bar, both of which have big log fires in the winter. Pub snacks and good sandwiches available.

Among the many ales on hand pump are Theakstons Best, Fullers London Pride, Marstons Pedigree, Morlands Old Speckled Hen and six guest beers. Seats outside in the big garden.
NB: Voted Northants Pub of the Year in 1994 (for its ales).

OPEN: 11.30 - 2.30; 5.30 - 11 (12 - 3; 7 - 10.30 Sun).
Real Ale. No food Sunday.
No children. No dogs.

OUNDLE

Ship Inn   Tel: 01832 273918

West Street, Oundle, Northants PE8 4EF
Free House. Frank Langbridge, licensee

Heavily beamed bars, one with a blazing fire and one panelled snug which is no-smoking. Choice of bar food, ranges from soups, sandwiches, ploughmans, salads, steak & kidney pie, lasagne to curries. Roasts and pies only on Sundays. A busy, popular pub. Tetleys, Wadworths 6X, Marstons Pedigree, Bass and a guest beer.

OPEN: 11 - 3; 6 - 11 (11 - 11 Sat).
Real Ale.
Children welcome. Dogs on leads.
Bedrooms.
Live music Fri or Sat.

PITSFORD

The Griffin   Tel: 01675 481205

25 High Street, Pitsford, Northants NN7 9ND
Free House. Mr & Mrs A Worthington, licensees

This stone-built pub, about three miles north of Northampton, takes its name from the heraldic emblem of the Earls of Strafford who, during the 18th century, were Lords of the Manor for both Boughton and Pitsford and created a wonderful Gothic folly in nearby Boughton Park. Popular during the early evening with local doctors, lawyers, accountants and farmers having a pre-dinner drink before wending their way home. This gives the Griffin a 'clubby' atmosphere in the early evening. Friendly and relaxing, the Pitsford Young Farmers Club and, of course, many local people use it too. Only bar snacks are served. Theakstons Best Bitter, XB and Old Peculiar on hand pump.

OPEN: 12 - 2.30; 6 - 11.
No food Monday lunchtime.
No children. Dogs in bar only.

SHUSTOKE

Griffin Inn   Tel: 01675 481205

Nr Coleshill, Birmingham B46 2LB (at Furnace End E of Shustoke)
Own Brew. Michael Pugh & Sydney Wedge, licensees

An old-fashioned, 300 year old village pub with its own small brewery set up last year in what used to be a coffin shop. There is a large, beamed bar and a roomy conservatory where children are allowed. Good choice of bar food ranges from sandwiches, various fish dishes, steak & kidney pie to steaks. There are a dozen or so hand pumps for a wide choice of beer - the guests changing every couple of days. The Griffin's own bitter has recently been christened, and the first-named, M Reg GTI reflects the motoring interest of the landlord. Not sure what interest Gravediggers' Mild indicates, something to do with the coffins, no doubt. The Sunbeam Alpine Tiger Club meets monthly. Seats outside in the garden and on the terrace.

OPEN: 12 - 2.30; 7 - 11.
Real Ale. Lunchtime meals & snacks (not Sun).
Children in conservatory. Dogs on leads.

WOOTTON WAWEN

Bulls Head   Tel: 01564 793511

Stratford Road
Free House. John Willmott, licensee

Over 300 years old, this heavily timbered, attractive black & white inn is proving increasingly popular since becoming a free house. There is an imaginative menu: a good choice of seafood, excellent sausages, home-made quiche, daily specials and vegetables in season. Marstons, Morlands, Wadworths 6X, Fullers London Pride, a range of wines. Seats in the garden.

OPEN: 12 - 3; 6 - 11.
Real Ale. Restaurant.
Well behaved children.
No dogs.

NORFOLK

BLAKENEY

Kings Arms
Tel: 01263 740341

Westgate Street, Blakeney, Norfolk
Free House. Howard & Marjorie Davies, licensees

Blakeney is a yachting centre with a main street of brick and flint houses. Near the quay and in the bracing sea air of one of East Anglia's most picturesque villages, the 18th century Kings Arms - once three fishermen's cottages - is among the most popular pubs in the area. It is simply furnished and the walls of the bars are decorated with lots of photographs of the licensees' theatrical careers and original paintings by local artists. A wide range of bar food is available: home-made pies, seafood pasta, local crabs and other fish, vegetarian dishes and daily specials. There are two no-smoking areas in the pub. Norwich, Webster and Ruddles Bitters plus the local Woodfordes Wherry. Fosters and Carlsberg lagers. Seats on the terrace at the front of the pub and in the large garden. There is also a separate children's area.

OPEN: 11 - 11.
Real Ale. Meals all day weekends.
Children welcome. Dogs on leads. Self-catering flatlets.

BLICKLING

Buckinghamshire Arms
Tel: 01263 732133

Blickling, Nr Aylsham, Norfolk NR11 6NF (off B1354 N of Aylsham)
Free House. Danny & Wendy Keen, licensees

Once the servants' quarters of Blickling Hall - which now belongs to the National Trust - this 17th century listed building has three pleasant and comfortable bars, all with open fires. If you are lucky enough to stay here, you get a wonderful view of floodlit Blickling Hall from two of the bedrooms. Good selection of bar food: home-made soups, sandwiches, ploughmans, game pies, baked gammon and home-made puds. Adnams Southwold, Woodfordes Wherry and Baldrick ales, plus a good selection of wines. There are picnic tables on the lawn. You can walk through Blickling Park all year round.

OPEN: 11 - 3; 6 - 11.
Real Ale. Restaurant.
Children in Restaurant. No dogs. Bedrooms.

BURNHAM MARKET

Hoste Arms
Tel: 01328 738257

The Green, Burnham Market, Norfolk PE31 8HD
Free House. Pauline Osler & Paul Whittome, licensees

A handsome seventeenth century hotel, The Hoste Arms overlooks the green in the beautiful Georgian village of Burnham Market, in the heart of Nelson's Norfolk. Inside there are two very welcoming bars, one of which has a grand piano the landlord will play when he's in the mood - usually when there's live jazz on Monday and Friday evenings. The bar menu, available both at lunchtime and in the evening, served in both bars and the conservatory, could include: pasta, soups, venison pie, steaks, home-cooked ham and daily specials from the blackboard. In the evening, the restaurant, which is partly non-smoking, serves a daily changing à la carte menu. Woodfordes Wherry, Ruddles and Websters, Hook Norton Old Hooky and guest beers. Seats in the garden and at the front of the pub among the flower tubs.

OPEN: 11 - 11 (11 - 3; 6 - 11 winter).
Real Ale. Restaurant.
Children welcome. Dogs on leads. Bedrooms.
Live Jazz Mon & Fri.

COLKIRK

Crown   Tel: 01328 862172

Crown Road, Colkirk, Fakenham, Norfolk NR21 7AA
Greene King. P Whitmore, tenant

A straightforward village pub, friendly and comfortable, serving good, interesting food without pretention. Cosy fires in the public and lounge bar. There is also a dining room. Menu includes soup, prawns and mushrooms in garlic, paté, lots of fresh fish and salads. Good puds too. Small but interesting wine list. Greene King Abbot and Rayments ales. Tables at the back of the pub.

OPEN: 11 - 3 6 - 11.
Real Ale. No food after 1.30 Sun.
Children in lounge & dining area. Dogs on leads.

ERPINGHAM

Saracens Head   Tel: 01263 768909

Wolterton, Nr Erpingham, Norfolk, off A140 Nr Wolterton Hall
Free House. Robert Dawson-Smith, licensee

You need a good map to find the Saracens Head, but persevere, the hunt is worth it. The secret is to find Wolterton Hall; the pub is not far away. When you get there you'll find interesting, unusual snacks and a selection of main dishes which change for both lunch and dinner; Monday to Friday there is a special, very reasonable, two-course lunch with, I quote, "no chips, peas or fried scampi." Special feast nights are held throughout the year: Mediterranean feast night, for example, venison, seafood or French feast. You can even organize your own if you are so inclined. The everyday changing-menu could include: duck and orange soup, sautéed wild mushrooms, ham in a sherry sauce, mussels in cider and cream, grilled fillet of trout, braised local pigeon, vegetarian croûte and lovely puddings. And that's just lunch! The main dinner course could be roast local pheasant, pot roast leg of lamb with herbs and cream or grilled fresh salmon in a white wine sauce. Seats in the delightful courtyard and the walled garden. There is even a special evening garden menu. Adnams ales and several guest beers; a good choice of wines.

OPEN: 11 - 3; 6 - 11.
Real Ale.
Well behaved children welcome.
No dogs. Bedrooms.

NORTH CREAKE

Jolly Farmers   Tel: 01328 738185

1 Burnham Road, North Creake, Norfolk NR21 9JW
Pubmaster. Peter Whitney, tenant

A favourite with the locals (being the only pub in the village), this is a friendly two-bar establishment with a big welcoming fire in winter. Good choice of home-made dishes, fresh fish, ploughmans, filled rolls, pork in cider, steak & kidney pie, coq au vin, steaks, etc. Greene King IPA, Abbot and Ind Coope Burton ales. Choice of wines. Seats outside in the garden.

OPEN: 11.30 - 2.30 (3 Sat); 6 - 11.
Real Ale. Restaurant.
Children in restaurant. Dogs on leads.

REEDHAM

Ferry Inn
Tel: 01493 700429

Reedham Ferry, Norwich, Norfolk NR13 3HA
Free House. David Archer, licensee

As the name implies, this pub has rather watery connections. The ferry plying to and fro across the river belongs to the pub and is able to carry three cars. They also have a launching ramp for boats up to 35 ft long. After all that excitement you can either anchor yourself in the bar or on the terrace to enjoy all that the pub has to offer. There is a wide range of dishes: freshly prepared sandwiches, ploughmans, fresh fish and home-made pies, a changing seasonal menu using local produce, a children's menu and a selection of vegetarian dishes. Woodfordes Nelson's Revenge, Charles Wells Eagle and Adnams ales plus guest beers. Also country wines.

OPEN: 11 - 3; 6.30 - 11 (11 - 2.30; 7 - 11 winter).
Real Ale. Restaurant.
Children until 9 pm. Dogs on leads.

SNETTISHAM

Rose & Crown Inn
Tel: 01485 541382

Old Church Road, Snettisham, Norfolk PE31 7LX
Free House. Anthony Goodrich, licensee

Find the pretty hanging baskets and you have found the Rose & Crown. A rambling, beamed old pub, with big fireplaces and four bars. Very popular with families as it is geared up to accommodate children and keep them happy. Well served bar food in ample proportions: sandwiches, ploughmans, lots of salads (rare beef, seafood, etc), wide choice of vegetarian dishes and grills. A children's menu and a selection of barbecue dishes. Greene King IPA, Abbot, Adnams, Bass and guest beers on hand pump. Seats on the terrace and in the garden. Family room, and a well equipped children's play area outside.

OPEN: 11 - 3; 5.30 - 11 (11 - 11 summer Sat).
Real Ale. Restaurant.
Children in own room & eating areas. No dogs. Bedrooms.

STIFFKEY

Red Lion   Tel: 01328 830552

Wells Road, Stiffkey, Wells next Sea, Norfolk NR23 1AJ
Free House. Adrienne Cooke, licensee

This white brick and flint building has only fairly recently been brought back to life after having been closed down, along with other village pubs, by one of the big national brewers during the 60's. Now a busy, jolly place, it is furnished with pine tables and settles, and serves good, home-cooked food. The blackboard menu is changeable but there are always generously filled sandwiches, a paté, ploughmans, grilled fish and baked crab. Woodfords Ales, Greene King IPA, Abbot and guest beers. Seats on the terrace.

OPEN: 11 - 3 (2.30 winter); 6 - 11 (5.30 - 11 Sat).
Real Ale. Restaurant (closed Sun).
Children welcome. Dogs on leads.

STOW BARDOLPH

Hare Arms   Tel: 01366 38229

Stow Bardolph, Norfolk PE34 3HT
Greene King. Trish & David McManus, tenants

A nice old country pub, very much part of the village, busy and friendly. It has a large comfortable bar, adjacent to the conservatory, where a wide variety of food is served throughout the week. Bar food could include: sandwiches, soups, home-made paté, game pie, prawn and dill tartlets, chicken with crab, pork marsala, and Madeira chicken. The restaurant menu is more extensive. All the dishes are home-cooked, using local seasonal produce, local game, fresh fish, lamb and beef. Imaginative puds. Greene King ales. Good selection of wines. Tables in the garden among the peacocks.

OPEN: 11 - 2.30; 6 - 11.
Real Ale. Restaurant (not Sun eves).
Children in Conservatory. No dogs.

THORNHAM

Lifeboat Inn   Tel: 01485 512236

Thornham, Norfolk PE36 6LT
Free House. Nicholas & Lynn Handley, licensees

A charming, rambling 16th century smugglers' inn and restaurant. Low beamed ceilings, quarry-tiled floors, old oak furniture, blazing fires in winter and tempting home-cooked food. The bar menu ranges from soup, stuffed Thornham mushrooms, Lifeboat toasties, Brancaster mussels, to Lifeboat fish pie. Summer buffets in the garden. An à la carte menu is available in the restaurant. Greene King ales, Adnams, Woodfordes Wherry and guest beers. Good range of wines.

OPEN: 11 - 11.
Real Ale. Restaurant.
Children welcome. Dogs on leads. Bedrooms.
Folk/Country/Jazz Fri & Sun eves.

TITCHWELL

Manor Hotel   Tel: 01485 210221

Titchwell, Kings Lynn, Norfolk PE31 8BB
Free House. Ian & Margaret Snaith, licensees

Close to the RSPB Titchwell Reserve and situated in a coastal area of tremendous interest, this comfortable hotel with its bars, children's room and pretty no-smoking restaurant opening onto a sheltered lawn, provides not only bar meals, morning coffee and afternoon teas, but a daily changing menu in the garden restaurant. Using local produce, they specialise in dishes using the local fish and seafood. Lobster is available all year, oysters from the local beds, game in season. Bar food includes soups, chicken, mushroom and ham pie, bowls of steaming mussels and crab salad. There are Sunday buffets during the summer. Greene King Abbot and IPA on hand pump. Tables on the lawn.

OPEN: 12 - 2; 6.30 - 11.
Real Ale. Restaurant.
Children welcome.
No dogs.
Bedrooms.

UPPER SHERINGHAM

Red Lion   Tel: 01263 825408

Holt Road, Upper Sheringham, Norfolk NR26 8AD
Free House. Jason Baxter, licensee

Over 300 years old, these flint cottages have only fairly recently been converted into the village pub. With two attractive bars, the Red Lion has become popular for its reliable, tasty home-cooked food. The blackboard menu changes frequently, but there could be local game, local fish and delicious soups; all the herbs are home grown as are most of the fruit and vegetables. Special three-course Wednesday suppers. Sunday roasts. This is another 'chip-free' zone. Greene King Abbot, Adnams Broadside and guest ales, also quite a number of malt whiskies.

OPEN: 11 - 3; 7 - 11 (closed Sun eves winter).
Real Ale.
Children in eating area.
Dogs on leads.
Bedrooms.

WARHAM ALL SAINTS

Three Horseshoes   Tel: 01328 710547

The Street, Warham All Saints, Norfolk NR23 1NL
Free House. Iain Salmon, licensee

Within this pretty village of flint cottages you will find the 18th century Three Horseshoes. The village pub, still with its gas lighting and stone floors, retains the atmosphere of the 1920s, though one has to emphasise that the attitude to pub food has taken a great leap forward. There's a good choice of home-cooked bar food based on fresh, local produce: game terrine, potted smoked fish, cheesy mushroom bake and rabbit pie. A daily selection on the blackboard complements the printed menu. All dishes are cooked to order. Greene King IPA and Abbot, plus guest ales. House wines. Tables on the grass outside. Loos outside too!

OPEN: 11 - 3; 6 - 11.
Real Ale. No-smoking restaurant.
Children in eating area.
Dogs on leads.
Bedrooms.
Occasional live music Sat evenings.

NORTHUMBRIA (DURHAM), NORTHUMBERLAND, CLEVELAND & TYNE & WEAR

BLANCHLAND

Lord Crewe Arms   Tel: 01434 675251

Blanchland, County Durham DH8 9SP (Nr Derwent Reservoir)
Free House. A Todd, Peter Gingell, Ian Press, licensees

Someone should write about the most haunted pubs in the country - this one has a tragic ghost. She's the sister of a Jacobite, Tom Forster (whose family originally lived here), and still haunts the building, asking people to deliver a message to her long-dead brother. Built in the 13th century, there is still evidence of its historic past, and the layout of the village is much the same as it was before the dissolution of the monasteries, when Blanchland Abbey dominated the surrounding area. The cloister garden is still evident and is now listed as an ancient monument. After that history lesson and having made your way to the Crypt Bar, you will find a good choice of bar food, daily specials and home-made cakes for afternoon tea; they also do Sunday lunches. Vaux ales, brewed in Sunderland. Seats in the enclosed garden. NB: they say there is sometimes music in the restaurant but not the bar, so avoid the restaurant.

OPEN: 11 - 3; 6 - 11.
Real Ale. Meals & snacks. Evening restaurant, also Sun lunch.
Children welcome.
Bedrooms.

CORBRIDGE ON TYNE

Angel Inn   Tel: 01434 632119

Corbridge on Tyne, Northumberland NE45 5LA
Scottish & Newcastle. Mandy McIntosh Reid, manageress

Founded in Saxon times, the village is situated on one of the country's best salmon rivers, and the Angel Inn - originally the Head Inn - is the oldest building in the village. An important posting stop, the weekly mail coach would deliver the Newcastle paper which the landlord would then read out to the villagers. Now the different demands of the 20th century have again made it a desirable, popular stopping place, providing all you could wish for in the way of food, drink and hospitality. The bar menu changes daily; monthly, in the no-smoking restaurant. Good, substantial dishes with a northern theme, using fresh local produce: local lamb, salmon, Cumberland sausages, home-made soups and puddings. Theakstons ales and Youngers on draught. Choice of wines.

OPEN: 12 - 2.55; 5 - 11. Teas: 3 - 5.
Real Ale. Restaurant.
Children welcome. Dogs on leads.

COTHERSTONE

Fox & Hounds   Tel: 01833 650241

Cotherstone, Co Durham DL12 9PF (on B6277)
Free House. Michael & May Carlisle, licensees

Not far from Barnard Castle and surrounded by some wonderfully empty countryside. We forget how lucky we are to have all that space "up north". Overlooking the village green, this 18th century pub has a reputation for serving good, imaginative food. Well worth a stop, not only for the food, but for the setting, the attractive beamed bars, winter fires, and well kept ales. Varied bar menu - all home-made, children's dishes and a Sunday roast. John Smiths Bitter and regional ales. A choice of over 50 wines. Good walks nearby.

OPEN: 11.30 - 2.30; 6.30 - 11.
Real Ale. Restaurant.
Children in Restaurant. No dogs. Bedrooms.

CRASTER

Jolly Fisherman   Tel: 01665 476461

Craster, Alnwick, Northumberland NE66 3TR
Vaux. William & Muriel Silk, licensees

An attractive unspoilt fishing village noted for its Kippers. The only pub in the village, so it's understandably popular. Full of local fishermen, lifeboatmen, landbased locals and those travelling through. Situated above the harbour, with views of the rocky coastline - this is a wild and rugged part of the country. No surprise when we say that seafood sandwiches are favourites here: local crab, salmon and prawn - other simple dishes too. Ales are Vaux Samson Bitter, Extra Special and Double Maxim. Seats in the garden. The nearby ruins of the 14th century Dunstanburgh Castle, perched 100ft above the shore, can only be reached by walking along the coastal path.

OPEN: 11 - 3; 6 - 11.
Real Ale. Snacks only.
Children welcome. Dogs on leads.

DIPTON MILL

Dipton Mill Inn   Tel: 01434 606577

Dipton Mill Road, Nr Hexham, Northumberland NE46 1YA
Free House. Geoff Brooker, licensee

Dipton Mill Inn, with just a few cottages for company, is situated in peaceful countryside just two miles outside Hexham. The Inn, originally a 17th century farmhouse, and the cottages next to it, were extended about a hundred years ago into what you see today. A small pub, with only one main bar - and off this, a room which houses the bar billiards table. Hot food is served at lunchtime and also in the early evening during the summer. A typical menu is: soup, beef in ale pie, chicken breast in a sherry sauce, always salads and sandwiches, a choice of savoury flans and a selection of puddings. Ales are mainly from their own brewery where they brew three beers: Shire bitter, Devil's Water and Whapweasel. (Whapweasel is named after a burn on the fells.) Very beautiful countryside. The old mill stream runs through the garden, and another stream runs alongside the pub. Seats in the attractive garden. You are in good walking country.

OPEN: 12 - 2.30; 6 - 11.
Real Ale. Lunchtime meals and snacks.
Children in Games Room. No dogs.

HALTWHISTLE

Milecastle Inn	Tel: 01434 321372

Military Road, Nr Haltwhistle, Northumberland NE49 9NN
Free House. Ralph & Margaret Payne, licensees

Not far from one of the 'milecastles', each of them a Roman mile apart on Hadrian's Wall, which at this point crosses the southern edge of the Northumberland National Park. The Milecastle Inn is fairly isolated, and is one of those places you are only too pleased to see when travelling across the moors, or walking the hills. It has a small snug interior, with a good fire, short, well chosen menu, plus well-kept ales. Filling home-made soups, hearty pies, lots of game (in season), quite a list of "dishes of the day", and local ales from the Hexham Brewery. Malt whiskies and a good wine list. Seats outside at the front of the pub and in the enclosed garden at the back. Muddy walking boots outside only - where the pub starts you stop - unless in socks.

OPEN: 12 - 2.30. 6.30 - 11.
Real Ale. Restaurant (closed Sun, Mon, Tues evenings).
Children over 5 if eating. No dogs.

HEDLEY ON THE HILL

Feathers   Tel: 01661 843607

Stocksfield, Northumberland NE43 7SW
Free House. Marina & Colin Atkinson, licensees

I know this information is at the end, but I want to emphasise that this pub is not open during the day except at weekends and Bank Holidays. We have all done it - turned up at the right place at the wrong time. Sandwiches usually available weekday evenings but the food at weekends would appear to be ample compensation for the lack of it during the week. Interesting home-made soups, peppered steaks, smoked salmon roulade, chicken in tarragon, vegetarian dishes, children's meals and good puddings. Local ales - usually from the Hexham Brewery, Boddingtons always available and one guest. A selection of malt whiskies.

OPEN: 6 - 11 weekdays, 12 - 3; 6 - 11 Sat.
Daytime opening weekday Bank Holidays only.
Real Ale. Weekend meals. Evening sandwiches.
Children in eating area and family room till 8.30. Dogs on leads.
Folk night twice a month.

MATFEN

Black Bull   Tel: 01661 886330

Matfen, Newcastle-upon-Tyne NE20 0RT (off B6318 NE Corbridge)
Free House. Colin & Michelle Scott, licensees

Another pub which is more of a "dining pub" - nothing wrong with that as there is still the well-frequented bar for just a drink, snack and chat. During the summer, this is one of those pubs you can't miss. Find the wonderful floral display and somewhere behind it you will find this attractive pub. Nicely presented bar food: soups, paté, filled Yorkshire puddings, stuffed pancakes, salads, steak & kidney pies, game pies, steaks and puddings. There is also an extensive, changing, restaurant menu. Part of the restaurant is no-smoking. Theakstons Best and several guest ales. Seats outside at the front of the pub among the flowers.

OPEN: 11 - 3; 6 - 11 (11 - 11 Sat).
Real Ale. Restaurant.
Children in eating area. No dogs. Bedrooms.

NEW YORK

Shiremoor House Farm   Tel: 01912 576302

Middle Engine Lane, New York, Northshields, Tyne & Wear NE29 8DZ
Sir John Fitzgerald Ltd. M W Garrett & C W Kerridge, licensees

This is a lovely place, which was developed from renovated old farm buildings. Without losing any of the character, they have been turned into a well appointed pub and restaurant catering for everyone - not only someone wanting a pint and bar snack, but also for the family who want high-chairs, bottle warmers, etc. For the grown-ups, there is the traditional bar menu, with the addition of more interesting dishes: roast duck julienne, breast of chicken in garlic and brandy sauce, beef stroganoff, steaks, daily specials and home-made puddings. Bass, Theakstons Best and Old Peculiar, Stones Best and guest beers. Tables on the grass by the farm courtyard among the flowers.

Open 11 - 11.
Real Ale. Restaurant. (Food all day Sunday.)
Children in eating areas. No dogs.

NEWCASTLE-UPON-TYNE

Crown Posada   Tel: 01912 321269

31 The Side, Newcastle-upon-Tyne, NE1 3JD
Free House. Malcolm McPherson, manager

An interesting old city centre pub which leans architecturally towards the Victorian with its stained glass mirrors, tulip lamps and painted ceilings. One long bar, with a snug to one side, serves lunchtime sandwiches and snacks. The ales are: Theakstons Best, Boddingtons Bitter, Butterknowle Conciliation Ale, Hadrians Gladiator and guest beers. If you want to catch up on the day's events the daily papers are kept in the snug for you to read.

OPEN: 11 - 11 (Sat: 11 - 4; 7 - 11).
Real Ale. Lunchtime snacks (not Sun).
No children. Dogs on leads if well behaved.

NEWCASTLE-UPON-TYNE

Tap & Spile   Tel: 01912 761440

33-37 Shields Road, Byker, Newcastle-upon-Tyne NE6 1DJ
Pubmaster. Christopher Spinks, manager

They keep quite a selection of beers, so this is the place to come if you want to try a few of the more unusual ales. Lunchtime sandwiches, crisps and nuts too no doubt. More a chap's place this I think - so if you want quiet and a good pint the Tap & Spile is the place to be. Five regulars: Marstons Pedigree, Ruddles Best, Thwaites Craftsman, Jennings Cumberland, Hadrians Gladiator and up to nine changing guests. Westons farm cider and some country wines.

OPEN: 12 - 3; 6 - 11 (all day Fri & Sat).
Real Ale.
Dogs on leads.
Live Jazz Mon.

NEWTON ON THE MOOR

Cook & Barker Inn   Tel: 01665 575234

Newton on the Moor, Felton, Morpeth, Northumberland NE65 9JY
Free House. Lynn & Phil Farmer, licensees

High above sea level, and with wonderful views of the Northumbrian coast, this is a good place to stop if you're travelling on the A1. All the locals have probably beaten a path here anyway. A good, solid, stone village pub, which has been updated and re-organised. Now you have a large beamed bar for drinks and snacks, plus a stone walled restaurant in what was the forge. Good soups, beef with ginger and spring onions, hot beef and onion sandwiches, lamb's liver with vegetables, mixed grills, steaks, grilled trout and home-made puddings. Timothy Taylors Best and Landlord, Theakstons Best and XB plus Boddingtons - all on hand pump. Seats in the garden and on the terrace.

OPEN: 11 - 3; 6 - 11.
Real Ale. Evening Restaurant.
Children in eating area.
No dogs.
Bedrooms.

ROMALDKIRK

Rose & Crown Hotel   Tel: 01833 560213

Romaldkirk, Barnard Castle, Co Durham DL12 9EB
Free House. Christopher & Alison Davy, licensees

This is a fine old 18th century coaching inn with an interior which reflects its age. Beamed, panelled, polished and attractive, with the bonus of interesting and imaginative menus in the bar, and a no-smoking restaurant. Bread will be home-made, as is the chutney and pickled onions accompanying the ploughmans. Regional cheeses, meat from the local butcher, game from the surrounding moors and fish from the East Coast ports. Even the ice cream is home-made. Very good value daily lunchtime specials. Theakstons Best and Old Peculiar, varied wine list - half bottles, and by the glass. Tables outside overlooking the village green.

OPEN: 11 - 3; 5.30 - 11.
Real Ale. Restaurant (not Sun eves).
Children welcome.
Dogs on leads.
Bedrooms.

SHOTLEY BRIDGE

Manor House Inn   Tel: 01207 255268

Carterway Heads, Shotley Bridge, Consett, Northumberland DH8 9LY (A68 between Corbridge & Consett)
Free House. Mr A J Pell, licensee

On the A68 between Corbridge and Consett - on the tourist route to the Derwent Reservoir. This is a long, stone-built village pub with rather unfortunate modern windows. However, we are not judging a pub by architectural mistakes, only by what goes on inside. A friendly, efficient, well-run pub with an interesting blackboard menu. Food could include: leek and courgette soup with French bread, smoked chicken and brie croissants, moules marinières, baked sea trout and steaks. Home-made puddings. Butterknowle Bitter, Westons Beamish and three guest ales. Seats in the garden (wind permitting!).

OPEN: 11 - 3; 6 - 11.
Real Ale.
Well behaved children welcome.
Dogs in small bar only.

STOCKTON ON TEES

The Masham   Tel: 01642 580414

79 Hartburn Village, Stockton on Tees, Cleveland TS18 5DR
Bass. Dennis & John Eddy, tenant and manager

Hartburn village, a tree-lined backwater off the Darlington road, is attached to Stockton on Tees, but it is difficult for strangers to tell where one ends and the other begins. The pub, small and friendly, is a popular local meeting place. It has a bar, and bar area, three small rooms, and a garden at the back. Meals are not served, but sandwiches are available every day. Bass and a guest beer (usually Black Sheep) on hand pump, are particularly well kept. House entertainment (apart from the customers) is a TV in one of the small rooms for the big sporting events - rugby, cricket, etc; you can't hear the TV anywhere else in the pub - but the customers sometimes get carried away with enthusiasm! Seats and tables on the paved area in the garden and there is a secluded children's play area.

OPEN: 11 - 11.
Real Ale. Sandwiches only.
Children in family room. Dogs on leads.

WARENFORD

Warenford Lodge   Tel: 01668 213453

Warenford, Belford, Northumberland NE70 7HY
Free House. Raymond Matthewman, licensee

Stone-built, with mullioned windows, this is another pub with no obvious pub sign and with every appearance of being someone's private house; however, unless everyone has decided to walk, you will see a lot of parked cars, which means you're where you want to be. A very popular place to eat - you do have to book to be sure of a table in the evening . Lots of fishy dishes which could include: fish soup, marinated seafood salad and grilled herbed mussels. Also on the menu: chicken dishes, pepperpot steak, cold stuffed roast pork and some home-made puddings, including the ice cream. Newcastle Exhibition and McEwans Scottish ales plus a varied wine list. Seats in the garden.

OPEN: 7 - 11 (Sat & Sun 12 - 2; 7 - 11).
Evening Restaurant & weekend snacks & meals.
Not Mondays except Bank Holidays.
Children in Restaurant.
No dogs.

OXFORD

BINFIELD HEATH

Bottle & Glass   Tel: 01491 575755

Harpsden Road, Binfield Heath, Henley-on-Thames, Oxon RG9 4JT
Brakspears. Mike & Anne Robinson, tenants

Between Henley-on-Thames and Reading, this 15th century thatched pub has flagged floors, antique tables, settles and large log fires during the winter. An interesting choice of bar food: paté, Cumberland sausages, rump steak, mussels in garlic, lunchtime sandwiches and other dishes. The house specialities change from day to day. There is a large garden with 24 tables with their own thatched canopies to protect you from the noonday sun. Brakspears ales on hand pump and a good choice of malt whiskies.

OPEN: 11 - 3; 6 - 11.
Real Ale. No food Sun eves.
No children. Dogs on leads Sundays only.

BIX

Fox Inn   Tel: 01491 574134

Henley-on-Thames, Oxon RG9 6DB
Brakspears. Richard & Sue Wilson, tenants

Built in 1935 in "roadhouse style" to replace an old Fox Inn which was in the path of the dual carriageway into Henley. Now creeper covered, the pub is just a tiny part of this big building which boasts 51 doors! If the fancy takes you, you can ride up to the Fox, tie up outside, and enjoy a good lunch. Nobody has mentioned hay and nuts for your mount, so you will probably have to take your own. Very busy at weekends but peaceful during the week. Panelled lounge and public bar, log fire, and a good range of bar food: soups, ploughmans, sandwiches, pasties, daily specials such as casseroles and game in season, all quickly and cheerfully served. Roast Sunday lunch. Brakspears ales on hand pump. Water for the horse. Lots of seats in the garden.

OPEN: 11 - 3; 7 - 11.
Real Ale. No food Mon evening.
No children.
Dogs on leads.

BLOXHAM

Elephant & Castle   Tel: 01295 720383

Bloxham, Nr Banbury, Oxfordshire OX15 4LZ
Hook Norton. Charles Finch, tenant

You just have to look at a Cotswold stone pub and its wonderful warm colour to get the impression of a friendly welcome. Two bars: one a simply furnished public bar, the other a more comfortable lounge - both with good winter log fires. There are seats in the flower-filled courtyard where there is a summer barbecue on Saturday evenings and Sunday lunchtimes. Hook Norton ales with a changing monthly guest beer from small independent breweries. Good choice of malt whiskies.

OPEN: 10 - 3; 6 - 11 (5 - 11 Sat).
Real Ale. Restaurant. Bar Food lunchtimes only (not Sun).
Children in restaurant.
Dogs on leads.

BURCOT

Chequers
Tel: 01865 407771

Abingdon Road, Burcot, Oxon OX14 3DP
Free House. Mary & Michael Weeks, licensees

A charming thatched pub, dating back in part to 1550, with comfortable, unspoilt beamed bars. There is a no-smoking area called the Gallery, with an interesting collection of paintings. The blackboard menu changes daily and all the food is home-made including the bread. Garlic mushrooms, real steak & kidney puddings, vegetarian dishes, chicken in wine sauce and home-made ice creams. Attractive, flowery garden for summer lounging. Ruddles County, Ushers Best and guest beers on hand pump. A 6ft grand piano is kept at concert pitch and some very talented pianists queue up to play on Friday and Saturday evenings.

OPEN: 11 - 2.30; 6 - 11.
Real Ale. Restaurant. No meals or snacks Sun eves.
Children in eating area. No dogs.
Evening Fri/Sat pianist.

BURFORD

Angel
Tel: 01993 822438

14 Witney Street, Burford, Oxon OX18 4SN
Free House. Mrs Jean Thaxter, licensee

Ideally placed for an exploration of the Cotswolds. The stone-built Angel, with its pretty walled garden, has two dining areas, one partly no-smoking. The food leans towards the Italian: baked gnocci with Gorgonzola and crème fraîche, smoked salmon with prawns, mustard and dill sauce, Caesar salad with fresh anchovies, smoked haddock and prawns au gratin, venison, mushroom and red wine pie. Daily specials for the bar are listed on the blackboard, along with the fish dishes. Hampshires Pendragon strong ale, Marstons Pedigree and a guest beer on hand pump. Seats in the lovely sheltered garden.

OPEN: 11 - 2.30 (11 - 3 Sat); 6.30 - 11.
Closed Sun evening Nov - Mar.
Real Ale. Restaurant. Children in eating area of bar.
No dogs. Bedrooms.

BURFORD

Lamb   Tel: 01993 823155

Sheep Street, Burford, Oxon OX18 3LR
Free House. Richard de Wolf, licensee

A glorious example of a Cotswold inn, with honey-coloured stone walls covered in climbing roses and benches outside from where you can watch the world go by and enjoy your drink. Inside there are flagged floors, log fires, comfortably furnished bars and a pretty pillared restaurant. A courtyard and an attractive walled garden are behind the inn. Bar lunches: soups, ploughmans, filled pancakes, paté, and curries. Restaurant meals in the evening. Wadworths IPA and 6X on hand pump and Old Timer in winter.

OPEN: 11 - 2.30; 6 - 11.
Real Ale. Restaurant open eves; bar food lunchtimes.
Children welcome. Dogs on leads. Bedrooms.

BURFORD

Mermaid Inn   Tel: 01993 822193

High Street, Burford, Oxon OX18 4QF
Morlands. John Titcombe, lease

Another handsome Cotswold pub, 600 years old, with a long bar and two restaurants, the upstairs one for smokers, the one downstairs in the dining conservatory for non-smokers. Bar food includes sandwiches, Cumberland sausages with fried onion on garlic bread, omelettes, home-cooked ham and salads. Morlands ales on hand pump. There are tables on the very wide pavement in front of the pub.

OPEN: 10 - 11 (11 - 11 Suns & Winter).
Real Ale. Restaurants.
Children in restaurant (not small children). No dogs.
Pianist Fri & Sat evenings.

CHRISTMAS COMMON

Fox & Hounds   Tel: 01491 612599

Christmas Common, Oxon OX9 5HL
Brakspears. Kevin Moran, tenant

A good, solid, old-fashioned and friendly pub; just the place for a
quiet drink and a snack while out enjoying the glorious Chilterns. It
has a beamed bar with a big inglenook fireplace and a smaller
room where the serious drinking goes on. Traditional lunchtime
bar food of ploughmans, sandwiches, sausages, soups - good
solid fare. Brakspears ales from the cask. Seats outside to enjoy
the roses. Positively no music here of any kind. Anyone in their
cups fancying themselves as singers is promptly asked to leave!

OPEN: 12 - 2.30; 6 - 11.
Real Ale. Lunchtime snacks.
Children in games room till 9 pm. Dogs on leads.

CLIFTON

Duke of Cumberlands Head   Tel: 018693 38534

Clifton, Nr Deddington, Oxon OX15 0PE
Free House. Nick Huntington, licensee

Thatched. Built in 1580. Beamed, with huge fireplaces and a
comfortable lounge bar, it offers the added bonus of a French
restaurant and a constantly changing blackboard menu in the bar.
Dishes vary but they could be garlic mushrooms, salade niçoise,
good home-made soup and a fish dish. Roast Sunday lunch.
Good range of wines by the glass. Tables outside in the garden.

Adnams, Wadworths 6X, Hook Norton, Hampshires King Alfred and guest ales from Easter throughout the summer.

OPEN: 12 - 2.30; 6.30 - 11.
Real Ale. Restaurant (not Sun or Mon eves). No bar food Sun eves.
Children until 9 pm.
Dogs on leads.
Bedrooms.

CLIFTON HAMPDEN

Plough   Tel: 01865 407811

Clifton Hampden, Nr Abingdon, Oxon OX14 3EG
Courage. Yuksel Bektas, lease

A lovely 16th century thatched pub which is completely non-smoking. If you want a quick puff, go out into the car park. Food is served throughout the day. Run in the best traditions of a public house, what the customer wants, when he wants it, he will get. The landlord, Mr Bektas (in tails and white gloves) believes in service. In good food too. No frozen food vans out at the back here. One menu throughout the pub, informally in the bar, and more formally in the restaurant. The menu could include a variety of smoked fish, a pasta dish or two, salmon in mustard and white wine sauce and home-made puddings. Wonderful coffee (several varieties). Courage Best, Directors and Websters ales and a good wine list. A special place this.

OPEN: 11 - 11.
Real Ale. Restaurant (no-smoking). Food served all day.
Children welcome.
Guide dogs only.

CUMNOR

Bear & Ragged Staff
Tel: 01865 862329

19 Appleton Road, Cumnor, Oxon OX2 9QH
Morrells. George Daly, licensee

Not far from the High Street, you'll easily find this large ivy covered old inn. Inside there are flagstone floors, beams, log fires and comfortable chairs. It has a very busy lunchtime trade. There is a separate restaurant area, one section of which is no-smoking. The usual bar snacks, daily specials, Sunday roasts and a barbecue during the summer. Morrells Bitter and Varsity. Choice of wines and malt whiskies

OPEN: 11 - 11.
Real Ale. Restaurant.
Children in eating areas. Dogs on leads.

FINSTOCK

Plough Inn
Tel: 01993 868333

The Bottom, Finstock, Oxon OX7 3BY
Free House. Keith Ewers, licensee

Recently taken over by the Ewers brothers: one shows at Crufts, so there are lots of dog prints in the no-smoking restaurant. Thatched, with a cosy beamed bar, a log-burning stove in the big inglenook fireplace and comfortable furnishings. Their speciality is a steak & kidney pie with red wine/guinness and a crusty top, but the menus are changing all the time. Bar food could include grilled bass, quiche, vegetarian pie, steaks and home-baked ham. Hook Norton Old and Best, Adnams Broadside and guest beers. Farm ciders, choice of wines and a range of malt whiskies. Tables outside in the garden.

OPEN: 12 - 3; 6 - 11. All day Sat.
Real Ale. Restaurant.
Children welcome. Dogs on leads. One bedroom.

HAILEY

King William IV
Tel: 01491 686675

Hailey, Nr Ipsden, Wallingford, Oxon OX10 6AD
Brakspears. Brian Penney, tenant

A small, old-fashioned, family-run pub. No fancy meals, just good honest bar food: ploughmans, pasties, filled rolls, soup at lunchtime, (only filled rolls available in the evening). Seats outside at the back with a view of the rolling countryside, and where there is a fascinating collection of old farm machinery. Keeping in the mood, you can hitch a lift on a horse and cart which plies between the pub and Nettlebed. Brakspears ales drawn from casks in front of the customers. Farm ciders.

OPEN: 11 - 2.30; 6 - 11.
Real Ale.
Children in eating area lunchtimes. No dogs.

HOOK NORTON (nr)

Gate Hangs High
Tel: 01608 737387

Banbury Road, Nr Hook Norton, Oxon OX15 5DS
Hook Norton. Stuart Rust, tenant

A toll once had to be paid on cattle and horses passing through this gate, but not on geese. To give the birds unimpeded passage, it was hung high enough for them to pass under, whilst stopping the larger animals - and that is how the pub got its name, or so the landlord believes. In the middle of nowhere, but nevertheless very popular, the pub has no restaurant, just a room with tables, and a bar. There is a variety of home-made bar food with changing daily specials. Also an evening blackboard menu. Hook Norton Ales and a guest beer, a good choice of wine and selection of malt whiskies. There are seats in the garden. The Hook Norton brewery isn't far away and well worth a visit.

OPEN: 11.30 - 3; 6.30 - 11.
Real Ale. Restaurant. No meals or snacks Sun eves.
Children in eating area & restaurant.
Dogs on leads.

ISLIP

Swan Inn Tel: 01865 372590

Lower Street, Islip, Kidlington, Oxon OX5 2SB
Morrells. Mr Michael Watkins, tenant

A small pub by the River Ray, a tributary of the Cherwell. Family-run, friendly, it has a reputation for well-cooked bar food. They specialise in a variety of home-made pies which could be pheasant, rabbit or duck, home-baked ham. Their ham, egg and chips is very popular. Morrells Varsity Bitter, Graduate and College Ale. Mulled wine in the winter. Seats on the verandah at the front of the pub.

OPEN: 11 - 2.30 (11 - 3 Sun); 6 - 11.
Real Ale. Mulled wine in winter. No food Sun & Mon eves.
Children welcome.
Dogs on leads.

MOULSFORD

Beetle & Wedge Tel: 01491 651381

Ferry Lane, Moulsford, Oxon OX10 9JF
Free House. Richard & Kate Smith, licensees

You are in *Wind in the Willows* country here and if you are looking for a very civilised day by the river, this is the place to be. Very elegant, it has nevertheless, an informal boathouse bar with traditional real ales, and a charcoal fire on which a selection of dishes is grilled - fresh fish and game in season. There are also soups and a variety of salads and casseroles, plus puds. In good weather the boathouse bar moves onto the terrace, just a few feet from the river. There are also tables by the jetty. Lunch is served by the Water Garden on fine, summer days. Only the finest, fresh, local produce is used in this very appealing riverside hotel. Wadworths 6X, Adnams and Badger Tanglefoot on hand pump. Extensive wine list. For the truly energetic who want to work up an appetite for lunch - rowing boats are for hire nearby.

OPEN: 11.30 - 2.30; 6 - 11.
Real Ale. Restaurants (not Sun eves); one no-smoking.
Children welcome.
No dogs.
Bedrooms.

NUFFIELD

Crown   Tel: 01491 641335

Nuffield, Henley, Oxon RG9 5SJ
Brakspears. Ann & Gerry Bean, tenants

Just the place to stop and recharge the batteries whilst walking the Ridgeway Path. Collapse on the seats at the front of the pub in summer or in the beamed bars with their roaring log fires in winter, ordering from the extensive menu of home-made bar food: soups, salads, sandwiches, paté, sausage and bean casserole, gammon steaks, steak & kidney pie, leek tart, vegetarian dishes, daily specials and home-made puds. The only thing that isn't home-made is the bread. Brakspears ales on hand pump and a good choice of wines.

OPEN: 11 - 2.30; 6 - 11.
Real Ale.
Children in family room, lunchtimes only.
Dogs on leads.

OXFORD

Turf Tavern
Tel: 01865 243235

4 Bath Place, off Holywell Street, Oxford OX1 3SU
Whitbread. Trevor Walter, manager

Set in an attractive courtyard in the middle of Oxford, the pub has two comfortable, low-beamed rooms, and is well known for always having between 20 and 30 different guest ales on offer - even though it is a Whitbread pub. The uncomplicated bar menu lists baps with various fillings, both hot and cold, roasts, steak & mushroom and other pies, and a vegetarian dish or two. Seats in the very attractive courtyards. Wadworths 6X and Brakspears plus various guest ales. Farm cider and mulled wine is available in winter.

OPEN: 11 - 11.
Real Ale.
Children in one bar only. Guide dogs only.

ROKE

Home Sweet Home
Tel: 01491 838249

Roke, Nr Wallingford, Oxon OX10 6JD
Free House. Jill Madle, Peter & Irene Mountford

Certainly someone's home in the past, as this was originally a row of cottages. It's now a smart pub with two beamed bars, one of which leads into the restaurant. Quite an extensive choice of food throughout the pub - the sandwiches have lots of different fillings. There is a wide range of salads and substantial dishes may be chosen from the changing blackboard menu. A more elaborate menu is available in the evening restaurant. Brakspears Ordinary and Royal Oak ales. There is a pretty garden with picnic tables at the front of the pub.

OPEN: 11 - 3; 5.30 - 11.
Restaurant.
Well behaved children welcome. Dogs on leads, only in the bar.

SHENINGTON

Bell Inn   Tel: 01295 670274

Shenington, Nr Banbury, Oxon OX15 6NQ
Free House. Jennifer & Steven Dixon, licensees

Very much the local, probably since it was built in 1722 on the edge of the village green. A well beamed, traditional interior with some pine panelling and good log fires. There is a changing blackboard menu, all the food is home-cooked using the best local seasonal produce. Good soups, quiches, salmon in cucumber sauce, mushrooms in creamy paprika, celery and nut bake and puds. Boddingtons, Hook Norton and Flowers ales. A good wine list. Tables at the front of the pub overlooking the village green.

OPEN: 12 - 2.30; 7 - 11. (12 - 3; 6.30 - 11 Sat.)
Real Ale. Restaurant.
Children welcome.
Dogs on leads.
Bedrooms.

SHIPTON-UNDER-WYCHWOOD

Lamb   Tel: 01295 670274

High Street, Shipton-under-Wychwood, Oxon OX7 6DA
Free House. Mr & Mrs L Valenta, licensees

Situated on the outskirts of the village, this old, honey-coloured, stone-walled Cotswold Inn with stone-tiled roof, has been catering for the traveller for several hundred years and continues to be as popular as ever. There is a good cold buffet, home-made soups and other traditional bar dishes. In the evening the blackboard menu offers a more extensive range of dishes: local game in season, fresh fish from Cornwall, the ducks from Minster Lovell and carefully-chosen beef and lamb. The home-made fruit pies are said to be excellent. There are "wine-of-the-week" suggestions on the blackboard; also a good wine list. Hook Norton, Wadworths 6X, cider and Guinness on draught. There are tables in the garden.

OPEN: 11 - 3; 6 - 11.
Real Ale. Restaurant (not Sun eves).
No children.
No dogs.
Bedrooms.

SHIPTON-UNDER-WYCHWOOD

Shaven Crown Hotel Tel: 01993 830330

High Street, Shipton-under-Wychwood, Oxon OX7 6BA
Free House. Trevor & Mary Brookes, licensees

Originally a hospice for nearby Bruern Abbey, the 14th century Shaven Crown was built around a medieval courtyard garden and is an attractive place to sit and enjoy a drink and meal on a summer's day. The comfortable beamed bar, with a log fire in winter, offers a wide range of bar snacks: smoked salmon mousse, whitebait, curried meatloaf, steak sandwich, home-baked ham and vegetarian nut roasts. There is a more extensive menu in the evening restaurant: pancakes filled with salmon & spinach in white wine sauce, deep-fried Camembert, Normandy pheasant, chicken with apricot stuffing and fennel sauce, fish dishes, steaks and interesting puddings. Hook Norton ale and guest beers. The wine list varies from week to week. Those architecturally minded among you, do try to see the medieval hall, now the Residents' Lounge, with its double-collar braced roof, still in perfect condition after six hundred years.

OPEN: 12 - 2.30; 7 - 11.
Real Ale. Restaurant.
Children welcome but not under 5 in evening restaurant.
Dogs on lead, not in hotel rooms.
Bedrooms.

SOUTH STOKE

Perch & Pike Inn

Tel: 01491 872415

South Stoke, Oxon RG8 0JS
Brakspear. Michael & Jill Robinson, tenants

On the Ridgeway between Goring and Wallingford, this is an attractive and popular small flint-built pub. Log fires in winter, always fresh flowers and candles on the table in the evening. Proper napkins, too, if you are eating. The menus are unusual and varied, changing every couple of weeks: interesting summer salads, imaginative hot dishes and mouth-watering sweets. The specials change daily, the beef is Aberdeen Angus and everything is fresh, seasonal and home-cooked. Brakspears ales, wines by the glass. Seats outside in the pretty garden which is within walking distance of the river.

OPEN: 12 - 2.30; 6 - 11.
Real Ale. Restaurant. No meals or snacks Sun eves.
Children in eating area.
Dogs on leads. Stables available.

STEEPLE ASTON

Red Lion

Tel: 018693 40225

South Street, Steeple Aston, Oxon OX6 3RY
Free House. Colin Mead, licensee

It isn't often, when writing about a pub, that you can say "this is the place for a decent glass of wine". The landlord is very keen on his wines and in consequence keeps an interesting, inimitable cellar. Bar food is limited to lunchtimes only: home-made soups, ploughmans with local cheeses, sandwiches, winter hotpots and summer salads. There's a more ambitious and creative menu in the evening restaurant. Hook Norton Bitter, Wadworths 6X, draught Budweiser and Guinness. Over 100 wines are kept and there are regular wine-tastings and promotions. Seats on the sunny terrace at the front of the pub amid the flowers.

OPEN: 11 - 3; 6 - 11.
Real Ale. Evening restaurant (closed Sun & Mon).
Lunchtime meals & snacks (not Sun).
Children in restaurant.
Dogs on leads.

SWINBROOK

Swan Inn
Tel: 01993 822165

Swinbrook, Nr Burford, Oxon OX18 4DY
Free House. H V Collins & C Y Collins, licensees

Not far from the River Windrush, you will find the wisteria covered 16th century Swan Inn. It has only a small bar, but it is very popular with walkers and locals. Traditionally furnished, with stone-flagged floors and winter fires. Home-cooked bar food and a more ambitious evening menu. Bass, Morlands Bitter and cider from Hereford. Benches outside - muddy boots outside too.

OPEN: 11.30 - 2.30; 6 - 11.
Real Ale. Dining room (not Sun eve). No snacks Sun eve.
No children. No dogs.
No dirty boots in dining room.

TOOT BALDON

Crown Inn
Tel: 01865 343240

Toot Baldon, Nr Nuneham, Courtenay, Oxon OX44 9NG
Free House. Liz & Neil Kennedy, licensees

Busy, friendly, this is a country pub with good home-cooked food. There is a small eating area with only 30 seats so it is best to book if possible, to make sure of a table - or just get there early. A good choice of bar food with changing and quite exciting specials on the blackboard menu: e.g. smoked salmon and prawn pasta or carbonnade of beef. Morlands Original, Charles

Wells Bombardier, Fullers London Pride and one guest ale. Seats outside on the terrace where there is a barbecue in summer.

OPEN: 11 - 3; 6.30 - 11.
Real Ale. Restaurant. No meals or snacks Mon eve.
Children welcome. Dogs on leads.

WATLINGTON

Chequers Inn   Tel: 01491 612874

Love Lane, Watlington, Oxon OX9 5RA
Brakspear. John & Anna Valentine, tenant

A useful place to be aware of as it is not far from Junction 6 on the M40 - just the right place to get away from the motorised hoards. It's a rambling old pub with a lovely garden and comfortable low-ceilinged rooms with some interesting pieces of furniture. A copious and varied menu: sandwiches, ploughmans, vegetable moussaka, salads, fish kebabs, steak & kidney pie, and gammon are just a few of the dishes on offer. Brakspears ales on hand pump. There is a conservatory and seats in the garden among the fruit trees.

OPEN: 11.30 - 2.30; 6 - 11.
Real Ale.
Children restricted to own area, none under 14.
Dogs on leads.

WITNEY

Royal Oak   Tel: 01993 702576

17 High Street, Witney, Oxon OX8 6LW
Free House. Brian Simpson, licensee

Nothing frightfully exciting about Witney, the home of the blanket, but it is interesting to see the woollen mills that have spread themselves down the Windrush valley. The 16th century Royal

Oak is the oldest pub in the town. Stone built with a stone tiled roof, it is well beamed inside and has the feel of a country pub. One bar serves two areas. There is a short bar menu: home-made soup, filled rolls, toasted sandwiches, hot dog and onions, steak pie, filled jacket potatoes, fish and chips and ham and chips. The ales are Wadworths 6X, Morlands and Archers Best Bitters. Picnic tables in the big flowery courtyard.

OPEN: 10.30 - 2.30; 5 - 11 Mon - Wed. 10.30 - 11 Thurs - Sat. 12 - 3; 7 - 10.30 Sun.
Real Ale. No food Sunday.
Children in garden.
Dogs on leads.

WYTHAM

White Hart   Tel: 01865 244372

Wytham, Nr Oxford, Oxon OX2 8QA
Ind Coope. Louise Tran, licensee

An attractive, creeper-covered pub in the pretty, thatched village of Wytham (the whole of which is owned by Oxford University). It has a flagstone floor and a part-panelled bar with open fires. Bar food includes a huge choice of salads, filled baked potatoes, lots of fish dishes - swordfish, halibut, tuna and others. Most of the food is prepared to order. Daily specials. Ind Coope Burton, ABC, Tetleys and one guest beer. Seats in the very lovely walled garden.

OPEN: 11 - 11.
Real Ale. Food 12 - 2; 7 - 9.30.
Children welcome.
No dogs.

SUFFOLK

ALDEBURGH

Cross Keys   Tel: 01728 452637

Crabbe Street, Aldeburgh, Suffolk IP15 5BN
Adnams. G Prior, licensee

The Cross Keys is in what you might term an idyllic situation at the height of summer: only the promenade separates the courtyard at the back of the pub from the beach. Sitting in the courtyard you can have a drink or a meal and watch the world go by. Inside, the two bars, each with a cosy stove to warm things up, are a refuge from the cold easterly winds which blow during the winter. Familiar bar food plus good open sandwiches, vegetarian dishes and lots of fish. Adnams Traditional ales. There are some interesting things to see in Aldeburgh. The church has a John Piper window commemorating Benjamin Britton, the founder of the Music Festival, and there's a half-timbered 16th century Moot Hall which is now a museum.

OPEN: 11 - 3; 6 - 11 (11 - 11 Sat).
Real Ale. No food winter Sun eves.
Dogs on leads.

SUNDAY OPENINGS

All-day Sunday opening came in too late for us to check every pub. Assume that tied houses are open all-day; free houses on the wishes of their licensees.

BLYFORD

Queens Head   Tel: 01502 478404

Southwold Road, Blyford IP19 9JY
Adnams. Tony Matthews, tenant

Situated opposite the church, this old thatched pub is one to make
a note of if you are wandering the lanes of Suffolk in the early
morning, as they serve breakfast from 8.30. A good variety of
lunchtime bar snacks, and a greater, more adventurous, selection
of meals during the evening. All Adnams ales. A no-smoking
family room. Tables outside in the garden where there is an
activity area for the children.

OPEN: 11 - 3; 6.30 - 11.
Real Ale. Restaurant.
Children in eating area & no-smoking restaurant.
No dogs.

DUNWICH

Ship Inn   Tel: 01728 648219

St James' Street, Dunwich, Nr Saxmundham, Suffolk IP17 3DT
Free House. Stephen & Ann Marshlain, licensees

Visiting Dunwich today, it is hard to believe that in Henry II's reign it
had 15 religious establishments and a flourishing shipbuilding
industry. The village you see today is all that remains of the
prosperous medieval centre that was gradually washed away by the
sea over the intervening centuries. The Ship Inn, originally the haunt
of smugglers, has a comfortable bar with a wood-burning stove in a
big fireplace, and plenty of fishing and nautical bric-à-brac distributed
throughout the pub. As well as a dining room, it has a family
conservatory. Bar snacks at lunchtime only. During the evening the
restaurant menu applies throughout the pub. It is renowned for its
own fish and chips, and many other fish dishes, but you can still get
soups, pies, salads, ploughmans and good puddings. Adnams ales.
Seats on the terrace and in the sheltered garden.

OPEN: 11 - 3 (11 - 3.30 Sat); 6 - 11 (6.30 - 11 winter).
Real Ale. Evening Restaurant.
Children not in bar. Dogs on leads.
Bedrooms.

EARL SOHAM

Victoria   Tel: 01728 685758

Earl Soham, Suffolk IP13 7RL
Own Brew. Clare & John Bjornson, licensees

A pub where the beer is brewed on the spot. Not only can you sample the goods on the premises, you can even take some home with you. Traditionally furnished, and with pine panelling, tiled floors, big open fires and pictures of our dear Queen Victoria. The pub is very popular and gets quite busy. It has a good selection of bar food, soups, curries, chilli, salads and vegetarian dishes plus a Sunday roast. The ales are called Victoria Bitter, Albert - Strong Ale, and Gannet which is a mild. Seats at the front of the pub and on the lawn at the back.

OPEN: 11.30 - 2.30; 5.30 - 11.
Real Ale.
No dogs.
Folk music Tues & Fri eves.

FRISTON

Old Chequers   Tel: 01728 688270

Aldeburgh Road, Friston, Nr Saxmundham, Suffolk IP17 1NP
Free House. David Grimwood, licensee

This is a pleasing old village inn, not far from Saxmundham and Snape, with beams, and a couple of wood-burning stoves to keep it cosy during the winter. No sandwiches here, but you'll certainly find home-made soups and hunks of French bread. There is a fixed price hot or cold buffet at lunchtime, and during the evening there's a blackboard menu with a choice of dishes - more restaurant meals than bar food. Adnams and guest ales on hand pump. A selection of house wines sold by the glass. Tables set out at the back of the pub.

OPEN: 11.30 - 2.30; 6.30 - 11 (7 - 11 winter).
Real Ale. No food Sun eves.
Children lunchtimes only. No dogs.

GREAT GLEMHAM

Crown Tel: 01728 663693

The Street, Great Glemham, Nr Saxmundham, Suffolk IP17 1DA
Free House. Roger Mason, licensee

Between Framlingham and Saxmundham, deep in the lovely Suffolk countryside. Inside the pub is a large beamed bar which has two huge fireplaces filled with blazing logs during the winter. Lots of food available, ranging from filled rolls to lasagne, steak & kidney pie, vegetarian dishes, and a children's menu. Adnams ales, Bass and Greene King Abbot. Choice of wines and a selection of malt whiskies. Tables on the lawn at the corner of the pub during the summer.

OPEN: 12 - 2.30; 7 - 11.
Real Ale. Restaurant (no meals or snacks Mon).
Children in restaurant. No dogs.
Bedrooms.

HORRINGER

Beehive Tel: 01284 735260

The Street, Horringer, Suffolk IP29 5SD
Greene King. Gary & Dianne Kingshott, tenants

In what must be a very desirable location, sharing a boundary with glorious Ickworth Park, you will find the pretty village of Horringer and the attractive rambling Beehive pub. Inside there are lots of low-beamed nooks and crannies - plenty of room in which to sit and sample the imaginative food. The printed menu changes about three times a year, but there could be curried vegetable pancake, chicken and mushroom stroganoff, steak sandwiches (lovely rare beef inside), wide choice of fish dishes from the specials board and lots of home-made puddings. Greene King IPA and Abbot ales plus a short wine list. Seats on the terrace at the back of the pub and also in the garden.

OPEN: 11.30 - 2.30; 7 - 11.
Real Ale. No food Sun evening.
Children welcome. Dogs on leads.

HOXNE

Swan   Tel: 01379 668275

Low Street, Hoxne, Suffolk IP21 5AS
Free House. Tony & Francis Thornton-Jones, licensees

Very near here is the site of King Edmund's murder in 670 AD by the marauding Danes. His body was later buried on the site of the town named after him - Bury St Edmunds. Legend has it that part of the tree he was tied to before execution forms a section of the screen in a nearby church. The Swan, a little younger than the martyrdom, has its own ecclesiastical connections in that it was built by the Bishop of Norwich in the 15th century and much of the interior of The Swan dates back to that time. Better than average bar menu: filled pancakes, spinach and garlic terrine, omelettes and grills. There is a specials board, among which fillet of pork in brandy and cream sauce, cod and prawn gratinée, are just a few of the dishes that may be on offer - good puds too. Greene King Abbot ale, Adnams Bitter, Old Ale and Tally Ho in winter. Well chosen wine list and a selection of wines by the glass. Seats outside in the large sheltered garden which boasts a croquet lawn for the mildly energetic.

OPEN: 12 - 2.30 (12 - 3 Sat); 5.30 - 11. (12 - 3; 7-10.30 Sun.)
Real Ale. Restaurant.
Children in eating area. Dogs on leads.

LAMARSH

Red Lion   Tel: 01787 227918

Bures, Lamarsh, Suffolk CO8 5EP
Free House. John & Angela O'Sullivan, licensees

Particularly attractive on a summer's evening if you just want to sit and let time drift by, watch the river, look at the view and contemplate life. Built in the 14th century, it has lots of beams, pretty flowers inside and a friendly, helpful staff. The menu is very changeable, as it depends on what inspires the chef that day. Be assured that it will be imaginative, varied and well cooked. Courage Directors, Greene King IPA, John Smiths, Marstons Pedigree and Wadworths 6X ales. Wines by the glass and a selection of malt whiskies. Life on the river can get very exciting when the young farmers hold their annual raft race on Whit Bank Holiday weekend.

OPEN: 11 - 3; 6 - 11. (11 - 11 Sats.)
Real Ale. Restaurant.
Children in eating area. Dogs in barn.
Occasional live music.

LAVENHAM

Swan   Tel: 01787 247477

High Street, Lavenham, Suffolk CO10 9QA
Free House (Forte). M R Grange, licensee

Wonderful Lavenham. An unspoilt, carefully preserved medieval town, with magnificent timbered houses and the church of St Peter and St Paul dominating the horizon. Dating back to the 14th century, the Swan, heavily beamed inside and out, with a minstrels' gallery in the no-smoking restaurant, is very much the smart hotel. At its heart though, is a small, friendly bar, still with its mementos from the time when it was a local for the American 48th

Bomber Group, stationed here during the last war. Lunchtime sandwiches, salads and bar snacks are served from a buffet in the Garden Bar which overlooks the courtyard garden. John Smiths and Greene King IPA ales, a number of malt whiskies and cognacs. Seats in the courtyard.

OPEN: 11 - 3; 6 - 11.
Real Ale. Restaurant.
Children welcome. Dogs on leads in bar.
Pianist every night. Bedrooms.

LAXFIELD

Kings Head   Tel: 01986 798395

Gormans Lane, Laxfield, Nr Woodbridge, Suffolk IP13 8DG
Free House. Adrian Read, manager

Laxfield, with its long wide village street and interesting half-timbered Guildhall, was the birthplace of William Dowsing, a fervent follower of Oliver Cromwell. "Destroyer" Dowsing was mainly responsible for the destruction of some of the most beautiful artefacts and interiors in our churches during the time of the Civil War. Bearing in mind the village's relationship with a follower of Oliver Cromwell, 'The King's Head' is aptly named. Low, thatched and unspoilt, nothing much has changed over the years; beer is still drawn from the cask in the tap room. Food though, has moved with the times. Popular, hearty bar food using the best local produce; a blackboard menu which could offer: home-made soups, hot beef sandwiches, chicken pie, liver and bacon, all with fresh vegetables, and puds such as fruit crumbles and apple pie. Adnams Ales, Greene King Abbot and a couple of guest beers. Country wines and local cider. Seats in the sheltered garden where there is a croquet and bowling green.

OPEN: 11 - 3; 6 - 11.
Real Ale.
Children in eating area. Dogs on leads.
Occasional folk nights.

LEVINGTON

The Ship Inn   Tel: 01473 659573

Church Lane, Levington, Nr Ipswich, Suffolk IP10 0LQ
Pubmaster. William & Shirley Waite, tenants

On the edge of an attractive village overlooking the River Orwell, popular with locals, townies and visiting yachtsmen, the pub has a decidedly nautical air. Prints, pictures, nets and even a compass under the counter. Is that to check where you are? Simple, well chosen bar food: ploughmans, quiche, sausages in cider sauce, lots of salads and a vegetarian dish or two. Daily specials offering more substantial dishes and good puds. Flowers Original, Bass, Tolly Cobbold Bitter and Greene King IPA drawn from the cask. Country wines and some wines by the glass. Seats in front of the pub overlook fields and the river.

OPEN: 11.30 - 3; 6 - 11.
Real Ale. Restaurant.
No children under 14. No dogs.
Folk music first Tues in month.

ORFORD

Jolly Sailor   Tel: 01394 450243

Quay Street, Orford, Nr Woodbridge, Suffolk IP12 2NU
Adnams. Philip Attwood, tenant

Orford is at the end of the road, so to speak - any further and you would have to become a sailor, jolly or otherwise, as you would be in, or on, the River Or. An old smugglers' inn, the Jolly Sailor is reputed to be built out of the timbers of ships wrecked nearby. Inside, there are several small rooms, warmed by a big stove in winter. Well chosen bar food, local fish and chips, home-cooked ham, omelettes and ploughmans. The dining room is no-smoking. Adnams range of ales. There are tables in the large garden.

OPEN: 11 - 2.30; 7 - 11.
Real Ale.
Children in dining room.
Dogs on leads in middle bar.
Bedrooms.

PIN MILL

Butt & Oyster   Tel: 01473 780764

Pin Mill, Nr Chelmondiston, Ipswich, Suffolk IPN 1JW
Pubmaster. Dick & Brenda Mainwaring, tenants

Overlooking the River Orwell and originally a bargeman's retreat, this 17th century riverside pub is still popular with sailors and landlubbers alike. It used to be the 'done thing' to sail here for lunch - probably still is. If so, what better place to be than sitting at one of the tables on terra firma watching the negotiation from yacht to dinghy and vice versa after a good lunch. Traditional bar food with a selection of blackboard specials. The ploughmans is very generous and there will be a vegetarian dish or two. Tolly Original Bitter and Mild plus two guest beers.

OPEN: 11 - 11. (11 - 3; 7 - 11 winter.)
Real Ale.
Children welcome away from main bar. No dogs.
Occasional piano & folk dancing.

RATTLESDEN

Brewers Arms   Tel: 01449 736377

Lower Road, Rattlesden, Nr Bury St Edmunds, Suffolk IP30 0RJ
Greene King. Ron Cole, tenant

Deep in the country between Stowmarket and either Bury St Edmunds or Lavenham, depending really where in Suffolk you start from - you could say you were in the middle of the triangle. A jolly, popular, 16th century village pub with a reputation for imaginative, well-cooked food, it has a creative changing menu; nevertheless, a simple filled roll, bowl of soup and other bar snacks are always available. Greene King ales, quite a few local wines and a choice of malt whiskies. There are seats in the pretty rose-filled garden which has a boules pitch.

OPEN: 12 - 2.30 (12 - 3 Sat); 7 - 11.
Real Ale. Pub closed Sun & Mon evening. Last week June, 1st week July.
Well behaved children.
Dogs in one bar & garden.
Jazz Thurs eve & monthly Sun lunchtime.

SNAPE

Golden Key   Tel: 01728 688510

Priory Road, Snape, Nr Saxmundham, Suffolk IP17 1SG
Adnams. Max & Susie Kissick-Jones, tenants

Close to Snape Maltings and the site of the Aldeburgh Festival, you will find this charming 15th century pub. It has a large main bar, divided into public (tiled floor) bar and lounge (carpeted). Lots of sustaining, well prepared bar food: home-made soups, paté, filled rolls, sausage and onion pie, smoked haddock, quiche, fresh fish, steaks and roast on Sunday. Adnams ales, local farm ciders and a choice of malt whiskies. Seats at the front of the pub, also in the colourful garden at the back.

OPEN: 11 - 3; 6 - 11 (extensions during Aldeburgh Festival).
Real Ale.
Children in eating area.
Dogs on leads.

SOUTHWOLD

Crown Hotel
Tel: 01502 722275

High Street, Southwold, Suffolk IP18 6DP
Adnams. Anne Simpson, manager

Originally a posting inn, this very attractive Georgian hotel has been renamed three times during its lifetime. At first it was called the Nag's Head; after rebuilding in 1715 it became 'The New Swan' (not to be confused with The Old Swan in the marketplace); then in 1829 it took on a new identity and was called 'The Crown'. Now restored, it is very handsome - an elegant Georgian town house - combining pub, wine bar, restaurant and small hotel. It has an extensive wine list, imaginative daily changing bar food and a restaurant where they serve a very reasonably priced three-course lunch. Flagship of the nearby Adnams Brewery - the ales are kept in the best condition and the impressive wine list (wine merchants as well) is on display in the cellar. Lots of wines by the glass, including classic vintages selected monthly. Do note the wonderful wrought iron inn sign attached to the front of The Crown Hotel.

OPEN: 10.30 - 3; 6 - 11 (closed first week Jan).
Real Ale. Restaurant.
Children in eating area & restaurant.
Dogs in one bar.
Bedrooms.

STOKE BY NAYLAND (Nr Colchester)

Angel
Tel: 01206 263245

Polstead Street, Stoke by Nayland CO6 4SA
Free House. Peter Smith, licensee

This attractively restored 16th century inn is at the main crossroads of the village situated in the heart of 'Constable country'. The casual drinker is still catered for in the small bar, but on the whole it is a serious eating pub. A blackboard menu operates throughout the bars and restaurant; the selection of reasonably priced dishes can change twice a day. As the Angel is hugely popular, it is best to book to be sure of a table. Lots of fish dishes, local game in season, roast duckling, home-made steak & kidney puddings and traditional Sunday roasts. Greene King Abbot ale, Adnams Bitter, Nethergate - either Bitter or Old Growler. Lots of interesting wines. Seats outside on the terrace.

OPEN: 11 - 2.30; 6 - 11.
Real Ale. Restaurant.
No children in the bar.
No dogs.

TOSTOCK

Gardeners Arms   Tel: 01359 270461

Church Road, Tostock, Nr Bury St Edmunds IP3 9PA
Greene King. Reg Ransome, tenant

Situated near the village green, this pleasant, beamey old pub delivers the sort of service you hope for, but don't necessarily get elsewhere - flexible eating times, well presented home-made bar food and well kept ales. The usual well tried selection of bar snacks and daily specials. A greater variety of grills and other dishes is available during the evening, when it can get very busy. Greene King Abbot, IPA and Rayments ales. Seats in the attractive garden.

OPEN: 11.30 - 2.30 (11 - 2.30 Sat); 7 - 11.
Real Ale. Restaurant (not Sun lunch). No snacks Mon/Tues eves.
Children in eating area of bar.
Dogs on leads.

WALBERSWICK

Bell   Tel: 01502 723109

Walberswick, Southwold, Suffolk IP18 6TN
Adnams. Mark Stansnall, tenant

Once a flourishing port on the mouth of the River Blyth, Walberswick is now a favoured residential area for artists and craftsmen. There are no street lights, pavements or buses. Just lots of unspoilt countryside and that wonderful expanse of East Anglian sky. 600 years old, the Bell, with its worn stone floors and beamed bars, is a favourite meeting place for locals and visitors. Bar food offers soups, sandwiches, ploughmans, plus, as you would expect, local fish and chips, lots of salads in summer and more substantial dishes during the cold months. Adnams Traditional ales. Tables in the sheltered garden (depending on the wind direction!).

OPEN: 11 - 11 (11 - 4; 6 - 11 winter).
Real Ale. Evening restaurant; Children in room off bar.
Dogs on leads.
Regular folk evenings.
Bedrooms.

SURREY

ALBURY HEATH

King William IV
Tel: 01483 202685

Little London, Albury Heath, Guildford, Surrey GU5 9DB
Free House. Mike & Helen Davids, licensees

Set in lovely walking country, this friendly little pub is a welcome stopping place for a quiet pint and a sandwich or two. Its rooms are small with flagstone floors, and in one there is a huge inglenook fireplace, with an equally huge log fire in the winter. Short, reasonably priced bar menu: ploughmans, pies, home-cooked ham and eggs and a Sunday roast. Every month they have a special fish evening. All the fish is brought in fresh from Billingsgate, and there is quite a variety to choose from. Boddingtons, Whitbreads Castle Eden and the local Hogs Back ales. Regularly changing guest beers. Seats in the pretty front garden.

OPEN: 11 - 3; 5.30 - 11.
Real Ale. Restaurant (not Sunday).
Children welcome.
Dogs on leads.

BETCHWORTH

Dolphin Inn
Tel: 01737 842288

The Street, Betchworth, Surrey RH3 7DW
Youngs. George Campbell, manager

An unspoilt village pub dating back to the late 16th century. Still with its beams, flagstone floors and panelled walls. Near excellent walking country, so it is understandably popular and gets very busy. Interesting, varied bar food: sandwiches, filled baked potatoes, ham on the bone, steak, and other pies, grills and daily specials. Youngs range of ales, including the seasonal "Winter Warmer". Seats at the front, side, and back of the pub.

OPEN: 11 - 3; 5.30 - 11.
Real Ale.
No children.
Dogs on leads.

EFFINGHAM

Sir Douglas Haig   Tel: 01372 456886

The Street, Effingham, Surrey KT24 5LU
Free House. Laurie Smart, licensee

This is a slightly doubtful entry as they do switch the music on after 9 pm, presumably to empty the pub: any earlier, do please let us know, and they'll get the chop. Virtually rebuilt several years ago, it remains a solidly reliable pub where you will be adequately fed and assured of a good pint. The bar menu includes home-made favourites with lots of fresh vegetables, and daily specials. They serve a roast lunch on Sunday. Boddingtons, Fullers London Pride, King and Barnes Festive, Gales HSB and Badger Tanglefoot. Seats on the lawn and the terrace.

OPEN: 11 - 3; 5.30 - 11 (11 - 11 Sat).
Real Ale. No food Sun evening.
Dogs on leads.
Bedrooms.
N.B: Music is put on after 9 pm.

ELSTEAD

Woolpack   Tel: 01252 703106

Elstead, Surrey GU8 6HD
Friary Meux (Allied). Jill Macready, lease

Originally built sometime in the 18th century to store bales of wool after shearing, the building was later licensed and it has since evolved into the pleasant country pub you find today. Inside, the main bar is decorated with a number of artefacts which relate to its woolly past. Familiar pub stalwarts such as home-made pies, ploughmans, casseroles, grills and ham on the bone, also daily specials and Sunday lunches. The puddings are another speciality - really home-made. Children's portions available. Greene King IPA ale and one other from the cask. A selection of wines by the bottle and by the glass. Family room opening onto the garden, and a children's play area. Seats in the garden for the grown-ups.

OPEN: 11 - 2.30 (3 Sat); 6 - 11.
Real Ale. Restaurant.
Children in family room & restaurant.
Dogs on leads.

OXTED

Haycutter   Tel: 01883 712550

Broadham Green, Oxted, Surrey RH8 9PE
Ind Coope. Barry Aldridge, tenant

This charming old building, full of character, is set on the edge of Broadham Green. Inside there is a "U" shaped bar which encourages general chat, but if you want to get away from the friendly repartee there are lots of corners for more private conversations. The bar is decorated with Barry Aldridge's collection of hats and historical photographs. A wide choice of bar food is available ranging from soup, grilled sardines, prawns in garlic butter, omelettes, steaks, fish dishes, salads to the humble sandwich. Youngs, Friary Meux, Burton Bitter and Wadworths 6X ales. A short wine list. Seats in the garden to take advantage of the attractive Surrey countryside.

OPEN: 11 - 11.
Real Ale. No food Sundays.
Children in dining area.
Dogs on leads.

PIRBRIGHT

Royal Oak   Tel: 01483 232466

Aldershot Road, Pirbright, Aldershot, Surrey GU24 0D4
Whitbreads. John Lay, manager

A very pleasant 16th century beamed, rambling old pub. Lots of flowers both inside and out during the summer; big log fires in winter. There is an interesting variety of bar food: steaks and grills, a vegetarian dish or two, beef in a port and onion sauce, not forgetting traditional bar snacks. Quite a selection of ales are offered, occasionally some from the smaller, less well known breweries: Boddingtons, Flowers Original, Marstons Pedigree, Youngs Special, and a number of guest beers. Seats among the flowers at the front, or in the quieter garden at the back. Good walking country.

OPEN: 11 - 11.
Real Ale. Restaurant.
Children in restaurant.
No dogs.

SHAMLEY GREEN

Red Lion   Tel: 01483 892202

Shamley Green, Surrey GU5 0UB
Free House. Ben Heath, licensee

Overlooking the village green and summer cricket matches, this listed 17th century pub has a comfortable, well furnished, polished interior. An interesting, reliable blackboard menu could offer: home-made soup, ploughmans, stuffed mushrooms, peppered chicken breast, seafood tagliatelle, home-baked ham and eggs, salads and some vegetarian dishes, properly cooked vegetables and home-made puddings. A more substantial menu is available in the restaurant. Greene King Abbot Ale, King and Barnes Sussex, Flowers Original and guest beers. Choice of wines. Tables in the garden.

OPEN: 11 - 11.
Real Ale. Restaurant.
Children welcome.
No dogs.

SHERE

White Horse Inn   Tel: 01483 202161

Middle Street, Shere, Nr Guildford, Surrey GU5 9HS
S & N. Mike Wicks, manager

A pretty, flowery 14th century timbered pub. Rambling beamed rooms with undulating floors and huge, handsome inglenook fireplaces. During the renovation of the building, some fascinating objects came to light; centuries ago these articles were buried in the walls in the hope that they would ward off the evil spirits. They are now on display in the pub. Old-style pub favourites and daily specials on the menu. Theakstons and Ruddles Best and County Ales. Seats outside in the attractive courtyard and garden. Lots of good walks nearby.

OPEN: 11.30 - 11.
Real Ale.
Children in eating area.
Dogs on leads.

THURSLEY

Three Horseshoes   Tel: 01252 703268

Dye House Lane, Thursley, Godalming, Surrey GU8 6QD
Free House. Steve and Ann Denman, licensees

Between the Devil's Punchbowl and Thursley Common, Thursley is a tiny village in the middle of this huge, wonderful nature reserve. Inside the Three Horseshoes - a Grade II listed building - the pleasant bar has log fires in the winter and an ample supply of newspapers, guides and Parish magazines for you to read whilst enjoying your pint or two. Surrounded by a network of footpaths, it is a favourite meeting place for ramblers, - not more than six at once unless pre-warned (just think of all those ruck-sacks and boots). Relaxed and friendly, the pub - with sparkling new kitchens and a new extension to the restaurant - serves good, home-made food: soups, sandwiches and other snacks, curries, lamb wellington, bangers and mash and daily specials. Gales HSB, BBB, Fullers London Pride, Tennants, Carling and Kaliber, plus a wide range of country wines. Barbecues in the lovely large garden, which has a Gazebo with views over the surrounding countryside.

OPEN: 11 - 3; 6 - 11 (11 - 3.30; 6 - 11 Sat). (12 - 3.30; 7 - 10.30 Sun.)
Real Ale. Restaurant.
Children over 5 in restaurant.
Dogs in garden only.

WALLISWOOD

Scarlett Arms   Tel: 01306 627243

Walliswood, Surrey RH5 5RD
King & Barnes. Mrs Pat Haslam, tenant

Once a pair of 17th century cottages, the Scarlett Arms is a small, charming, unspoilt, popular, country pub. Inside there are beams, polished flagstones, solid, well-used furniture, and a timeless friendly atmosphere. Sometimes it is standing room only, but there are plenty of seats in the garden. Generous portions of good reliable bar food: sandwiches, ham, egg and chips, rabbit pie, curries, ham and mushrooms in a cheese sauce. Thursday is the day for a roast. King and Barnes Festive, Broadwood, Sussex and Mild, Old Ale in winter.

OPEN: 11 - 2.30; 5.30 - 11.
Real Ale.
No children.
Dogs on leads and very welcome.

WEST CLANDON

Onslow Arms   Tel: 01483 222447

West Clandon, Nr Guildford, Surrey GU4 7TE
Free House. Alan Peck, proprietor

When it is suggested that you "drop in for a drink" it isn't often you can take the invitation literally; here you can - if you have your own helicopter. One of the grander pubs in the heart of the Surrey countryside, it provides a perfect setting for a relaxing meal and a drink. Wonderfully opulent hanging baskets make the Onslow Arms difficult to miss. Inside there are a wealth of oak beams, gleaming copper and brass and comfortable furnishings. You have a choice of a carvery, cocktail lounge and an extended Cromwell bar - the locals' favourite. An extensive selection of well prepared bar food could include: sandwiches, chicken and mushroom pie, steak, kidney and oyster pie, quiche, huge choice of cold meats and salads from the carvery, fish dishes and a vegetarian dish or two. A more elaborate menu features in the restaurant. Ales could include Courage Best and Directors, Fullers London Pride, Boddingtons, Flowers IPA, Youngs Special, and guest beers from the West Country. Seats at the front of the pub, and in the glorious, flowery, award-winning courtyard and garden.

OPEN: 11 - 2.30 (3 Sat); 5.30 - 11.
Real Ale. Restaurant partly non-smoking. No food Sun eve.
Children in eating areas.
No dogs.

SUSSEX

ASHURST

Fountain Inn
Tel: 01403 710219

Ashurst, Nr Steyning, W Sussex BN44 3A
(N of Steyning on B2135)
Free House. Maurice Caine, licensee

Originally a farmhouse, this 16th century building was gentrified during Georgian times, when a new façade was added to make it appear grander than it really was. Turn right into the tap room with its flagstones, big fireplace, comfortable furnishings and well kept ales and into the larger carpeted room for the well-chosen bar food. Choice of soups, smoked salmon, Cajun chicken, vegetarian meals, duck breast in cherry sauce, steaks and a variety of fish dishes. Very popular, therefore very busy, so book for evening meals. Seats on the terrace and in the pretty garden. There are usually six ales available, among which could be Fullers London Pride, John Smiths, Youngs Special and changing guest ales.

OPEN: 11 - 2.30; 6 - 11.
Real Ale. Restaurant. No food Sun eves.
Children in restaurant till 8 pm. Dogs in garden only.

CHRISTMAS

Many pubs have varying opening times on Christmas Day. A few DO open all day. Some don't open at all; others open at mid-day only.

BERWICK

Cricketers Arms   Tel: 01323 870469

Berwick, Polegate, E Sussex BN26 6SD
Harveys. S P Bayley, manager

A pleasing unspoilt country pub in a peaceful village at the foot of the South Downs, south of the A27. Once two cottages, now a pub with an extension, which accounts for the mix of brick and stone. A friendly, busy place with a heavily beamed bar and good winter log fires. Home-made pub food - "nothing flash" to quote the landlord. Several daily specials, plus ploughmans and sandwiches. Harveys Bitter and seasonal ales from the cask. Seats in the attractive garden.

OPEN: 11 - 2.30; 6 - 11.
Real Ale. Food every lunchtime & Fri & Sat eves.
No dogs.

BILLINGSHURST

Blue Ship   Tel: 01403 822709

The Haven, Billingshurst, W Sussex RH14 9BS
King & Barnes. J R Davie, tenant

Tucked away in the middle of the country, this little unspoilt pub is originally 15th century, with Victorian additions. Very popular, particularly at weekends, it has a good choice of traditional bar food - ploughmans, sandwiches and home-made soups, a fish dish or two, cottage pie, steak & kidney pie and good puds. King & Barnes Sussex and Broadwood from the barrel. Tables outside in the garden and in front of the pub under the honeysuckle.

OPEN: 11 - 3; 6 - 11.
Real Ale. No food Sun or Mon eves.
Children in rooms without bar.
Dogs on leads.

BLACKBOYS

Blackboys Inn   Tel: 01825 890283

Blackboys, Nr Uckfield, E Sussex TN22 5LG
Harveys. Patrick Russell, tenant

Overlooking the attractive village pond, this pub had to be largely rebuilt after a serious fire a few years ago. Luckily the rambling beamed ground floor didn't suffer too much. Full of interesting bits and pieces, antique furniture and a big log fire in winter. There are window seats from where you have a view of the pond. Bar food is listed on the blackboard above the bar: sometimes home-made soups, usually ploughmans, fish, stuffed pancakes, steak & kidney pie and Cajun chicken. Seats outside and by the pond. Harveys ales, usually a choice of four.

OPEN: 11 - 3; 6 - 11 (12 - 3; 7 - 10.30 Sun).
Real Ale. Restaurant.
Children in restaurant. Dogs on leads.

BROADWATER

Cricketers   Tel: 01903 233369

66 Broadwater St West, Nr Worthing, W Sussex BN14 9DE
Bass Charrington. R Humphreys, licensee

Now within the boundaries of Worthing, Broadwater parish dates back to Saxon times and once governed the villages of Broadwater, Worthing and Ottington. Formally the Brewers' Arms, the pub was renamed in 1878. Always a popular meeting place. Cricket has been played on the green since early in the 18th century, and as you might expect, the pub is the home of the local team. Home-cooked bar food, a table d'hôte and an à la carte menu. They specialise in seafood. Bass, Fullers London Pride, Harveys and Bass Worthington.

OPEN: 11 - 3; 6 - 11.
Real Ale. Restaurant every lunchtime & Wed - Sat eves.
Children in family room. Dogs on leads.

BURPHAM

George & Dragon   Tel: 01903 883131

Burpham, Nr Arundel, W Sussex BN18 9RR
(off A27 E of Arundel)
Courage. James Rose & Kate Holle, tenants

In an attractive village, not far from Arundel Castle, the pretty George and Dragon, built in 1742, is popular for its food and real ales. There is one spacious bar and a smart, elegant dining room. Bar food, available both at lunchtime and in the evening, varies from home-made soups, sandwiches, mushrooms in garlic, ploughmans and jacket potatoes to the daily changes on the blackboard - avocado and fresh Jersey crab, vegetarian chilli and Irish stew for example. Home-made puddings too. Dinner is served in the restaurant. Ales available include Arundel Best, Harveys Best, Youngers, Cotleigh and Ashvine. From the garden there are views towards the castle and River Arun. The pub has a resident ghost of a girl who was jilted on her wedding day and murdered by her fiancé in one of the upstairs rooms. Lovely walks nearby.

OPEN: 11 - 2.30; 6 - 11 (closed Sun eves winter).
Real Ale. Restaurant (no food Sun eves).
No dogs.
Occasional jazz evenings.

BYWORTH

Black Horse   Tel: 01798 42424

Byworth, Nr Petworth, W Sussex GU28 0HO
Free House. Paul Wheeler-Kingshott & Jenny Reynolds, licensees

Byworth is a quiet village not far from Petworth. The pub, built on the site of an old priory, has a Georgian façade which is hiding a much older building. Friendly busy bars with a good choice of changing bar food - all freshly made. Bar menu ranges from soups, filled potatoes, salads, ploughmans, steak & kidney pudding, chicken in tarragon sauce, pastas, spare ribs, steaks, and fish when available. Tables in the flowery courtyard, or in the large garden, which has views across the valley. Ales do change but could include Fullers London Pride, Gales HSB and guest ales which change in spring and summer. Also a good wine list.

OPEN: 11 - 3; 6 - 11.
Real Ale. Restaurant.
Children welcome.
Dogs on leads.

CHARLTON

Fox Goes Free   Tel: 01243 811461

Charlton, Nr Goodwood, W Sussex PO18 0HO
(village off A286 Chichester-Midhurst)
Free House. Paul Palombi, licensee

This rambling old pub has been selling ales since 1588. Four very different rooms - each with its own character - one of which is a no-smoking dining room. With an Italian licensee the move is going to be towards more Italian oriented dishes along with the traditional bar food. Ales are the William Younger range and Ballards Best, also a changing guest ale. Good range of wines. Seats outside in the sheltered garden which has views over the South Downs. There is also a children's play area.

OPEN: 11 - 3; 6 - 11 (7 - 11 winter).
Restaurant.
Children in family room.
Dogs on leads.

CHIDDINGLY

Six Bells   Tel: 01825 872227

Chiddingly, Nr Lewes, E Sussex BN8 6HE (off A22 Uckfield-Hailsham)
Free House. Paul Newman, licensee

Situated opposite the church, this 18th century pub is jolly, unassuming, friendly and not the quietest of places when the bands play. There is live music: Tuesday, Friday, Saturday evenings and Sunday lunchtimes, in a separate building admittedly, but I think you could say the joint jumps. Pub grub only, all good, home-made and very reasonable. Soups, chilli, curry, spare ribs in barbecue sauce, lasagne, filled potatoes, etc. Puddings too. John Smiths and Courage Directors ales on hand pump. Seats out in the garden and good long walks nearby.

OPEN: 11 - 3; 6 - 11.
Real Ale.
Dogs on leads.
Live Jazz, Blues, etc. Fri, Sat & Sun eves.

CHIDHAM

Old House at Home   Tel: 01243 572477

Cot Lane, Chidham, Nr Chichester, W Sussex PO18 8SU
Free House. Andy Simpson, Terry Brewer, licensees

Slightly off the beaten track, and beautifully situated in the glorious West Sussex countryside. You should beat a path to the door if you want to enjoy the good home cooking and well-kept beers at this friendly, popular pub. They offer a good range of bar snacks - home-made soups, including Old House shellfish soup with French bread. Chef's specials on the blackboard, lots of fresh fish, steaks and other dishes. Well stocked cellar. They have their own Old House beer, Ringwood Best, Badger Best and Old Thumper plus a guest ale. Seats on the terrace and in the garden.

The pub can get extremely busy, so to be sure of a table you should book, particularly in the evenings.

OPEN: 11.30 - 2.30 (12 - 3 Sat); 6 - 11.
Real Ale. Restaurant.
Children welcome.
Dogs on leads.

COWBEECH

Merrie Harrier   Tel: 01323 833108

Cowbeech, Nr Hailsham, E Sussex BN27 4JQ (off A271)
Free House. C P Conroy, J H Conroy, licensees

The licensees are very keen to emphasise the food in this rather jolly white weatherboarded pub. There is a dining area and a modern no-smoking conservatory, but drinkers are not forgotten in the beamed bar with its well kept ales. Wide ranging lunchtime food - filled rolls, ploughmans, home-made soups, fresh fish, etc. A more extensive menu is available in the evening. Don't expect the speed of the microwave - all food is cooked to order. Good plentiful Sunday roast. Harveys Best and Boddingtons on hand pump. Good choice of wines. Seats in the garden, also by the fish pond and on the terrace.

OPEN: 11 - 3; 6 - 11.
Real Ale. Restaurant.
Children welcome lunchtime. No dogs.

DANEHILL

Coach & Horses   Tel: 01828 740369

Danehill, Nr Haywards Heath, E Sussex RH17 7JF
Free House. Peter Hayward, licensee

Just outside the village, in the heart of the Sussex countryside and set in large gardens which have spectacular views towards the South Downs. The old pub has a public and saloon bar, plus dining area, each with its own log fire. Bar snacks include toasted French bread with various toppings, grilled field mushrooms and bacon on wholemeal toast, home-made sweetcorn and mushroom quiche, ploughmans, sandwiches, seafood platter and children's portions. The evening menu could include smoked chicken and avocado salad, mushrooms en croûte, grilled sea bass, grilled noisettes of English lamb and home-made puddings. Harveys Best and a weekly changing guest beer. Farm cider during the summer. Short wine list and wines by the glass. There is an enclosed children's play area.

OPEN: 11 - 2.30; 6 - 11 (12 - 2; 7 - 10.30 Sun).
Real Ale. Children welcome.
Dogs on leads away from dining area.

DITCHLING

Bull   Tel: 01273 843147

2 High Street, Ditchling, E Sussex BN6 8SY
Whitbread. John & Jannette Blake, tenants

Virtually on the border between East and West Sussex, Ditchling has many fine old buildings, including the Bull Inn. The red-brick house in the High Street was where the sculptor Eric Gill lived and worked for many years. The Bull, a 14th century coaching inn, is a popular village local. Two bars in the pub, the main bar having some fine old furniture; the second is more simply furnished. There is also a no-smoking restaurant. Good wholesome bar food - garlic mushrooms with crispy croûtons, tiger prawns in filo pastry with salad garnish, home-cooked gammon ham, home-made beef lasagne, a vegetarian dish, fish when available, steaks and home-made puddings. Morlands Old Speckled Hen, Flowers Original, King & Barnes Sussex, Brakspears and Boddingtons ales. Seats outside on the terrace and in the pretty garden, which has fine views towards Ditchling Beacon.

OPEN: 11 - 11.
Real Ale. Restaurant (not Sun eves).
Children in restaurant. Dogs on leads.
Bedrooms.

EAST DEAN

Tiger Inn   Tel: 01323 423209

The Green, East Dean, Eastbourne, E Sussex BN20 0DA
(village off A259 Eastbourne-Seaford)
Free House. J Davies Gilbert, licensee

A good resting point if you are energetically walking the South
Downs Way. The white-painted old pub amid the pretty cottages
that border the village green makes for a very attractive setting,
especially in summer. Inside the Tiger Inn is a comfortable low-
beamed bar with good winter fires and a children's room upstairs.
Interesting bar food which could include venison casserole, garlic
mushrooms, macaroni cheese with tomatoes, ploughmans or fish
and chips. Seats outside, from where you can admire the scenery.
Beers do change but could include Timothy Taylors, Youngs
Special, Harveys Best and Adnams.

OPEN: 11.30 - 2.30; 6.30 - 11.
Real Ale. No food Sun eves.
Dogs on leads.
Occasional Morris dancers.

ELSTED

Three Horseshoes   Tel: 01730 825746

Elsted, Midhurst, W Sussex GU2N 0JX (W of Midhurst, off A272)
Free House. Andrew & Sue Beavis, licensees

There are generous quantities of changing bar food here to help
stoke up the walkers and cyclists on the South Downs Way. A
very traditional 16th century pub, originally serving the drovers
travelling the South Downs. Cosy, low-beamed rooms, full of old
furniture, with big fireplaces blazing with logs in the winter. A
changing blackboard menu could offer: home-made soups,
ploughmans, casseroles, steak pies, steak in red wine sauce, and
fresh fish. Filling puddings. Ales, which are kept behind the bar,

could include: Ballards Best, Flowers Original, Fullers London Pride and Gibbs Mew. They try to have some ales from smaller independent breweries. Farm cider. Seats in the pretty garden which has a marvellous view of the South Downs.

OPEN: 11 - 3 (2.30 winter); 6 - 11.
Real Ale. Restaurant (no food winter Sun eves).
Well behaved children in eating areas.
Dogs on leads.

ELSTED MARSH

Elsted Inn   Tel: 01730 813662

Elsted Marsh, Midhurst, W Sussex GU29 0JT
Free House. Tweazle Jones & Barry Horton, licensees

Deep in the West Sussex countryside and well worth the journey for the very good ales and imaginative food. White-painted, Victorian, built when there was a railway station, now all alone, but certainly not forgotten. There are two traditionally furnished bars and a separate dining room seating 30. All the food is cooked on the premises using local seasonal produce: soups, sandwiches, prawns in garlic, home-cooked gammon, salads, venison stew, spinach roulade, chicken breast in a cream and caper sauce, fresh fish and home-made ice creams. Ballards Ales, founded in 1980, used to be brewed in this pub but have now moved to Myewood; however, the pub keeps a full range of Ballards Ales, Gibbs Mew and a couple of the more unusual beers as guests. Tables outside in the large garden. Folk music, a monthly band and barn dances during the summer.

OPEN: 11 - 3; 5.30 - 11 (6 - 11 Sat).
Real Ale. Restaurant.
Children in eating area & restaurant. Dogs on leads.
Folk Music and monthly band. Barn dances summer.
Bedrooms.

FINDON

Gun Inn   Tel: 01903 873206

High Street, Findon, W Sussex
Whitbread. Ian Cooper & Valerie Cleake, managers

In a beautiful situation, surrounded by woods and rolling hills, Findon is a charming, unspoilt, downland village. Dating from the 16th century, The Gun is a homely and welcoming port of call. The low beamed lounge bar contains beams that are reputed to be from old sailing ships. The sea is not far away, nor is the great earthwork of Cissbury Ring, an Iron Age hill-fort which rises 600ft above sea level. Generous helpings of home-cooked bar food. Up to seven real ales, among them: Morlands Old Speckled Hen, Flowers Original and IPA, Boddingtons and guest beers. You are in horsey country here - Josh Gifford's racing stables are nearby.

OPEN: 11 - 11.
Real Ale.
Children in family room. No dogs.

FIRLE

Ram Inn   Tel: 01273 858222

Firle, West Firle, Lewes, E Sussex BN8 6NS
(off A27 Lewes-Polegate)
Free House. Michael & Keith Wooller, licensees

Lots to see and do near here: Glyndebourne, a little more than an interval away: Firle Place, an imposing and apparently 18th century mansion disguising an old Elizabethan house to look at; and when you have had your pint and lunch, a quick dash up Firle Beacon, 713ft high on the Downs, should put you right for the rest of the day. The Ram has a main bar and a cosy snug, which is non-smoking. Fresh local produce is used in the daily changing menu. Good home-made soups, filled pitta bread, spicy chicken wings, salmon steaks, home cooked ham and interesting puddings. Charringtons IPA and Harveys BB plus guest beers. A good choice of wines. There is a big walled garden to sit in.

Open: 11 - 3; 7 - 11 (6 - 11 summer Sat).
Real Ale.
Children in non-serving bars.
Dogs on leads.
Bedrooms.
Live Folk once a week. Piano Sat eves.

FLETCHING

Griffin   Tel: 01825 722890

Fletching, E Sussex TN22 3NS (village off A272)
Free House. David & Nigel Pullan, licensees

One of the most appealing villages in East Sussex, Fletching dates back to Saxon times and has a particularly fine church. Some of the knights killed in the Battle of Lewes in 1264 are said to lie buried in full armour below the nave. The Griffin pub, a mere 400 years old, is all a village local should be. There is a heavily beamed main bar, a public bar with pool table and other games for those so inclined, and an attractively decorated restaurant. The very popular bar food changes daily and there is a shorter à la carte menu in the restaurant. The bar menu could include home-made soups, ploughmans, quiches, local sausages with onion gravy, salmon fishcakes and grilled fish. They do regular themes, and one dish evenings. Harveys, Badgers, Tanglefoot and Fullers London Pride, also Groslsch Lager (for those that don't know, it is a full strength German lager), and a very good wine list. Splendid views of the Sussex countryside from the garden.

OPEN: 12 - 3; 6 - 11.
Real Ale. Restaurant (not Sun eves).
Children welcome.
Dogs on leads.
Piano Fri/Sat eves & Sun lunchtime.

FLETCHING

Rose & Crown   Tel: 01825 722039

Fletching, East Sussex
Free House, Roger & Sheila Haywood, licensees

Nearly as old as the neighbouring Ashdown Forest, this pretty Sussex village is lucky to have two pubs, both blissfully quiet. The brick built 16th century Rose & Crown has one heavily beamed comfortable bar with a splendid inglenook fireplace and a restaurant offering a choice from either the à la carte or the table d'hôte menu. Bar snacks too: home-made soup, grilled jumbo prawns in garlic butter, gammon steak, fish omelettes, ploughmans and several vegetarian dishes. Home-made puddings and ice creams. Harveys Ales and Ind Coope Burton. Seats in the garden.

OPEN: 11 - 2.30; 6 - 11 (12 - 2; 7 - 10.30 Sun).
Real Ale. Restaurant. Children in restaurant only.
Dogs in bar only.

FULKING

Shepherd & Dog   Tel: 01273 857382

Fulking, Nr Henfield, W Sussex BN5 9LU
Free House. Anthony & Jessica Bradley Hull, licensees

Wonderfully situated at the foot of the South Downs, this 14th century pub has been continually popular. Originally sustaining the local shepherds and presumably their dogs - hence the name. If you want to sit inside and gaze at the view from the windows you need to arrive early to be sure of a seat. A cosy bar with rustic artefacts, and a changing bar menu: lovely fresh fish, steaks, vegetarian dishes, sandwiches, ploughmans and home-made puddings. Courage Directors, Harveys Best, Websters and guest beers from the smaller breweries. There are seats in the very pretty garden. If you have had too good a lunch, there are some energetic walks on the South Downs nearby.

OPEN: 10 - 12.30; 6 - 11.
Real Ale.
Dogs on leads.

GORING BY SEA

Bull Inn   Tel: 01903 248133

Goring Street, Goring by Sea, W Sussex BN12 5AR
Scottish & Newcastle. Barrie Wellmann & David Thurston, managers

Probably dating back to the 15th century, local smugglers were certainly making full use of the facilities by the 18th century. Still retaining much of its character, the pub, situated by the cricket green in the leafy Sussex countryside, now has the excitement of the local teams battling it out on a summer's day. One large bar, divided into different areas, one of which is used for dining. During the summer food is also served in the large garden, where there are enough picnic tables to seat 80. Short reliable menu: soup, ploughmans, home-made curry, omelettes, fish, gammon, steaks and salads. Sweets from the blackboard. Theakstons Bitter, lagers and wines by the glass.

OPEN: 11 - 2.30; 5.30 - 11.
Real Ale.
Dogs on leads.

GUN HILL

Gun Inn   Tel: 01825 872361

Gun Hill (Nr Horam), Heathfield, E Sussex TN21 0JU
Free House. R J Brockway, licensee

There were thriving iron foundries in this area during the 17th century; they used the trees of the Ashdown Forest to heat the iron ore and forge the guns. This explains why today the forest is mainly gorse, virtually treeless, and why the Gun is so named. The building which pre-dates the foundries, is now an attractive flower-bedecked country pub with rambling, beamed, rooms. It's very popular with the walkers from the Wealden Way - muddy boots and all. Lots of room to eat inside, big fires, a no-smoking area, good value food and well kept beers. Soups, salads, ploughmans, pork in cider sauce, beef Wellington and lots of fresh fish when available. Flowers IPA, Marstons Pedigree and Harveys. Farm cider and wines by the glass. There is a big sheltered garden which has seats and a children's play area.

OPEN: 11 - 11 (11 - 3; 6 - 11 winter).
Real Ale.
Children until 9 pm. Dogs on leads.

KIRDFORD

Half Moon Inn   Tel: 01403 820223

Kirdford, Nr Billingshurst, W Sussex RH14 0NA
Whitbread. Anne Moran, lease

In another pretty Sussex village, between Petworth and Billingshurst, this friendly, busy local dates back to the 17th century. The menu relies heavily on fish - all the easily recognisable species, also more exotic imported fish whose names don't easily trip off the tongue. Regular bar food too - salads, omelettes, ploughmans, steak & kidney pies, paté, sandwiches and there could be fish soup. The restaurant is no-smoking. Flowers IPA, Boddingtons, Fullers London Pride and Gales HSB on hand pump. Farm ciders. A short good wine list.

OPEN: 11 - 3; 7 - 11.
Real Ale. Restaurant (meals & snacks only in restaurant Fri/Sat eves).
Children until 9 pm.
Dogs, maybe.
Occasional live music.

KINGSTON, Nr Lewes

Juggs
Tel: 01273 472523

Kingston, Nr Lewes, E Sussex (off A27, W of Lewes)
Free House. Andrew Browne, licensee

The Juggs here aren't the sort of jugs you would put water in; these juggs were vessels the local women carried on their heads - full of fish brought from the nearby port to Kingston. Not far from Brighton, this small, pretty, tile-hung, rose-covered pub dates back to the 15th century. It has a rambling beamed main bar with a log fire, and a small no-smoking dining room in what used to be a hay store. The bar and restaurant share the same menu, and food includes a variety of sandwiches, locally made sausages, a vegetarian dish, pitta bread with a selection of fillings, steak & kidney pudding (speciality of the house), daily specials and a children's menu. King & Barnes, Harveys Sussex and guest beers on hand pump. Tables outside in the courtyard, on the sunny terrace and on the lawn.

OPEN: 11 - 2.30; 6 - 11.
Real Ale. Restaurant (not Sun lunchtime).
Children in two family rooms. Dogs on leads.

LEWES

The Lewes Arms
Tel: 01273 473152

Mount Place, Lewes, E Sussex BN7 1YH
Beards of Sussex. Matthew Dartan, licensee

Built at the beginning of the 18th century in the county town of East Sussex. Situated on a steep hill overlooking the River Ouse, Lewes is full of fine buildings from all periods. Off the busy main street, and just below the Castle Mound, the Lewes Arms is a pleasant, friendly, old-fashioned town pub. Two bars and a cosy snug. Food is all home-made: sandwiches and interesting hot snacks: pastas, De Ville Chicken - a speciality - vegetable au gratin, tagliatelle and hot Mexican food. The menu is contantly changing. Well kept ales: Harveys Best Bitter, Fullers London Pride, Courage Directors and Buchanans Original, plus seasonal ales.

OPEN: 11 - 11.
Real Ale. Lunchtime food only.
Children in games room.
Dogs on leads.

LEWES

Shelley's Hotel Bar   Tel: 01273 472361

137 High Street, Lewes, E Sussex BN7 1XS
Free House. Graeme Coles, licensee

Originally a private house owned by the poet's aunts, now an attractive hotel in the centre of the town. Recently overhauled and refurbished, £1.5 million has been spent bringing it up-to-date without losing any of the atmosphere or character from this splendid 16th century building. Within the hotel there is a 'Victorian' bar serving a selection of interesting bar snacks, quite a substantial menu which could include: home-made soup, seasonal fish stew, grilled goat's cheese, sandwiches, filled baguettes and toasted sandwiches. One real ale - the local Harveys - other beers are all bottled. Choice of wines. Seats in the garden.

OPEN: 11 - 3; 6 - 11.
Real Ale. Lunchtime snacks only.
Children not in bar.
No dogs.

LICKFOLD

Lickfold Inn   Tel: 01798 861285

Lickfold, Nr Lodsworth, Petworth, W Sussex GU28 9EY
Free House. Ron & Kath Chambers, licensees

Surrounded by lovely walks, this very attractive inn dates back to 1450 and has interesting, beamed, interiors, contemporary panelling and huge open fires. Lickfold, the village whose name means the garlic enclosure, was the home of Walter de Lykfold in 1332, and wild garlic still grows by the stream, not far from Lickfold Bridge. Talking of garlic naturally draws our attention to the bar menu, chalked on the blackboard and available only during lunchtime. There is a restaurant menu in the evening. Bar food includes a selection of sandwiches, ploughmans, tasty stews and pies and fish in season. There are Sunday lunchtime roasts. Here they rotate the ales but, there are usually about 8 on offer: Badgers Tanglefoot and Best, Ballards Best, Fullers London Pride, Harveys Best and Adnams, amongst others. There is also a resident ghost which the landlady has seen and says she is quite harmless. Psychic customers have felt her presence and one had a very strange experience in the gents' lavatory! Lots of seats in the large well planted garden.

OPEN: 11 - 2.30 (3 Sat); 6 - 11 (closed Mon eves).
Real Ale. No food Sun or Mon eves.
No children. Dogs on leads.

LODSWORTH

Halfway Bridge   Tel: 01798 861281

Lodsworth, Nr Petworth, W Sussex GU28 9BP
Free House. Sheila, Edric, Simon & James Hawkins, licensees

Built as a coaching inn early in the 18th century, halfway between Petworth and Midhurst, the Halfway Bridge is still serving the traveller with imaginative food and good ales. Lots of room in the comfortable, spacious bars and attractive dining room. An extensive blackboard menu lists food ranging from mushrooms in cream and tarragon, garlic stuffed mussels, lamb's liver and bacon, steak, kidney & ale pie to grilled fish and home-made puds. Sunday roasts. Tables in the garden during the summer and on the sheltered terrace at the back of the pub. Brakspears, Flowers Original and Gales HSB on hand pump. Also changing guest beers. Farm cider and wine by the glass.

OPEN: 11 - 3; 6 - 11 (closed winter Sun eves).
Restaurant not Sun evening.
Children over 10 in restaurant. Dogs on leads.

LURGASHALL

Noahs Ark   Tel: 01428 707346

Lurgashall, Nr Petworth, W Sussex GU28 9ET
Greene King. Kathleen & Ian Kennedy, tenants

On the edge of the village green which is also used as the local cricket pitch (a good six will land you on the bricks in front of the pub), this very pretty building, which was built as a pub in 1537, is extremely popular with locals, cricketers and non-cricketers alike. Apparently Cromwell trained his New Model Army nearby, worshipped in the village church and no doubt drank in the pub. Two bars, both with lovely fires in the winter, also two menus. Bar food includes toasties, ploughmans, chicken or ham salads, liver & bacon, vegetarian tagliatelle. In the restaurant: Langoustine, salmon, steaks, etc. Tables in the front of the pub overlook the church and village green. Rayments Special Bitter, Greene King IPA, Best Bitter and Abbot Ale. During the summer they occasionally have concerts and a theatre group performing in the garden.

OPEN: 11 - 2.30; 6 - 11.
Real Ale. Restaurant (no food Sun eves).
Children in family room & restaurant. Dogs on leads.
Occasional bands, concerts, theatre in garden during summer.

OVING

Gribble Inn   Tel: 01243 786893

Oving, Chichester, W Sussex PO20 6BP (E of Chichester)
Own Brew (Badger). Ron & Anne May, managers

So named after a Mrs Gribble who, years ago, used to live in this
16th century thatched cottage - now the local pub. Set in a very
attractive cottage garden and with its own brewery (tours can be
arranged), the pub has a heavily beamed bar with big log fires
and a no-smoking family room. Familiar home-cooked bar food -
soups, ploughmans, sandwiches, salads, ham and eggs, steak -
also Sunday lunches. Seats outside amongst the apple trees. The
pub's own skittle alley, along with the brewery, is on the other side
of the car park. Tanglefoot and Badgers Best and Own brew Pig's
Ear Wobbler in the winter, Gribble Ale, Reg's Tipple, Black Adder
and the newest - Plucking Pheasant.

OPEN: 11 - 2.30; 6 - 11 (all day Sat).
Real Ale.
Children in family room. Dogs on leads.

PUNNETTS TOWN

Three Cups Corner   Tel: 01435 830252

Punnetts Town, Nr Heathfield, E Sussex TN21 9LR
Free House. Leonard & Irenie Smith, licensees

Yet another ghostly pub, although here the landlady hasn't seen
the ghost, but has just felt its presence. Thought to be 17th
century, this is a very friendly unspoilt local with a big, low-
beamed bar and huge log fire in the winter. Traditional bar food
includes sandwiches, steak or chicken pie, locally made sausages
and filled baked potatoes. There is a no-smoking eating area.
Ales change every 2-3 weeks. When QUIET PINT queried, they
had Arkles, Tanners, Harveys and Buchanan. There are seats in
the garden and this is also good walking country.

OPEN: 11 - 3; 6.30 - 11.
Real Ale.
Children in eating area & family room.
No dogs.

RUDGWICK

Blue Ship   Tel: 01403 822709

The Haven, Rudgwick, Horsham, W Sussex
King & Barnes. John Davie, tenant

A small unspoilt Sussex pub. On entering the public bar you could
be forgiven for thinking you had slipped back a century or two.
Flagstone floors, scrubbed deal tables, in winter a roaring fire in
the big inglenook fireplace and farm dogs waiting patiently under
the benches. No bar as such; drinks are served through the hatch.
Food is all home-cooked; the blackboard menu changes
constantly - ham, egg and chips is a speciality. Everything they
serve is very wholesome. King and Barnes Broadwood and
Sussex ales, Old is available during the winter. There are
wonderful views from the garden over the surrounding
countryside. It can get very crowded.

OPEN: 11 - 3; 6 - 11 (12 - 3; 7 - 10.30 Sun).
Real Ale.
Children welcome.
Dogs on leads.

RUDGWICK

Thurlow Arms   Tel: 01403 822459

Baynards, Rudgwick, Horsham, W Sussex
Free House. Julian Gibbs, licensee

Tucked away down a side road, opposite the disused Baynards
Park railway station, now a private house, this old pub has seen

some changes in its lifetime. Not only was it moved in the late 18th century 500 yards to its present site, but since then it has been a private house, railway hotel, pub, private house again and now a pub once more. Traditional bar snacks are served, and there is a blackboard menu. Fresh fish is delivered daily and could include: john dory, lemon sole, mussels, skate wings or cod; there is frequently a choice of eight or more - other dishes too. King and Barnes Sussex, Hall and Woodhouse Badger, Hardtackle, Tanglefoot and Wadworths 6X plus Over Draught, which is the pub's own brew. There are tables in the garden and the old railway track offers a lovely walk to Cranleigh.

OPEN: 11 - 3; 6 - 11 (12 - 3; 7 - 10.30 Sun).
Real Ale. No food Sun eves.
Children welcome but not in bar. Dogs on leads.

RYE

Mermaid Inn   Tel: 01797 223065

Mermaid Street, Rye, E Sussex TN31 7EU
Free House. Robert Pinwill, licensee

Thought to be one of the loveliest smugglers' inns in the county. Probably dating back to the 12th century. Certainly by 1300 the Mermaid was brewing its own ale and charging a penny a night for accommodation. Rebuilt in 1420, the pub looks much the same today as it did then, wonderfully beamed and panelled, with a really vast inglenook fireplace. Two very comfortable lounges, a bar and also a restaurant. Traditional bar food and a more elaborate restaurant menu. Local Potters Pride and Morlands Old Speckled Hen on hand pump. House wines and sherries. Brass band concerts occasionally in the car park during summer.

OPEN: 11 - 11.
Real Ale. Restaurant.
Children welcome.
Dogs on leads.
Bedrooms.

SIDLESHAM

Crab & Lobster
Tel: 01243 641233

Mill Lane, Sidlesham, Chichester, W Sussex PO20 7NB
Free House. Brian Cross, licensee

Just outside Chichester, built as a pub in the 18th century, the Crab & Lobster backs onto the bird sanctuary in Pagham Harbour. There are two bars, a main bar with a fine log fire in winter and a slightly posher lounge bar. Bar food includes a variety of sandwiches, steak & kidney pie, gammon & eggs, salads and, as you might expect, quite a number of fish dishes plus home-made puddings. Seats in the very pretty garden at the back of the pub. Gales Best, BBB, and Arundel Stronghold on hand pump. Country wines.

OPEN: 11 - 2.30 (3 Sat); 6 - 11 (closed Sun eves Jan & Feb).
Real Ale. No food Sun eves.
Dogs on leads.

SUTTON

White Horse Inn
Tel: 01798 869221

Sutton, Nr Pulborough, W Sussex RH20 1PS
Free House. Howard & Susie Macnamara, proprietors

This 18th century building has served as the village ale house since 1746. Nestling at the foot of the South Downs in the lovely village of Sutton, the White Horse has a friendly, welcoming atmosphere. Lots of traditional scrubbed pine furniture in the bar, which extends through into the dining room. A good variety of country dishes, using fresh seasonal produce, are served in the restaurant and as a light meal in the village bar. The blackboard menu changes daily: cod and chips, liver and bacon being very popular, but there is quite a choice of exotic fare. Arundel, Courage Best and Directors, Youngs and Batemans ales. Tables in the attractive garden.

OPEN: 11 - 3; 6 - 11.
Real Ale. Restaurant.
Children welcome.
Dogs on leads in public bar only.
Bedrooms.

TICEHURST

Bull   Tel: 01580 200586

Three Legged Cross, Nr Ticehurst, E Sussex TN5 7HH
Free House. Josie Wilson Moir, licensee

For a pub so hidden away, the 13th century Bull is extremely busy. Rambling rooms, huge fireplaces, interesting food and a good choice of ales. There is a summer buffet, home-made soups, sandwiches, chicken en croûte, fresh salmon, steaks, fresh trout and home-made puddings. A more elaborate and extensive menu is available during the evening. The garden is particularly attractive in summer when the roses are out. There are two pétanque pitches and a sockby pitch - half soccer and half rugby - with a knock-out competition each year. Plenty of room for the children to play. . George Crown Best, Old Speckled Hen, Worthington Best, Rother Valley and guest beers.

OPEN: 11 - 3; 6.30 - 11.
Real Ale. Restaurant. No meals Sun or Mon eves.
Children in eating area & restaurant. Dogs on leads.

TICEHURST

Bell Hotel   Tel: 01580 200234

High Street, Ticehurst, Wadhurst, E Sussex
Free House. Mrs Pamela Tate, licensee

Situated in the village square, this pub has been run by the same family for over forty years. Parts of the Bell date back to 1296, but it is better known as a 14th century coaching inn. The public bar has the pool table, juke box and fruit machine, but the lounge bar is unspoilt and free of any distraction - lots of ancient timbers and a hugh inglenook fireplace ablaze with logs in the winter, all you'll hear is friendly chatter and the clink of glasses. There is a fascinating display of between 300 and 400 bells in and around the lounge bar. Bar snacks and meals are freshly cooked to order from the menu. Shepherd Neame, Harveys and Whitbread ales. Seats in the garden.

OPEN: 11 - 3; 6 - 11.
No food Sun eves.
Children welcome.
Dogs on leads.
Bedrooms.

WEST ASHLING

Richmond Arms   Tel: 01243 575730

Mill Lane, West Ashling, Chichester, W Sussex PO18 8EA (out of village towards Hambrook)
Free House. Bob & Christine Garbutt, licensees

For those of you interested in boxing history and wanting to sample a wide selection of beers, this simple friendly country pub is the place to be. The skittle alley - now used as a family room - is reputed to have been used for the last bare-knuckle fight in the country. As for the beers, four or five are available permanently: Timothy Taylors Landlord, Boddingtons, Wadworths 6X and Morlands Old Speckled Hen, another five or six are guest beers, many of them from the smaller, less well known breweries, offering a taste of the more unusual ales. Farm ciders and country wines too. There is a blackboard menu listing the usual bar snacks plus lasagne, chilli, baked potatoes and the daily specials.

OPEN: 11 - 3; 5.30 - 11 (all day summer Sats).
Real Ale.
Children welcome. Dogs on leads.
Tues Quiz nights.

WEST CHILTINGTON

Elephant & Castle   Tel: 01798 813307

Church Street, West Chiltington, W Sussex
King & Barnes. Charles Hollingworth, tenant

Not immediately visible, but if you find the church, the Elephant & Castle is just behind it. Dating back to the 16th century, this popular friendly pub has its own golf society - they enthusiastically follow all matches on the satellite television. Bar snacks include: ploughmans, sandwiches, filled baked potatoes and quite a choice of main dishes: liver and bacon, steaks, grilled trout, gammon, salmon, steak and kidney pie plus daily specials. Among the normal English fare you will find a few South African dishes. King and Barnes Festive, Broadwood and Sussex. Good selection of malt whiskies. Wonderful views from the large garden, which has swings and slides for children.

OPEN: 11 - 4; 6 - 11 (Mon - Thurs); 11 - 11 (Fri & Sat); 12 - 3; 7 - 10.30 (Sun).
Real Ale.
Children welcome.
Dogs on leads.

WINEHAM

Royal Oak   Tel: 01444 881252

Wineham Lane, Wineham, Nr Heathfield, E Sussex BN5 9AY
Whitbread. Tim Peacock, tenant

This attractive, unchanging, part-timbered, part tile-hung 14th century cottagey pub, with its low beams, huge inglenook fireplace and cosy back snug, is all you could wish for in a country pub. Ales straight from the cask. Food is limited to a good range of sandwiches and home-made soup in winter. Pompey Royal, Harveys BB, Wadworths 6X and Boddingtons in the summer. Tables on the lawn at the front of the pub next to the old well.

OPEN: 11 - 2.30; 5.30 - 11 (6 - 11 Sat).
Real Ale.
Children in family room.
Dogs on leads.

WILTSHIRE

BOWDEN HILL

Rising Sun
Tel: 01249 730363

Bowden Hill, Nr Laycock, Wilts SN15 2PP
Free House. Anthony & Julie Page, licensees

Situated high on a hill above Laycock, with views on a clear day across five counties and the Avon Valley, the Rising Sun is a small, stone-built, 17th century pub. It has flagstoned floors, open fires and a good choice of interesting bar food, ranging from sandwiches to coq au vin with stuffed pancakes. Moles Ales from Melksham and well-kept guest beers. Seats in the terraced gardens which are at a premium on a good clear day, so if you want to admire the view arrive early and bag a space.

OPEN: 11.30 - 3; 6 - 11 (12 - 3; 7 - 10.30 Sun).
Real Ale.
Children in eating area.
Dogs on leads.

DEVIZES

Bear
Tel: 01380 722444

The Market Place, Devizes, Wilts SN10 1HS
Wadworths. W K Dickenson, tenant

Before being converted into such an attractive, dependable-looking old coaching inn, the Bear was the home of Sir Thomas Lawrence, the 18th century portrait painter. It's at its glorious best in summer, when wonderful flowery eyebrows bloom extravagantly over the bay windows and the handsome pillared doorway. Inside is what you would expect - beamed, panelled and polished. Traditional bar food and a more extensive menu served in the Lawrence Room Restaurant. There is also the elegant Marston Lampton Restaurant, if you are really pushing the boat out. Wadworths ales, which are brewed locally. Morning coffee. Tables in the courtyard.

OPEN: 10 - 11 (10 - 3; 6 - 11 winter).
Real Ale. Restaurant (closed Sun eve).
Children in eating area.
Dogs on leads.
Bedrooms.

EBBESBOURNE WAKE

Horseshoe Inn   Tel: 01722 780474

Ebbesbourne Wake, Nr Salisbury, Wilts SP5 5JF
Free House. Andrew & Patricia Bath, licensees

It's tucked away in a fold of the Wiltshire Downs, well away from the rush of the modern world, and covered in rambling honeysuckle and roses. The bars are traditionally furnished, have open fires and walls decorated with country artefacts. Good value bar food, all "cooked that day," is listed on the blackboard: pies, quiches, patés, fresh fish, plus the stalwarts - sandwiches, ploughmans and a hot dish or two. Sunday: roast lunches. Adnams Broadside, Ringwood Best and Wadworths 6X from casks behind the bar, plus farm ciders and a choice of malt whiskies. Seats in the pretty, flowery garden overlook the Ebble Valley.

OPEN: 11.30 - 3; 6.30 - 11.
Real Ale. Restaurant. No meals/snacks Mon eve.
Children in top bar & restaurant.
No dogs.
Bedrooms.

HINDON

Lamb Inn
Tel: 01747 820605

Hindon, Salisbury, Wilts SP3 6DP
Free House. John & Paul Croft, licensees

This interesting old stone coaching inn, on the most important corner site in the village, is considerably older than its Georgian frontage. It pre-dates the coaches, and in the 15th century served as a court house for the local assizes. The big, old, beamed bar with a huge inglenook fireplace has plenty of room for you to enjoy a drink and sample the short, well chosen bar menu from the blackboard. There is a no-smoking restaurant with an evening table d'hôte menu: fresh asparagus, steamed cushion of salmon with prawn and brandy sauce, or fillet of beef with peppercorn sauce. A similar à la carte menu is available at lunchtime. Wadworths 6X, Boddingtons, Oakhill, Ringwood Best and Hook Norton on hand pump. Picnic tables outside.

OPEN: 11 - 11.
Real Ale. Restaurant.
Children welcome. Dogs on leads.
Bedrooms.

KILMINGTON

Red Lion
Tel: 01985 844263

Kilmington, Warminster, Wilts
Free House. Chris Gibbs, licensee

Like the marvellous nearby gardens at Stourhead, the Red Lion is owned by the National Trust and is an ideal base for the many good, country walks that radiate from it - so there will be lots of serious walking boots around. Comfortable, appealing bars, with winter log fires and simple but satisfying bar food which could include home-made soups, home-cooked ham, ploughmans, game pies and a vegetarian dish. Marstons Pedigree and a guest beer. Farm ciders. Seats in the large garden.

OPEN: 11 - 3; 6.30 - 11.
Real Ale.
Children in eating area 'til 9 pm.
Dogs on leads. Bedrooms.

LITTLE BEDWYN

Harrow   Tel: 01672 870871

Little Bedwyn, Nr Marlborough, Wiltshire SN8 3JL
Free House, Luis and Angela Lopez, licensees

The village had to buy the Harrow and run it, or lose it altogether.
So a couple of dozen locals got together, bought it, and installed
Angela and Luis Lopez to run it. Angela is English; Luis hails from
Granada, so, although the food on offer is predominantly English,
a number of Spanish specialities appear on the bar and no-
smoking restaurant menus. Garlic soup in winter, gazpacho in
summer, tapitas in the bar and paella on Sundays. Hook Norton
Bitter, Foxley Best and a couple of guest ales. Good selection of
wines from Spain and from the New World. Seats in the pretty
enclosed rear garden. Not far from the Kennet and Avon canal.

OPEN: 11 - 2.30, 5.30 - 11 (6 - 11, Sat).
Real Ale. Restaurant.
Children welcome. No dogs.

LOWER CHICKSGROVE

Compasses Inn   Tel: 01722 714318

Tisbury, Lower Chicksgrove, Nr Salisbury, Wilts SP3 6NB
Free House. Sarah Dunham & Tony Lethbridge, licensees

No proper inn sign here, so look out for the thatched roof; then, if
you see a car park and signs of activity you know you've come to
the right place. Not Monday to Wednesday though, as it's closed.
A very popular 14th century pub, offering a well chosen changing

menu of home-cooked bar food, a good selection of beers and a barbecue on summer Sundays. Plenty of room in the beamed main bar which has lots of country and farming bits and pieces hanging from the beams and on the walls. Bass, Adnams, Wadworths 6X plus a guest beer. Seats in the garden and in the courtyard. There is a children's play area.

OPEN: 12 - 3 (11.30 - 3 Sat); 6 - 11. Closed Mon - Wed.
Real Ale. Restaurant.
Children in eating area. Dogs on leads.
Bedrooms.
Occasional live music.

LOWER WOODFORD

Wheatsheaf Tel: 01722 73203

Lower Woodford, Nr Salisbury, Wilts SP4 6NQ
Badger. Peter & Jennifer Charlton, tenants

If you happen to go to the Wheatsheaf on an evening when there's a meeting of the local rugby club, you may think we have mistakenly classified this pub as quiet. Don't be misled, that is only the rugby club's record player - it is not permanent wallpaper music. An extension has recently been completed so there is now more room for you to enjoy your drink and to sit down for a meal. A wide selection of bar food is available ranging from soups, open sandwiches, chicken curry, basket meals, salmon, trout and steaks, to a full vegetarian menu. Badger ales, Tanglefoot and Hard Tackle. Hofbrau Lager. Seats in the big garden and on the terrace.

OPEN: 11 - 11 (11 - 2.30; 6.30 - 11 Mon & Tues + Winter).
Real Ale. Restaurant.
Children in eating areas.
Dogs on leads.

RAMSBURY

Bell   Tel: 01672 20230

The Market Square, Ramsbury, Wilts SN8 2PE
Free House. Graham Dawes, licensee

A popular village pub with a reputation for serving imaginative, carefully prepared food. The same concise menu features in both the restaurant and the bar, offering soups, paté, single course snacks, fish dishes, steaks, lots of fresh vegetables, school puds and proper ice creams. Sunday roast. There is also a daily changing blackboard menu. Wadworths range of ales plus a couple of guest beers. Lots of malt whiskies. Seats in the garden and good walks not far away.

OPEN: 12 - 3 (11 - 3 Sat); 6 - 11.
Real Ale. Restaurant.
Children in eating area & restaurant. Dogs on leads.

SALISBURY

Haunch of Venison   Tel: 01722 322024

1 Minster Street, Salisbury, Wilts SP1 1TB
Courage. Antony & Victoria Leroy, lease

There is a salutary lesson in this pub for anyone contemplating cheating at cards. Next to the 600 year old fireplace, thought to date back to the pub's early days, is a mummified hand, discovered earlier this century, holding some 18th century playing cards. Was this some awful 18th century gamblers' retribution? Inside, the pub is heavily beamed, with timbered and panelled walls and open fires. Good traditional bar food: sandwiches, ploughmans and a variety of pies, and salads. Over 140 malt whiskies. Courage Best and Directors ales served from a pewter bar counter. A charming pub, not to be missed.

OPEN: 11 - 11.
Real Ale. Restaurant. No meals/snacks Sun evening.
Children away from bar. Dogs on leads.

WINGFIELD

Poplars Inn   Tel: 01225 752426

Wingfield, Nr Trowbridge, Wilts BA14 9LN
Wadsworth. Mike & Sue Marshall, licensees

Originally a shop; before that two cottages. Now it's the village pub. Licensed at the beginning of the Second World War, it is a traditional early Georgian building, situated in the centre of the village, with the unusual addition of its own cricket field. Just a paddock for many years, it was then decided to convert it into a cricket pitch. Locals sit and drink and watch the local teams play. The usual range of bar food, from cheese rolls to steaks. Wadsworths range of ales.

OPEN: 11 - 3; 5.30 - 11 (12 - 3; 7 - 10.30 Sun).
Real Ale.
No children under 14. Dogs on leads.

WYLYE

Bell Inn   Tel: 01985 248338

High Street, Wylye, Warminster, Wilts BA12 0QP
Free House. Steve & Ann Locke, licensees

Next to the church, not far from Stonehenge and situated in a picturesque valley between Salisbury and Warminster, The Bell has been catering for the traveller since 1373. A traditional stone building with an interior reflecting its great age. The home-cooked bar food, from a continually changing menu includes daily specials, children's dishes and a selection of vegetarian meals, plus a Sunday roast. Wadsworths 6X, Badger ales plus a guest beer. 21 different varieties of fruit and country wines. Seats in the garden and on the terrace.

OPEN: 11.30 - 11 (11.30 - 2.30; 6 - 11 winter).
Real Ale. Restaurant.
Children in eating areas. Dogs on leads.

YORKSHIRE

APPLETREEWICK

Craven Arms   Tel: 01756 720270
Appletreewick, Nr Skipton, N Yorks BD23 6DA
Free House. Jim & Linda Nicholson, licensees

This is a pretty hillside village with some exceptionally fine
buildings: 17th century Mockbeggar Hall and, not far away, the
terraced gardens of Parcevall Hall. Overlooking the Wharfdale
Valley is the stone-built Craven Arms, a popular stopping place
for walkers enjoying the wonderful North Yorkshire countryside.
Traditionally furnished, beamed, cosy rooms with winter fires.
Ample portions of pub food: soups, sandwiches, ploughmans,
Cumberland sausages and onion gravy, vegetarian dishes, steak
& kidney pie and daily specials. Theakstons Best, XB and Old
Peculiar. Tetleys and Youngers as guest beers. Choice of wines
and a selection of malt whiskies. Seats at the front of the pub to
admire the view.

OPEN: 11.30 - 3; 6.30 - 11.
Real Ale. No food Mon evening.
Children welcome. No dogs.

AUGMENTING THE DIRECTORY

We know there are more pubs and wine bars eligible for inclusion in
THE QUIET PINT than are listed here. Please help us to find them for
our next edition by completing the nomination forms at the end of this
Book.

AUSTWICK

Game Cock   Tel: 01524 251226

Austwick, Nr Settle, N Yorks LA2 8BB
Thwaites. Alex McGwire, tenant

Not far from the A65, amidst the wildness of the Yorkshire dales -
a favourite stopping place for walkers and villagers alike. The pub
overlooks the main street; inside you have a simply furnished
friendly bar, separate dining room and a glassed-in terrace
sheltering you from the prevailing wind. Bar food includes the
well-tried favourites plus beef in ale pie, steaks, Game Cock
mixed grill and a children's menu. There is a no-smoking
restaurant. Thwaites ales. Outside there is a play area for
children.

OPEN: 11 - 3; 6.30 - 11.
Real Ale. Restaurant.
Children in restaurant. No dogs.
Bedrooms.

BECK HOLE

Birch Hall Inn   Tel: 01947 896245

Beck Hole, Goathland, Whitby, Yorks YO22 5LE
Free House. Colin Jackson, licensee

This area is closely associated with the dawn of railway travel.
Beck Hole Incline was part of the Whitby-Pickering Railway built
by railway pioneer George Stephenson, and where he located his
hydraulic engine to haul horse-drawn vehicles up to the old Bank
Top Station - which can still be seen. In Beck Hole itself, they built
a small ironworks in 1860 to exploit the rich, local ironstone veins,
but it closed after four years, so that the natural beauty of the
valley has not been impaired. It's down here that you'll find the
Birch Hall Inn, which also doubles as a village shop and boasts a

priceless and unique inn-sign painted by Algernon Newton RA in the 1940's. Algernon Newton was a very well known artist and this is not the usual medium for a conventional painter. The pub itself dates back to the 17th century; it has a small bar with a serving hatch and an open fire, an even smaller bar opening onto the garden, and a shop selling sweets, ices and soft drinks between the two bars. Just what a village pub should be - all things to all people. Local pork, turkey and ham pies, Beck Hole butties (northern sandwiches to you) with generous fillings of ham, cheese, paté or corned beef. Theakstons Best XB (Mild in summer), Black Sheep, local beers and guests - all from the cask. Family room, seats in the garden. A lovely part of Yorkshire, good walking country.

OPEN: 11 - 11 (summer). 11 - 3; 7.30 - 11 (winter).
Real Ale.
Children welcome. Dogs on leads.

BREARTON

Malt Shovel   Tel: 01423 862929

Brearton, Harrogate, N Yorks HG3 3BX
Free House. Les Mitchell, licensee

An unspoilt 16th century, family-run pub in a small remote village in North Yorkshire. Cosy, heavily beamed with panelled rooms and good winter fires. A popular meeting place which has a reputation for well-chosen, well-cooked food, with the attention to detail which lifts it above the ordinary. Concise, daily changing blackboard menus could include ham in parsley sauce, steak and mushroom pie cooked in a red wine sauce, haddock with a spicy batter coating, fresh salmon, a selection of salads and vegetarian dishes. All the puddings are home-made. Theakstons ales, Daleside Old Mill Traditional and Bitter plus a guest beer and farm ciders. Seats on the terrace at the back of the pub.

OPEN: 12 - 3; 6.45 - 11 (6.30 - 11 Sat). Closed Monday.
Real Ale. No food Sun evening or Mon.
Children welcome. Dogs on leads.

BURNSALL

Red Lion
Tel: 01756 720204

Burnsall, Skipton, N Yorks BD23 6BU
Free House. Elizabeth Grayshon, licensee

Lots to see in Burnsall. There is the impressive, five-arched bridge over the river, St Wilfred's Church which has a 16th century tower, Norman font, Jacobean pulpit and 10th century gravestones, the 15th century school, now the primary school, and finally - the whole point of being here - the 16th century Red Lion, originally a ferryman's inn on the bank of the River Wharfe. Lucky them, they have fishing rights over seven miles of the river. Inside, the pub has a panelled main bar and a no-smoking lounge bar with good no-nonsense bar food. Soups and sandwiches, local cheese for the ploughmans, gammon with free range eggs, lots of fish, game in season and good puddings. Tetleys Bitter, Theakstons Best and a guest beer. Choice of malt whiskies. Seats at the front and at the back of the pub.

OPEN: 11.30 - 3; 5.30 - 11 (5 - 11 Sat).
Real Ale. Restaurant.
Children welcome.
Dogs on leads (not in hotel rooms).
Bedrooms.

EAST WITTON

Blue Lion
Tel: 01969 24273

East Witton, Nr Leyburn, N Yorks DL8 4SN
Free House. Paul Klein, lease

A good, reliable-looking, old stone coaching inn. Built in the 19th century, evidence of its past can still be seen in the stone archway, designed to allow horse-drawn coaches to enter the stable courtyard. Only one bar. This has high-backed settles and a big log-filled fireplace. Popular, interesting home-made bar food from the blackboard menu. There is also a candlelit restaurant for residents. Theakstons Best, Timothy Taylors Landlord and Boddingtons on hand pump. Selection of wines and old English liqueurs. Seats outside the front of the pub and in the big, attractive garden at the rear.

OPEN: 11 - 11.
Real Ale. Restaurant (closed Sun evening).
Children welcome.
Dogs on leads.
Bedrooms.

FARNDALE

Feversham Arms   Tel: 01751 433206

Church Houses, Farndale, N Yorks (Nr Kirkby Moorside)
Free House. Fran & Ray Debenham, licensees

Situated in the lovely, remote Farndale Valley which is carpeted with miniature daffodils in springtime and is thought locally to be the inspiration behind Wordsworth's poem. A delightful, beautifully kept old pub. One wall of the small bar has a fine example of an old Yorkshire range. There is an à la carte menu in the restaurant, which is in a handsome converted old barn. Very generous portions, both in the restaurant and the bar - a hearty appetite is a necessity. All the food is home-cooked: gammon and egg pie, steak & kidney pie, soups and salads. One of the specialities in the restaurant is a fillet of pork en croûte stuffed with garlic and shallots, also tournedos Rossini. Sunday lunches (must book). Full Yorkshire breakfast if you stay. Tetleys ales; also stouts and lagers. Seats in the garden.

OPEN: 11 - 3; 5.30 - 11 (summer). 12 - 2.30; 7 - 11 (winter).
Real Ale.
Children welcome.
Dogs on leads.
Bedrooms.

GOATHLAND

Mallyan Spout Hotel

Tel: 01947 896206

Goathland, Whitby, N Yorks YO22 5AN
Free House. Judith Heslop, licensee

From the hotel it is a short walk down a steep track to the Mallyan Spout, a 70ft waterfall over a mossy cliff into the Esk Valley below. Situated on a pretty village green, with the local sheep as very efficient lawnmowers, the Mallyan Spout Hotel is an ivy-covered stone building. With years of experience at serving the discerning traveller, it has a reputation for solid dependability. Three lounges with big winter fires overlook the garden; a comfortable bar serves well kept ales and there is a very attractive restaurant. Bar food includes home-made soups, patés, home-made chutneys with the ploughmans, local salmon trout (in season), fish, plus daily specials. They host special gourmet weekends. Theakstons Best and local Malton Double Chance Bitter. Decent wine list and choice of malt whiskies.

OPEN: 11 - 11.
Real Ale. Restaurant.
Children welcome until 8.30.
Dogs on leads.
Bedrooms.

HEATH

Kings Arms

Tel: 01924 377527

Heathcommon, Nr Wakefield, W Yorks WF1 5SL
Clarks. David Garthwaite, manager

Overlooking acres of common land, this 18th century pub is in a very attractive setting and totally unspoilt. Small and flagstoned, its panelled bars are still lit by gas, and one of them has an old range which is lit in winter. A new conservatory provides more elbow room and opens onto the garden. Dependable bar food with daily specials and home-made puddings. Clarks Bitter and Festival Ale, Tetleys and Timothy Taylors Landlord. Lots of seats outside the front and the side of the pub.

OPEN: 11.30 - 3; 5.30 - 11.
Real Ale. Restaurant (not Sun evening).
Children welcome.
Dogs on leads.

HETTON

Angel Inn   Tel: 01756 730263

Hetton, Nr Skipton, N Yorks BD23 6LT
Free House. Dennis Watkins, licensee

Whilst you can definitely still get a pint and sandwich: (open - smoked salmon with cream cheese, smoked bacon and home-made chutney), you will understand when I say this isn't exactly one of your pint and a wad places. Food here is not just sustaining - it is an experience. Seafood filo parcels, char-grilled lamb, salmon en croûte, confit of duck and good puddings too. Special gourmet evenings are organised throughout the year. The three weeks prior to Christmas this year will be "Christmas in the hills of Northern Italy". All North Italian dishes with wine from Piedmont, Lombardy and Liguria, but we won't forget good English ale: Marstons, Black Sheep and Boddingtons. Quite a wine list and choice of malt whiskies. There is a no-smoking snug and seats outside on the terrace.

OPEN: 12 - 2.30; 6 - 10.30 (6 - 11 Sat).
Real Ale. Restaurant (closed Sun evening).
Well behaved children welcome.
Dogs outside only.

HUBBERHOLME

George Inn Tel: 01756 760223

Hubberholme, Nr Skipton, N Yorks BD23 5JE
Free House. Jerry Lanchbury & Fiona Shelton, licensees

Another of the many solid stone-built Dales pubs which can withstand all the weather this part of the world can throw at them. Luckily, they always seem to be in just the right place to sustain the traveller in this rugged terrain. On the banks of the River Wharfe, and virtually on the Dales Way, it is understandably a favourite with the big boot and hairy stocking brigade. Traditional, beamed and stone-walled bars serving substantial steak & ale pies, filled Yorkshire puddings, ploughmans with local cheese, steaks and daily specials. The dining room is no-smoking. Theakstons Best, Youngers Scotch and No.3 ales. A selection of Scotch whiskies and a choice of wines. Seats outside for the view and for gazing at the river.

OPEN: 11.30 - 4 (11.30 - 3 winter); 6.30 - 11 (11 - 11 Sat).
Real Ale. Restaurant.
Children in eating area.
Dogs on leads.
Bedrooms.

LEEDS

Whitelocks Tel: 01132 453950

Turks Head Yard, Offbriggate, Leeds LS1 6HB
Youngers. Julie Cliff, manager

If you want to see Victorian pub architecture at its best, this is the place. Stained glass windows, fine mirrors, red banquettes, and marble tiles on the bars. There is a panelled dining room at the back of the pub. Good choice of bar food: sandwiches, pies, sausages, filled Yorkshire puddings and Scotch eggs. Wallow in nostalgia by reading the pre-War prices which are still etched on the mirrors. Theakstons IPA and Youngers ales. A selection of wines. Seats outside.

OPEN: 11 - 11.
Real Ale. Restaurant (not Sun evening).
Children in restaurant. Guide dogs only.

LINTHWAITE

Sair Inn   Tel: 01484 842370

139 Lane Top, Hoyle Ing, Huddersfield, W Yorks HD7 5SG
Free house. Ron Crabtree, licensee

Two very important things to bear in mind here - this pub only opens in the evenings and you won't get fed. I am not saying there isn't a bag of crisps or nuts behind the counter, but that is all. You would only be here for the beer. This is what a Yorkshire pub used to be all about - serious beer. Traditionally furnished, big fires, flagstone floors and views across the Colne Valley. Own brew ales are: Linfit Mild Bitter and Special, Old Eli, Leadboiler, Autumn Gold, Enoch Stout and English Guineas (a stout) plus a guest beer. Farm ciders and some malt whiskies. The Huddersfield Canal - with its 25 locks and the longest canal tunnel in Britain - is not far away.

OPEN: 7 - 11 Weekdays. 12 - 3; 7 - 11 Sat, Sun & Bank Hols.
Real Ale.
Children away from bar. Dogs on leads.

LITTON

Queens Arms   Tel: 01756 770208

Litton, Nr Skipton, N Yorks BD23 5QJ
Free House. Tanya & Neil Thompson, licensees

When there are very few roads - perhaps one or two - in a vast expanse of countryside, you know you are in serious walking country. Here you are surrounded by fells, crags, peaks and all those places that have to be either walked up or over. Even more reason for wanting to know about the Queens Arms. A charming old stone pub giving shelter, warmth and sustenance in spectacular surroundings. Bar food includes the stalwarts: soup, sandwiches, ploughmans, filled baked potatoes and steak or rabbit pie - Danish sandwiches too. Youngers ales on hand pump. Wonderful views from the two-level garden.

OPEN: 12 - 3 (11.30 - 3 Sat); 6.30 - 11 (7 - 11 winter).
Real Ale.
Children in eating areas & own room.
Dogs on leads. Bedrooms.

MOULTON

Black Bull Inn
Tel: 01325 377289

Moulton, Nr Richmond, N Yorks DL10 6QJ
Free House. Audrey Pagendam, licensee

If and when you get to Moulton, remember the route is so complex that you cannot get onto the Northbound A1 without a map, probably a compass and detailed instructions - but why bother - after a decent lunch go the scenic way - the slower country route. Well worth the effort to get to the Black Bull. You'll find a lovely log fire in the bar where they serve hot and cold snacks; there is a seafood restaurant open in the evenings - no booking necessary; dining à deux? - a Pullman carriage from the Brighton Belle has just eight tables and an à la carte menu; for small parties there is a flowery conservatory complete with grape vine. Very impressive. In the bar there are home-made soups, smoked salmon sandwiches, paté, seafood pancakes, herby fishcakes, hot tomato tart with black olives and much more. Theakstons and Tetleys ales. Good choice of wines and sherries. Seats outside in the courtyard.

OPEN: 12 - 2.30; 6 - 10.30 (11 Sat). Closed Sun evening.
Real Ale. Restaurant (not Sun evening).
No bar meals Sun lunchtime.
Children in restaurant (over 7). No dogs.

MUKER

Farmers Arms   Tel: 01748 886297

Muker, Nr Richmond, N Yorks DL11 6QG
Free House. Chris & Marjorie Bellwood, licensees

An unspoilt popular old village pub, handy for walkers on the Pennine Way or anyone exploring the North Yorkshire moors. Inside it has flagstone floors so walking boots are acceptable. The furnishings are traditional and there's a good warming fire. Excellent value bar food: soups, filled baps, baked potatoes, ploughmans, gammon and egg, good filling pies and a children's menu. Butterknowle Bitter, Youngers and Theakstons ales on hand pump.

OPEN: 11 - 3; 6.30 - 11 (11 - 11 Sat). (7 - 11 winter evening.)
Real Ale.
Children in eating area. Dogs on leads.

OAKWORTH

Grouse Inn   Tel: 01535 643073

Oakworth, Nr Keighley, Yorkshire
Taylors. Joseph Procter, tenant

If you want a comfortable, interesting, old-fashioned pub with a friendly landlord in the middle of Bronté country, then this is it. Popular with walkers and tourists - Howarth is only two miles away - you will find good familiar bar food: Mrs Procter's soups, sandwiches, salads and daily specials. There is also a charming restaurant. Timothy Taylors ales include Golden Best, Dark & Mild, Best Bitter, Landlord, Ram Tam XXXX and Porter. Good walking country. The Keithley and Worth Valley Railway, which runs through 5 miles of the glorious Pennine countryside, is not far away (this was the line used in the film "The Railway Children").

OPEN: 11 - 3; 6.30 - 11. Closed Mon except bank holiday.
Real Ale. No food Mon.
Well behaved children. Dogs on leads.

REDMIRE

Kings Arms Hotel   Tel: 01969 622316

Redmire, N Yorks DL8 4ED
Free House. Nigel Stevens, licensee

This is an attractive small village with old stone houses surrounding the green and views of Penn Hill (1792 ft) and the River Ure. Superbly located within the village, the Kings Arms offers a wide choice of home-made bar food: soups, paté, omelettes, steak & kidney pies and daily specials. Fruit pies and crumbles to follow. A Sunday roast and freshly ground coffee. The restaurant is no-smoking. John Smiths, Theakstons Best, Hambleton Bitter and guest beers, (Shepherd Neame at the moment) or Websters Yorkshire and Tetleys. Panoramic views from the terrace and seats in the attractive garden.

OPEN: 11 - 3; 5.30 - 11.
Real Ale. Restaurant.
Children in eating area.
No dogs.
Bedrooms.
Live music last Fri of month.

RICHMOND

Black Lion   Tel: 01748 823121

Finkle Street, Richmond, N Yorks DL10 4QB
Pubmaster. Stephen J Foster, tenant

There are walks along the River Swale from this old market town, where the ruins of the Norman Castle dominate the skyline above the cobbled market place. The Black Lion Hotel is tucked in a side street, just opposite the market square. It's an old coaching inn with comfortable, heavily beamed bars, big fires, good familiar bar food and well kept ales. Food available includes: soups, paté, ploughmans, salads, leek bake, steaks, quiche and roast of the day. As the restaurant has music, stay in the bars. Camerons Strong Arm, Flowers IPA, Tetleys Imperial, Yorkshire wines and a choice of malt whiskies.

OPEN: 10.30 - 11.
Real Ale. Restaurant.
Children welcome.
Dogs on leads in bar only.
Music only in restaurant.

ROBIN HOODS BAY

Laurel Inn   Tel: 01947 880400

The Bank, Robin Hoods Bay, Whitby, N Yorks YO22 4SJ
Free House. David Angood, lease

Attractive and unspoilt, this fishing village was a haunt of smugglers (it even has a smuggling experience museum) and was named, so legend has it, as the place Robin Hood fought off another lot of those marauding Danes. There is also reputed to be a network of smugglers' tunnels under the houses in the village - probably the pubs too. This popular old pub, situated in the centre of the village, is more concerned now with the legitimate traveller. Inside there is a large, beamed main bar with an open fire. The only bar food available is a sandwich at lunchtime and soup during the winter. John Smiths, Ruddles Best, Marstons Pedigree and Theakstons Old Peculiar.

OPEN: 12 - 11.
Real Ale.
Children in family room.
Dogs on leads.

SAXTON

Greyhound Inn   Tel: 01937 557202

Main Street, Saxton, N Yorks LS24 9PY
Sam Smiths. Mr & Mrs McCarthy, managers

Not only the local inn, but also the post office (before opening times). A really old-fashioned tiny village pub, thought to be one of the smallest in England, and time has not changed it. Beer is still in casks and sandwiches have to be ordered during the week - however, at weekends they are always available - crisps and nuts too. The ale is Samuel Smiths Old Brewery Bitter. Pretty in the summer when the roses are out. Seats in the courtyard next to the church. Nearby is the Edwardian mansion at Lotherton Hall which consists of a museum and a bird park created to re-introduce birds to the wild. It is well worth a visit.

OPEN: 12 - 3; 5.30 - 11 (11 - 11 Sat).
Real Ale.
Children in games room.
Dogs in tap room only.

SETTLE

Royal Oak   Tel: 01729 822561

The Market Place, Settle, N Yorks BD24 9ED
Whitbread. Brian & Sheila Longrigg, tenants

An excellent centre for country walks. Limestone cliffs overhang this old market town, which has a handsome square, 18th and 19th century houses and lots of small courts and alleys. This big, low, stone building dates back to 1684 and has plenty of room in which to enjoy your bar food. Stay well away from the restaurant which has MUSIC. Bar snacks available include: soups, sandwiches (open or closed), local potted shrimps, steak & ale pie and other traditional dishes. Children's menu available. Boddingtons, Flowers Original and one guest ale. Range of malt whiskies.

OPEN: 11 - 11.
Real Ale. Restaurant.
Children welcome.
Dogs on leads.
Bedrooms.

SHEFFIELD

Fat Cat   Tel: 01142 728195

23 Alma Street, Sheffield S3 8SA
Own Brew. Steven Fearn, licensee

Opening in 1981, this was Sheffield's first real ale house, and in 1990 started brewing its own Kelham Island beer next door to the pub. Filling home-made soups, stews, pies and daily specials, plus a number of imaginative vegetarian dishes and usually, one fish dish. Good English puddings - crumbles and pies with cream or custard. Ten draught ales always available, five guest beers: Marstons Pedigree, Theakstons Old Peculiar, Timothy Taylors Landlord, two from Kelham Island which could be Wheat Beer or Fat Cat Pale Ale, draught cider and lots of Belgian bottled beers. Country fruit wines and small barrels of Kelham Island Beer to take away (ordered in advance). Seats in the courtyard at the back of the pub.

OPEN: 12 - 3; 5.30 - 11.
Real Ale. Lunch time meals, snacks only.
Children in one room only.
Dogs on leads.

WASS

Wombwell Arms
Tel: 01347 868280

Wass, N Yorks YO6 4BE
Free House. Alan & Lynda Evans, licensees

In a delightful situation. At the foot of the Hambleton Hills and near the ruined 12th century Byland Abbey where you can still see the remains of an entire monastic site. Charming 17th century inn serving an interesting selection of pub food. The day's selection is written on the blackboard and using only fresh local produce, could include sandwiches, ploughmans with local cheeses and home-made pickle, rabbit cooked with prunes and red wine, baked salmon in dill and lemon, local game, vegetarian dishes and good puddings. Timothy Taylors and Black Sheep plus a guest beer. Choice of wines.

OPEN: 12 - 2.30; 7 - 11 (closed Sun eve & all Mon Oct - April & one week Jan).
Real Ale.
Children in eating area (not under 5 in evening).
No dogs.

WATH-IN-NIDDERDALE

Sportsmans Arms
Tel: 01423 711306

Wath-in-Nidderdale, Pateley Bridge, Harrogate, N Yorks HG3 5PP
Free House. Ray Carter, licensee

High above Nidderdale are Brimham Rocks, fantastic shapes of sandstone outcrops shaped by centuries of wind and rain. There are magnificent views of the Nidderdale countryside from this comfortable 17th century old stone inn, set in its own grounds amidst picturesque wooded surroundings through which the river Nidd wends its way. More of an hotel than a pub; however, it does have a central bar which is popular with the locals and where you will find an interesting selection of bar food. Home-made soups, ploughmans with local cheese (you have a choice of nearly twenty, some local), lots of fresh fish, chicken in garlic butter - nothing fried - no chips here! Good puddings too. They do have a couple of real ales - Youngers Scotch Bitter and Theakstons, but the concentration is on the wine list. A choice of malt whiskies and several Russian vodkas. Seats outside from where you can appreciate your surroundings.

OPEN: 12 - 3; 6.30 - 11.
Real Ale. Evening restaurant (not Sun lunch).
Children welcome until 9 pm.
Dogs on leads & well behaved.
Bedrooms.

LONDON

THE AREA CONFINED BY THE M25

LONDON SW18

Alma   Tel: 0181 870 2537

499 York Road, Wandsworth
Youngs. Charles Gotto, tenant

First it was an hotel, built on the Old York Road a few years after the battle of Alma; now it is a popular pub. Green shiny tiles outside, opulent Victorian decor inside. Virtually opposite Wandsworth Town Railway station, it is a favourite stopping place with rugby followers after a match at Twickenham as they wend their way to the mainline station at Waterloo. Quite a lot of good natured "preparation" goes on before facing the hazards of a British Rail journey. Here you get friendly service in attractive surroundings. The pub has a central bar with a dining room at the back filled with interesting antique kitchen and restaurant artefacts. The bar menu offers sandwiches and soup, filled muffins (muffins Alma), croques monsieur, salads, fresh fish and daily specials. Youngs ales and a good choice of wines by the bottle or glass. Both Espresso and ordinary coffee. Youngs Brewery and their magnificent Shire horses are just around the corner.

OPEN: 11 - 11.
Real Ale. Restaurant. No food Sun eve.
Children in eating areas. Dogs on leads.

LONDON SW7

Angelsea Arms   Tel: 0171 373 7960

15 Selwood Terrace
Free House. Patrick Timmons, licensee

An early Victorian pub which isn't that small; but can get very crowded, and when it does, the party continues outside as it does with so many other popular London pubs - but here they don't need the pavement, they have their own spacious forecourt. A comfortable, friendly atmosphere inside the pub and efficient service, even with all those al fresco drinkers. Food is good pub grub - basically sandwiches (doorsteps - you have been warned), ploughmans, pies, a choice of three hot dishes and a roast on Sundays. A good range of ales: Fullers London Pride, Flowers Original, Harveys, Adnams, Boddingtons, Brakspears SB and Youngs Special - all on hand pump. A selection of malt and Irish whiskies.

OPEN: 11 - 3; 5 - 11 (7 - 11 Sat).
Real Ale. No food Sun eve.
Children lunchtime only. Dogs on leads.

LONDON EC4

Blackfriar   Tel: 0171 236 5650

174 Queen Victoria Street
Nicholsons (Allied). Mr Becker, manager

Originally built in the 1870's, it was not until it was redecorated at the turn of the century in a flamboyant art-nouveau style, that it merited a second glance. Now it is full of the most wonderfully florid Edwardian decoration, mosaics, marble walls, pillared fireplaces, mirrors and a bronze bas relief of monks - to remind you that you are on the site of the old Blackfriars monastery. Busy, busy, busy - and that's not just the customers. They have a simple lunchtime bar menu of filled rolls, baked potatoes with various fillings, and a few hot dishes. A favourite watering hole in early evening for the thirsty hordes refreshing themselves before the journey home. Tetleys, Brakspears, Adnams, Wadworths 6X and Nicholsons which is brewed by Allied - all on hand pump. No garden, but there is a good pavement for standing on.

OPEN: 11.30 - 10.00 weekdays. Closed weekends & Bank Holidays.
Real Ale. Lunchtime meals.
No children. No dogs.

LONDON SW13

Bulls Head   Tel: 0181 876 5241

373 Lonsdale Road, Barnes
Youngs. Dan Fleming, tenant

The reason they don't have piped music in the Bulls Head is that no-one would hear it anyway - certainly not during the evenings or Sunday lunchtimes when modern Jazz groupies congregate there. Midday is blissfully quiet as they gird themselves for another session. The top jazz groups, who come here to play, do have their own room, but jazz is not exactly quiet; they can certainly be heard throughout the pub, and frequently half-way down the road as well! Food in the bar is all home-made, including the bread, sausages and ice cream. At lunchtime there is a popular carvery and a selection of hot dishes. Youngs Bitter, Special, and nearly a hundred malt whiskies.

OPEN: 11 - 11.
Real Ale. Restaurant evenings only. No food Sun eve.
Children welcome. Dogs on leads.
Live jazz every evening in own room with bar.

LONDON SW11

Castle   Tel: 0171 228 8181

115 Battersea High Street, SW11 3JR
Youngs. Patrick & Laura Lewis (Charles Gotto)

Do not be deceived by the plain, rather uninspired look of the Castle pub in Battersea village. This is another of the four successful establishments run by the inspired Charles Gotto. One bar serves all areas, including the conservatory, which in turn opens onto the paved garden. The menu changes monthly, but there are daily blackboard specials, home-made soups, pasta, fish dishes, casseroles and an impressive cheese selection from Neal's Yard. Tables for the roast Sunday lunch must be pre-booked. Youngs ales, and a good selection of wines, many by the glass.

OPEN: 11 - 11; (12 - 3; 7 - 10.30 Sun).
Real Ale.
Children welcome. Dogs on leads.

LONDON SW3

Coopers Arms   Tel: 0171 376 3120

Flood Street, Chelsea
Youngs. Nick & Jill Markwell (Charles Gotto)

A stucco faced pub, built in 1874 - another in the four-part tenancy run by Charles Gotto. Outside there are cascades of flowers; inside more flowers, framed drawings by the cartoonist Jak and a selection of daily newspapers so you can catch up on world events whilst enjoying your drink. Quite a young crowd in the evenings; lunchtime is the local professionals' turn. The interesting, imaginative menu changes daily, but there could be: country paté, gazpacho, marinated and char-grilled or roast chicken, navarine of lamb, poached salmon fillet and grilled swordfish. Desirable desserts. Proper Espresso coffee, and that's rare - decent coffee, I mean. Youngs range of ales. Also an interesting selection of New World, French, German, Californian and other wines listed on the blackboard.

OPEN: 11 - 11 (11 - 3; 6 - 11 Sun).
Real Ale.
Children welcome. Dogs on leads.

LONDON W1

Dog & Duck   Tel: 0171 437 4447

Frith Street
Nicholsons (Allied). Mrs Gene Bell, manageress

A very small corner pub in the heart of Soho. At busy periods there is virtually standing room only, although an upstairs bar has recently been opened to cope with the overflow. As with a lot of well frequented Central London pubs, you will find the pavement serves as an extra room in good weather. Only sandwiches are served, but there is a good range of ales: Tetleys, Timothy Taylors Landlord, Nicholsons, brewed by Allied for the pub, and several guest beers. The Dog and Duck was the winner of the Courvoisier International Guide of Excellence.

OPEN: 12 - 11. Closed Sat & Sun lunchtimes. (6 - 11 Sat eve.)
Real Ale. No food weekends.
No children. No dogs.

LONDON W6

Dove   Tel: 0181 748 5405

19 Upper Mall, Hammersmith
Fullers. Brian Lovrey & Dale Neal, tenants

The Dove has an enviable riverside terrace on which to sit and watch the comings and goings on the river. Lunchtime is quiet-ish, but come evening, space is at a premium. You get to it via a quiet alley by Hammersmith Bridge. It is 17th century and claims to have the smallest bar in England - on the right as you go in - where five people are a crowd. The main bar is bigger, beamed and panelled, retaining much of its old charm and character. Well cooked lunchtime bar food: filled baked potatoes, various pies, salads, ploughmans and daily specials. Very well regarded Thai food is served during the evening. Fullers London Pride and ESB ales. Those patriotically minded among you might like to know that a copy of the score of Rule Britannia is on a wall of the bar. James Thompson, who wrote it, had a room here.

OPEN: 11 - 11.
Real Ale.
Children welcome. Dogs on leads.

DENHAM VILLAGE

Falcon Inn   Tel: 01895 832125

Denham Village, Nr Uxbridge, Middx
Whitbread. Don & Sue Petty, tenants

Small and cosy. There has been an inn on this site since 1670. Brick built, under a tiled roof and situated opposite a green which serves as an extra room in the summer. In winter there will be two big log fires at either end of the traditionally furnished bar. Only lunchtime food is available, the exception being Friday evenings when they serve a fish and chip supper. Familiar bar snacks: ploughmans, sandwiches and always a daily special. Brakspears ales, Morlands Old Speckled Hen and Pedigree, Flowers IPA, also the usual range of lagers.

OPEN: 11 - 3; 5.30 - 11 (12 - 3; 7 - 10.30 Sun).
Real Ale.
No Children. Dogs on leads.

LONDON EC2

Flying Horse   Tel: 0171 247 5338

52 Wilson Street
Dalkeith Inns. Michael Freeman, licensee/manager

In this area there is only one like it left - an old fashioned pub nestling between tall, modern office blocks, reminding all of us what the City of London used to look like. Long established, it is a busy, friendly, chatty drinking place. Only two bars but a real coal fire. Lunchtime bar snacks are simple and straightforward - just what the clients want: sandwiches, filled french bread and rolls filled with cuts off the hot roast. Ales include Youngs Bitter, Courage Best and Directors and Websters.

OPEN: 11 - 10 (closed Sat & Sun).
Real Ale.
No parking, no garden, no children, no dogs.

LONDON SE1

Founders Arms   Tel: 0171 928 1899

52 Hopton Street
Youngs. Mrs Jan Ray, tenant

In the shadow of Blackfriar's Bridge, next to the site of the new Tate Gallery, opposite St Paul's Cathedral and near the new Globe Theatre; culturally you are going to be spoilt for choice. Built only 16 years ago on the edge of the Thames, the Founders Arms is virtually all glass, with a terrace cut into the banks of the river from where you have a wonderful view of the City of London. Quieter after the weekday "happy hour" when, to quote our informant, "the city types have hit the road". Quite a choice of bar food: twelve different salads, cornish pasties, hand-raised pies, smoked trout and hot dishes of the day. The restaurant is à la carte, but specialises in fresh fish and steaks. All Youngs ales:

Bitter, Special, Ramrod and in winter, Winter Warmer. Every year, the pub sponsors a five-mile run along the river to raise money for the Guide Dogs for the Blind Association, and they welcome blind people into the restaurant.

OPEN: 11-11.
Restaurant.
Real Ale.
Children and dogs on leads.

LONDON SW10

Fox and Pheasant   Tel: 0171 352 2943

1 Billing Road
Greene King. Mrs Sian Angelo, licensee/manager

Not much has changed in this pub since it was built in 1848, except for the obvious concessions to the 20th century and a coat of paint at regular intervals, so with its well polished traditional furnishings, it has a nicely mellowed atmosphere appreciated by the customers of both the public and saloon bars. There really isn't a great difference between them, except that the saloon bar has a square of carpet and the public bar a darts board. As the Fox and Pheasant is situated on a private side road off the Fulham Road, there is no parking outside the pub. But it does have a small garden with five picnic tables which are very popular on a balmy summer evening. The bar menu is short and hearty: basket meals - chicken nuggets, plaice goujons, scampi, vegetable nuggets and sausage and chips. Ales include Greene King IPA, Rayments Special Bitter and Abbots. Water for the dog.

OPEN: 12 - 3. 5.30 - 11 (12 - 10.30 Sun).
Real Ale.
Children in garden.
Dogs on leads.

LONDON SW3

Front Page   Tel: 0171 352 0648

35 Old Church Street
Courage. Christopher Phillips & Rupert Fowler, lease

Turn off the busy Kings Road, look for the white painted pub with the hanging baskets and you've found the Front Page. Those of you familiar with the pub years ago will remember it as the Black Lion. Wonderfully airy inside, there are big ceiling fans to keep you cool when the temperature rises, and an open fire in winter to keep you warm. Never so full that you have to fight your way to the bar, just gently busy. Still very much a local and well frequented. Friendly staff and good dependable bar food. Dishes are listed on blackboards at either end of the bar: home-made soup, chicken paté, smoked salmon and scrambled eggs, salmon fish cakes, sausage and mash, various salads and puddings. John Smiths, Ruddles County, Boddingtons and Websters Yorkshire ales on hand pump. Also a choice of wines.

OPEN: 11 - 3; 5.30 - 11 (6 - 11 Sat).
Real Ale.
Children welcome lunchtimes. Dogs on leads.

LONDON SE1

George   Tel: 0171 407 2056

77 Borough High Street, Southwark
Whitbreads. John Hall, manager

What can you say about the 17th century George that hasn't been said before. We should all be grateful to the National Trust for saving it from almost certain destruction when, in 1937, it accepted this magnificent old coaching inn as a gift from London & North Eastern Railway. The original pub was destroyed in a fire that swept through Southwark in 1676 - ten years after the great fire of London - and what you see today is the replacement built in that year. It was one of the many inns in the area playing an important part in the long distance waggon trains plying to and fro from Kent, Sussex and Surrey to Southwark. Stage Coaches started using the George in 1732 and by the early 19th century, it had become one of the most important inns in Southwark, with huge stables and yards. It was these that attracted the LNER's predecessor, the Great Northern Railway, to buy the George in 1874 to use as a depot. By 1937, they had pulled down or sold off many of the old buildings, leaving the Inn, a couple of houses within the structure, and only one of the magnificent galleries to posterity in the care of the National Trust. Today the George caters for a totally different traveller. The remaining galleries of the South range look over the courtyard where you can sit and enjoy your food and drink, occasionally entertained by visiting Morris men or players from the nearby Globe Theatre - quite medieval. There is a simple menu of sandwiches, home-made pies and salads. Boddingtons, Greene King Abbot, Whitbread Castle Eden, Flowers Original, a guest beer and Farm Cider. If you don't know the pub, search it out, as it is not clearly visible behind the huge gates on Borough High Street.

OPEN: 11 - 11.
Real Ale. Restaurant (not Sun); lunchtime meals & snacks.
Children in eating area. No dogs inside - in courtyard only.

LONDON SW15

Green Man   Tel: 0181 788 8096

Wildcroft Road, Putney
Youngs. Karl Robson, manager

On the edge of Putney Heath, which was notorious in the 18th century as the haunt of highwaymen and vagabonds, nothing ever changes: by another name shall ye know them. The charming Green Man dates back to the 16th century, and has its own shady past, Dick Turpin being part of it. It is now busy looking after the needs of the law abiding modern man. Inside are two airy bars with views over the Heath. All summer they have a daily barbecue (weather permitting); also filled rolls and daily specials. Casseroles in winter. Youngs Bitter, Special and Premium. Seats in the flowery courtyards and in the newly laid out garden at the back where there is also a children's play area.

OPEN: 11 - 11.
Real Ale. No food winter eves.
Children in garden. Dogs on leads.

LONDON SW1

Grenadier   Tel: 0171 235 3074

Wilton Row
Watneys (Courage). Paul Gibb, licensee

Years ago - and now I show my age - you could drive through the mews and park outside the pub, no doubt much to the annoyance of the residents in the houses opposite. In the evenings it was one of "the places" and was heaving, the overspill continuing the party in the mews, leaning against the cars. Perhaps not so frightfully crowded now - you certainly can't drive up to the front door - but it is still very popular, so search it out; it has lost none of its charm or character. As the name suggests, it leans towards the military; the Duke of Wellington's officers used it as their mess in the 18th century. Painted patriotically in the colours of the Union Flag, a sentry box stands next to the front door, and a Guard's bearskin guards the bar. There is a small candlelit dining room where, naturally enough, you can order Beef Wellington. Good hearty bar food: soup, ploughmans, fish and chips, sausage and mash, scampi and chips and a vegetarian dish or two. The bitters change frequently, and they stock quite a range of lagers, cider, bottled beer and Guinness. The Grenadier has its own very special 'Bloody Mary', the recipe for which is passed on from landlord to landlord.

OPEN: 12 - 3; 5 - 11.
Real Ale. Restaurant.
Children in restaurant. Dogs on leads.

LONDON EC2

Hamilton Hall   Tel: 0171 247 3579

Liverpool Street Station
Wetherspoons. Dave Chapman & Bernice Hartnett, managers

Built at the turn of the century as the grand ballroom of the Great Eastern Hotel, it is now, still with its splendid, soaring Baroque decor, one of the expanding Wetherspoon chain of pubs which are proving so popular. Closed for over 50 years, Wetherspoon's converted the ballroom a few years ago, creating a comfortably furnished mezzanine floor, a great part of which is no-smoking. Reliable bar food with a choice of daily specials and puddings is served from 11 am to 10 pm every day. Beers in this chain are frequently cheaper than elsewhere. Greene King Abbot and IPA, Courage Directors, Theakstons Best and XB, Youngers Scotch and a guest beer, all on hand pump.

OPEN: 11 - 11.
Real Ale.
No children. No dogs.

LONDON WC1

Kings Arms   Tel: 0171 405 9107

11A Northington Street, London WC1
Bass. Clive & Linda Gilbert, tenant

This two hundred year old pub is in a Georgian area of London, off Theobalds Road and John Street, not far from Gray's Inn, one of the four Inns of Court. Within the gardens of Gray's Inn is a Catalpa tree, reputed to have been planted by Francis Bacon from a cutting brought into the country by Sir Walter Raleigh. The Kings Arms is a friendly, cosy pub - one of the few in London with a real coal fire in winter. Snacks and straightforward pub food are served in the downstairs bar: sausage and mash, liver and bacon, ploughmans, toasties and sandwiches. During the evening, the upstairs function room, which also has a bar, becomes a Thai restaurant. Bass, Fullers London Pride, Adnams Best Bitter and Everards Tiger Best Bitter (a Leicester brew) are the ales.

OPEN: 11 - 11 Mon - Fri. (Closed Sat & Sun.)
Real Ale.
No Children.
Dogs on leads.

LONDON WC1

Lamb   Tel: 0171 405 0713

95 Lamb's Conduit Street
Youngs. Richard Whyte, manager

Just off Theobalds Road, this is an old Victorian pub, full of atmosphere, with a friendly efficient staff. Inside, the pub still retains some of the original Victorian fittings. The U-shaped bar and glass snob screens are worth noting, also the old photographs of the Holborn Empire, a famous musical hall bombed in the last war. Usual bar snacks (no sandwiches Sunday) plus some worthwhile home-cooked daily specials, beef in red wine being a favourite. Choice of salads, and on Sundays there is a carvery in the restaurant. For the health conscious, there is a small no-smoking room where you can enjoy your pint without a fug. Youngs Bitter, Special and in winter, Winter Warmer. Some seats in the small courtyard.

OPEN: 11 - 11.
Real Ale.
Children in eating area.
No dogs.

LONDON WC2

Lamb & Flag   Tel: 0171 497 9504

33 Rose Street
Courage. Terry Archer & Adrian Zimmerman, lease

A busy, popular pub in an alley between Floral and Garrick
Streets. The Lamb and Flag, which dates back to the 17th century
still retains much of the character and atmosphere from that time.
Low ceilings, panelled walls - still with the original built-in
benches. Dickens knew this pub when he was working in nearby
Catherine Street and would still recognise it. It has two quite small
bars downstairs, and an upstairs dining room. Frequently crowded
in the early evening, you'll find the customers spilling out onto the
pavement enjoying a pre-prandial drink. Bar food includes roast
beef baps, paté, ploughmans with farmhouse cheeses and a
variety of hot dishes. John Smiths, Courage Best and Directors,
Wadworths 6X and a guest beer. They have a selection of malt
whiskies.

OPEN: 11 - 11.
Real Ale. Lunchtime meals (snacks 12 - 5 only). Not Sun.
No dogs.
Live Jazz Sun eves.

LONDON WC1

Museum Tavern   Tel: 0171 242 8987

Museum Street
Grand Met. John & Carmel Keating, managers

On an important corner site opposite the British Museum, this pub
was not always thus. Known as the Dog and Duck until the
Museum was built in 1761, it chose to emulate the atmosphere of
learning that the newly built Museum gave the area, and renamed
itself the British Museum Tavern. However, not satisfied with just a
change of name, the pub was rebuilt several times, the last being

in the mid 19th century. Largely unaltered since then, this is the building you see today. Students, scholars and tourists all come here. Karl Marx used it while he was studying at the British Museum. Very popular at lunchtime, or indeed anytime between 11 am and 10 pm - food is served all day. Traditionally furnished, it has a carvery at the end of the bar serving a variety of cold meats, salads, ploughmans, vegetarian dishes and a choice of hot daily specials. Courage Directors, John Smiths and Morlands Old Speckled Hen ales.

OPEN: 11 - 11.
Real Ale.
Children in eating area until 5 pm. No dogs.

LONDON EC4

Ye Olde Cheshire Cheese   Tel: 0171 353 6170

Wine Office Court (off Fleet Street)
Sam Smiths. Gordon Garrity, licensee

Like so much of London, the original Cheshire Cheese was burnt to the ground in the great fire of 1666; only the cellars remained. The present building, rebuilt on the original foundations two years later, is much as you see it today. After 300 years it was feeling a little shaky and in need of support, so it was recently made more secure and extended to cope with the demands of the 20th century. On four floors - not counting the cellars - there is a formidable number of dining rooms, four ground floor bars and the original panelled chop room which has famous literary connections. Anybody who was anybody in the literary world has crossed the threshold of this charming, timeless old pub. Only sandwiches are available in the cellar bar; elsewhere in the pub there is quite a choice of places to sit and eat: ask and ye shall be directed. Good hearty English fare on offer: soups, smoked salmon or black pudding are a selection of starters; lots of different fish dishes, salads, grills, steak kidney and mushroom pie, vegetarian dishes, bubble and squeak and various puddings. Sam Smiths Old Brewery and Museum on hand pump.

OPEN: 11.30 - 11. Closed Sun eve.
Real Ale. Restaurant (closed Sun eve).
Children welcome. No dogs.

LONDON EC1

Olde Mitre   Tel: 0171 405 4751

Ely Place
Taylor Walker (Allied). Don O'Sullivan, manager

This Olde Mitre takes its name from an earlier inn, built in
the 16th century to provide for the Bishop of Ely's staff. Rebuilt
during the mid 18th century, it remains much as it was, a
picturesque, delightful pub just off Hatton Garden, next to the
13th century St Ethelreda's Church. The small, panelled rooms
are crowded during weekday lunchtimes when they serve a
variety of sandwiches, scotch eggs, filled rolls and sausages -
simple but good. Ind Coope Burton, Friary Meux and Tetleys on
hand pump. There are seats among the plants in a delightful
small yard between the pub and the Church.

OPEN: 11 - 11. Closed Sat & Sun & Bank Hols.
Real Ale.
No children. No dogs.

LONDON EC2

The Old Monk   Tel: 0171 377 9555

128 Bishopsgate
Free House. Charles & Michelle Smythe, managers

This was originally a wine bar until it was taken over by Gerry
Martin earlier this year, adding to his embryonic empire.
Traditionally laid out and furnished, it has two biggish bars,
accommodating about 300 people. Popular with City businessmen, the bar food includes soups, filled jacket potatoes, omelettes,

chicken Kiev, filled enchilladas and a weekly special. Theakstons Best, XB and Old Peculiar, Wadworths 6X, Greene King IPA, Courage Directors and Marstons Pedigree ales.

OPEN: 11 - 11 (closed Sat & Sun).
Real Ale.
No children. Guide dogs only.

LONDON WC1

The Old Monk   Tel: 0171 831 01714

39-41 Grays Inn Road
Free House. Andrew Posner, manager

Once two shops, a wine bar five years ago, now celebrating its first birthday as a pub. One large open space with a U-shaped bar, comfortably furnished and with plenty of room to sit and eat. Bar snacks include soup of the day, garlic bread, jumbo sausages, selection of burgers, Mexican chilli and scampi. Scottish and Newcastle and Courage are the main suppliers of beer. Guest ales come from several micro-breweries now operating in the British Isles.

OPEN: 11 - 11 (12 - 3; 7 - 10.30 Sun).
Real Ale
No Children. Dogs when not too busy - weekends.

LONDON BARNET

The Old Monk & Holt   Tel: 0181 499 4280

193 Barnet High Street, Herts
Courage. Darren & Lisa Anderson, licensees

Between Hadley Common (to the left) and Barnet High Street (to the right). Once The Bell, this pub is another Gerald Martin has added to his budding chain of Monkish pubs. Comfortable, small and well-established, they serve a traditional pub menu consisting of soup, club sandwiches, filled jacket potatoes, various pies and fish and chips. Ales are Theakstons Best, Wadworths 6X, Courage Directors and Marstons Pedigree. Seats in the beer garden.

OPEN: 11 - 11 (12 - 3; 7 - 10.30 Sun).
Real Ale.
Children in Beer Garden before 9 pm.
No Dogs.

LONDON TWICKENHAM

Popes Grotto   Tel: 0181 892 3050

Cross Deep, Twickenham
Youngs. Stephen Brough, manager

Surrounded as you are here by Popes in various guises - mainly temporal - Alexander Avenue, Popes Grove and Grotto Road - what else could you possibly call a pub but Popes Grotto. Having said that, Walpole Road and Tennyson Avenue aren't a million yards away, so the literary choice was in fact wide open, but Alexander Pope did in fact live nearby. Popes Grotto is a comfortable, spacious pub with three bars and an attractive terraced garden at the back. Good, well chosen bar food ranges from soup, filled baked potatoes, king prawns in herbs and garlic, steaks, salads and daily specials. On Sundays they do a roast lunch. Ales are Youngs Bitter and Special, and Winter Warmer when appropriate.

OPEN: 11 - 3; 5.30 - 11 (11 - 11 Sat).
Real Ale.
Children in eating area until 9 pm.
Dogs on leads.

LONDON WC1

Princess Louise   Tel: 0171 405 8816

208 High Holborn
Free House. Joseph Sheridan, licensee

Named after the fourth daughter of Queen Victoria, the pub was built in 1872, but didn't become licensed until 1891, when it was bought and decorated by Arthur Chitty. Listed Grade II makes it a building of considerable note. The interior is a monument to the very best in late Victorian decoration. Polished granite pillars, gilt mirrors, ornate plasterwork, elaborate tiling and a huge mahogany U-shaped bar. The gents lavatory has a separate listing! Downstairs, a variety of well-filled, freshly made sandwiches are available all day. Upstairs they serve a selection of Thai food in the lounge bar. Beers change regularly but they usually have eight or nine on offer, and wines by the glass.

OPEN: 11 - 11 (12 - 3; 6 - 11 Sat).
Real Ale. No food weekends.
No children. Dogs on leads.

LONDON NW6

Queens Arms   Tel: 0171 624 5735

1 Kilburn High Road
Youngs. John Conroy, manager

Poor old pub: it has suffered quite a few upheavals in its lifetime. Quite literally during the last war, when it was bombed out of existence. Rebuilt after the war, it then burnt down in the 50's. Rebuilt yet again, this time in the style of a town house, it is up and flourishing. A favourite with local office staff and musicians from the London Orchestras who use the nearby St Augustine's Church for recording sessions. Two bars, a lounge and saloon combined, and public bar. Simple, first rate food served by courteous staff: ploughmans, sandwiches, steak and kidney pie, cottage pie and a daily special. Youngs Special, Ramrod and Bitter. The Queens Arms boasts a roof garden, which they have difficulty maintaining as some thieving lot keeps pinching the plants. (High trellis - that's what they need - thieves can't stand it because it is too unstable to climb over.) There are a few seats on the terrace at the front of the pub, surrounded by lots of flowers.

OPEN: 11 - 11 (Sat & Sun lounge bar closes from 4 - 7).
Real Ale.
Children at lunchtime only.
Dogs in public bar only.

LONDON W1

Red Lion   Tel: 0171 499 1307

Waverton Street
S & N. Raymond Dodgson, manager

Much has changed in the area since the Red Lion was built three hundred years ago. Then it was on a muddy lane alongside the grand Chesterfield House. Only an 'umble ale house, it was frequented by the "rougher" local traders from Shepherds Market, servants, and later the builders and masons who were slowly transforming the area in the 18th and 19th centuries into the London you see today. Its humble past forgotten, the Red Lion is now a very smart pub in a smart part of London. The small panelled bar serves sandwiches and hot daily specials. Greene King Abbot and IPA, Courage Best and Directors, Theakstons Best and XB and Wadworths 6X.

OPEN: 11 - 11 (12 - 3; 6 - 11 Sat).
Real Ale. Restaurant.
Children in eating area.
Dogs on leads.

LONDON SW18

Ship   Tel: 0181 870 9667

41 Jews Row, Wandsworth
Youngs. Charles Gotto & D N Haworth, licensees

The riverside terraces at the Ship are on two levels, and there is nothing nicer than to come here for lunch on a summery Sunday, enjoy a barbecued lunch and a pint, and watch the Thames slip by - along with hundreds of others. Incredibly popular, even though it is tucked away and not easy to find; consulting your A-Z should enable you to find your way. Walk if you can, as parking is a bit tight. It has a wonderfully airy conservatory opening onto the garden, and a public bar - the locals' favourite. Anything that can be barbecued will be, weather permitting; if not, it's back inside for the bar menu, which features soups, sandwiches, steak and kidney pie, casseroles, bouillabaisse, ploughmans with a choice of British cheeses and daily specials from the blackboard. Youngs range of well kept ales, a guest beer and a good selection of wines, many by the glass. Fantastic evening celebrations for the last night of the Proms; a huge television screen gives an opportunity to all budding Simon Rattles to practise their conducting, and the firework display on Guy Fawkes night is enough to satisfy all pyrotechnically-minded people.

OPEN: 11 - 11.
Real Ale. Restaurant.
Children in eating area. Dogs on leads.

LONDON SW10

Sporting Page   Tel: 0171 376 3694

6 Camera Place, Chelsea
Courage. Rupert Fowler, lease

It's off Park Walk and between the Fulham and Kings Road so take a bus as parking can be difficult. Once called the Red Lion, it has been transformed from a pub into more of a wine bar. Quite smart, decorated as you would expect with panels, prints and pictures depicting sporting "greats". The television will be on for all big sporting events. Well chosen bar food includes: soup, pasta, hot chicken salad, smoked salmon and scrambled eggs, home-made salmon fishcakes and hollandaise sauce - also steak sandwiches. Wadworths 6X, Websters Yorkshire Bitter, Boddingtons and John Smiths. There is a choice of house wines.

OPEN: 11 - 3; 5.30 - 11 (6 - 11 Sat).
Real Ale.
Children outside.
Dogs on leads.

LONDON SW1

Star   Tel: 0171 235 3019

Belgrave Mews West
Fullers. Bruce & Kathleen Taylor, managers

Situated in an attractive flowery mews off Belgrave Square, this has always been a haven from the noisy frenetic life of London just a few yards away. Three comfortably furnished rooms downstairs - and an upstairs room if it gets too crowded. Bar food includes lunchtime sandwiches, salads and favourite hot dishes such as fish and chips and steak pie. There is a greater selection during the evening. Fullers Chiswick, London Pride and ESB.

OPEN: 11.30 - 3; 5 - 11 (6.30 - 11 Sat). 11.30 - 11 Fridays & daily for 2 weeks before Christmas.
Real Ale.
Children if eating. Dogs on leads.

LONDON SW3

The Surprise
Tel: 0171 352 4699

6 Christchurch Terrace
Youngs. Grayburn Owen, tenant

The landlord thinks his pub was named after the ship *Surprise,* which brought Charles II back to England after the civil war and, as if to emphasise the point, the walls of the bars are hung with reproductions of nautical paintings. In complete contrast, the pub, well favoured by the racing fraternity, celebrates the "Sport of Kings" by festooning the rail over the bar with assorted members' badges from Newbury and other racecourses. Two bars: the saloon bar with the carpet, the public bar without. Those unfamiliar with the pub from their early days as impoverished young things struggling up life's ladder, use the carpeted side. The late impoverished young, now succesful City high flyers, still use the public bar, although they themselves are not necessarily local any more. Such loyalty! Food is served lunchtimes only, Monday to Saturday: gammon and eggs, pies cooked in the pub and a selection of pasta dishes. When winter sets in, steaks are added to the menu. If the kitchens are closed, you can get toasted sandwiches from the bar. Ales are Hancocks, Timothy Taylors Landlord as a guest, Bass and occasionally another guest beer in the winter.

OPEN: 11 - 11.
Real Ale.
Children, not encouraged.
Dogs on leads.

LONDON W9

Warrington Hotel   Tel: 0171 286 2929

93 Warrington Crescent
Free House. John Brandon, licensee

Listed Grade II, it is a wonderful relic of the Victorian Naughty
Nineties, with ceramic pillars at the entrance, mosaic steps, semi-
circular marble bar, sweeping staircase, high ceilings, cherubs
and art nouveau - what they used to call a gin palace. What is
extraordinary is that despite its music-hall associations - it was a
favourite with Marie Lloyd - and its present-day popularity, it has
no piped music. It was recommended for listing in THE QUIET
PINT by a local who told us "it has been free of muzak pollution
for many months since the infernal machine broke down. There
are no plans to replace it." Bar meals at lunchtime only. During the
evenings the food is Thai - and they say it's good. You have to
book. Ales are Fullers ESB, Brakspears Special, Ruddles County
and Youngs Special Bitter. The Warrington is lucky to have a
garden with 12 tables. Arrive early if you want one on a summer's
day.

OPEN: 11 - 11. (12.30 - 3; 7 - 10.30 Sun.)
Real Ale.
No children.
Dogs on leads.

LONDON W14

Warwick Arms   Tel: 0171 603 3560

160 Warwick Road London W14
Fullers. Peter Biggs, manager

At lunchtime, rumour has it that this charming late Georgian pub is
full of revenue men, a far better description - and probably more
polite than the usual definition - of the modern tax inspector; also
office workers from the DHSS. Comparing notes? Inside the

Warwick Arms, the bar fittings are at least a hundred years old, if not older, and the pump handles are Wedgewood - very smart! Not very big inside, the bar is decorated with two large detailed prints of the battles of Trafalgar and Waterloo. Bar food includes the traditional ploughmans, toasties and salads with the addition of hot dishes such as chicken Kiev and Chilli. Fullers ales: ESB, London Pride, IPA and Hock Ale.

OPEN: 11 - 11.
Real Ale.
Children not encouraged. Dogs on leads.

LONDON RICHMOND

White Cross Hotel	Tel: 0181 940 6844

Water Lane, Richmond
Youngs. Quentin & Denise Thwaites, licensee/managers

It really was an hotel until 16 years ago. Now it is just a pub in a super setting with a garden overlooking the Thames. The building dates back to 1835 and has one large bar with two fireplaces, one of which is directly under the picture window overlooking Richmond Bridge, and the question always is, "where's the chimney?" No free beer for the right answer! There is also a family room on the mezzanine floor which has a balcony overlooking the river. Sometimes during the summer there is live music in the garden. On one occasion they had a harpist on the balcony; dressed in a flowing white dress, she gave some of the clients a nasty shock - they thought they had suddenly joined the heavenly hordes. (Good strong beer here!) Food is all self-service from a buffet in the bar; various pies, vegetarian dishes, salads, lamb's liver in sherry sauce, chicken in a mushroom sauce and venison casserole with juniper berries are among the dishes on offer. Youngs Bitter, Special and Ramrod ales.

OPEN: 11 - 11 (12 - 10.30 Sun).
Real Ale.
Children in garden or family room.
Dogs very welcome.

LONDON SW6

White Horse   Tel: 0171 737 2115

21 Parsons Green, Fulham
Bass. Rupert Reeves, manager

A spacious Victorian building on the edge of Parsons Green. It has a wonderfully sunny terrace at the front of the pub which is the place to be for lunch, and to relax in the early evening. Big comfortable bar, hugely popular, so arrive in good time if you want a meal and somewhere to eat it. There is a blackboard menu with perhaps paté, salads, beef and ale casserole with dumplings, sausages, steak and kidney pie and other dishes using different ales as the marinade. An à la carte menu features during the evening. Sunday lunch is served upstairs. Quite a selection of well kept ales: Adnams Extra, Bass, Harveys Sussex and a guest beer. Many Belgian, Dutch and German beers.

OPEN: 11.30 - 3; 5 - 11 (all day Sat summer).
(11 - 4; 7 - 11 winter Sat.)
Real Ale.
Children in eating area (not evening). Dogs on leads.
Occasional jazz nights.

LONDON SW4

Windmill   Tel: 0181 673 4578

Clapham Common, Southside SW4 9DE
Youngs. Mr & Mrs Richard Williamson, managers

There really was a windmill here in the mid 17th century, but the fine building you see today wasn't mentioned in local records until 1729. The inn was later to be immortalised by J P Herring, who used it as the background in his painting "Return from the Derby", which now hangs in the Tate Gallery. Here you have a traditional pub within a smart hotel. Comfortable main bars which are understandably popular - sometimes it seems as though half

London has moved in on Monday evenings when it is "treat" night. Opera à la Carte in the conservatory; jazz nights in the back bar at least once a week; last but not least, good familiar bar food and well kept ales. Sandwiches, filled baguettes, ploughmans, salads, vegetarian dishes and daily specials. Youngs range of ales, a large choice of wines, some by the glass. Outside there is a barbecue going full pelt during the summer; seats here and among the tubs of flowers in a non-barbecue courtyard.

OPEN: 11 - 11.
Real Ale. Restaurant.
Children in no-smoking conservatory.
No dogs. Bedrooms.
Live Opera Mon; Jazz Sun; Cabaret Fri eve.

LONDON W8

Windsor Castle   Tel: 0171 727 8491

114 Campden Hill Road, Holland Park
Bass. Matthew O'Keefe, manager

The summit of Campden Hill is as high as the top of St Paul's Cathedral, and when the Windsor Castle pub was built on Campden Hill Road in 1828, it had uninterrupted views across country to Windsor Castle, nearly 20 miles away to the West. The views may have changed over the years, but not this charming old pub, which has three panelled bars - each with its own entrance and customers - and a small dining room. The pub fills up rapidly on summer evenings when its attractive, shady walled garden comes into its own. Interesting pub grub is served all day, and a tremendously popular roast beef and Yorkshire pudding for lunch on Sunday. Ales are Bass Charringtons IPA, Adnams Extra and Hancocks HB. Guest beers change monthly. There are also house wines, a very reasonable Champagne and various malt whiskies.

OPEN: 11 - 11.
Real Ale.
Children welcome. Dogs on leads (not in garden!).

SCOTLAND

ABERDEEN

Prince of Wales   Tel: 01224 640597

7-11 St Nicholas Lane, Aberdeen AB1 AIHF
Free House. Peter Birnie, licensee

Built on granite, out of granite quarried from Rubislaw Pit near Hazelhead Park, Aberdeen is known as the 'Granite City'. Its handsome buildings overlook the fishing harbour and docks. In a cobbled lane, just off the busy shopping centre, the old Prince of Wales, with its comfortable, popular, long main bar and side lounge, is just the place for a pint of well kept ale and a generous lunchtime snack. Draught Bass, Caledonian 80/-, Orkney Dark Island, Courage Directors, Theakstons Old Peculiar and Youngers No. 3 plus guest beers.

OPEN: 11 - midnight.
Real Ale. No lunchtime food Sun.
Children in eating area. No dogs.
Live music Sunday afternoons.

BROUGHTY FERRY

Fishermans Tavern   Tel: 01382 775941

12 Fort Street, Dundee DD5 2AD
Free House. Jonathan Stewart, licensee

Once an old fishing village, Broughty Ferry has now become a suburb of Dundee. However, there are still fishing boats in the harbour which is overlooked by the 15th century Broughty Castle, now a museum. The small, rambling old pub is known for its well kept ales and good traditional bar food which could include a home-made fisherman's pie, crab salads, other pies and daily specials. Belhavens 60/-, 80/- and St Andrew's, Maclays 80/- and a daily changing guest beer. If you look up river from the harbour you see the bridge over "the glorious River Tay".

OPEN: 11 - midnight.
Real Ale. Restaurant. Limited bar food Sun.
Children in eating area. Dogs on leads.
Bedrooms.
(Folk music Thurs eves.)

CLACHAN SEIL

Tigh an Truish Hotel   Tel: 01852 300242

Clachan Seil, By Oban, Argyll PA34 4QZ
Free House. Miranda Brunner, licensee

Known as the "Bridge over the Atlantic", the humpbacked stone bridge linking Seil Island to the mainland was designed by Thomas Telford in 1792. Also 18th century, the Tigh an Truish is a great favourite with locals, yachtsmen and tourists. In places like this you need your own seaweed to give you a personal weather forecast, but if the weather is awful you can tuck yourself inside the pub, near the fire, and enjoy the well-chosen bar food: soups, local oysters, seafood pie, local prawns, venison in cream and Drambuie, steak & kidney pies, lasagne - all home-made.

Specials on the blackboard. A children's menu and, to finish, malt whisky ice cream. (In winter perhaps not such a wide choice of food.) McEwans 80/- and a good choice of malt whiskies. Seats outside in the small garden.

OPEN: 11 - 11 (12.30 - 11 Sun). (11 - 2.30; 5 - 11 winter.)
Real Ale. Restaurant.
Children in restaurant/family room.
No dogs.

CLEISH

Nivingstone House Hotel   Tel: 01577 850216

Cleish, Nr Kinross, Tayside KY13 7L5
Free House. Allan Deeson, licensee

An attractive, solid, faintly baronial, small country hotel, set in 12 acres at the foot of the Cleish hills. A very comfortable (carpets and upholstered furniture) bar and friendly staff. Well presented lunchtime bar food ranges from soup and home-made paté to a dish of smoked salmon and prawns plus daily specials. There is a very elegant restaurant which has a reputation for serving imaginative, creative food. Yorkshire Bitter, over 50 malt whiskies and naturally, a good wine list. The seats at the front of the hotel overlook the sweeping lawns to the hills beyond.

OPEN: 12 - 2.30; 6 - 11 (6 - 11.45 Sat).
Real Ale. Restaurant. No bar meals eves.
Children welcome.
Dogs on leads.
Bedrooms.

CRINAN

Crinan Hotel   Tel: 0154 683261

Crinan, Argyll PA31 8SR
Free House. Nicholas Ryan, licensee

The Crinan Hotel is in a most spectacular position at the north end of the Crinan Canal, below wooded slopes and looking out over Argyll's rugged coastline. It's a great white building which, in this tiny hamlet, you can hardly miss. If it's a light lunch you are after, you have a choice of either eating in the public bar or having a sandwich in the coffee shop/bakery by the fishing-boat dock. Lots of fish included in the bar menu: local mussels, trout, princess clams, seafood stew, also honey roast ham, chicken stuffed with leeks and mushrooms. Lots of salads and daily specials. Bass and Caledonian 80/-, a choice of malt whiskies and a good wine list. During the evenings, when there is a shift of emphasis towards the restaurant, the atmosphere does become more formal. Seats outside on the terrace from where you can enjoy the view.

OPEN: 11 - 11 (11 - 2.30; 5 - 11 winter).
Real Ale. Restaurant. Bar meals lunchtimes.
Children in eating area of cocktail bar.
Dogs on leads.
Bedrooms.

EDINBURGH

Abbotsford   Tel: 0131 225 5276

3-5 Rose Street, Edinburgh EH6 2PQR
Free House. Colin Grant, licensee

A favourite place for the "lunchtime" crowd. Ideally placed, as it is parallel to Prince's Street, Scotland's greatest thoroughfare. Only one centrally situated bar in this efficient, well-run, Victorian pub. There is nevertheless, plenty of room for you to enjoy the well-kept ales and reasonably priced, varied choice of bar food. Soups, ploughmans, pork and cider casserole, roast beef, liver and onions, steaks, grills and puddings. Boddingtons, Caledonian 80/-, Deuchars IPA, Broughtons Greenmantle and one guest. Choice of malt whiskies.

OPEN: 11 - 2.30; 5 - 11 (Fri - Sat 11 - 11; closed Sun).
Real Ale. Restaurant.
Children in eating areas.
Dogs on leads.

EDINBURGH

Bannermans Bar   Tel: 0131 556 3254

212 Cowgate, Edinburgh EH1 1NQ
Free House. Douglas Smith, licensee

Busy, popular, and in the heart of the city, it is a favourite with locals and students - always full of a friendly, cheerful crowd. A well-liked, functional, traditionally furnished bar, offering a short reliable menu during lunchtimes and simple snacks in the evening. Filled rolls, soup, ploughmans, filled baked potatoes, vegetarian dishes and daily specials. Eight ales: Theakstons Best, Heather Ale, McEwans 80/-, Boddingtons, Caledonian 80/- and IPA, Belhaven St Andrew's and Youngers No.3. Good selection of malt whiskies and bottled Belgian beers.

OPEN: 11 - midnight (11 - 1 am Sat).
Real Ale. Lunchtime meals & snacks. Evening snacks only.
Children in eating area, daytime only.
Dogs if well behaved.
(Frequent eve folk bands.)

EDINBURGH

Bow Bar   Tel: 0131 226 7667

80 West Bow, Edinburgh
Free House. Bill Strachan, licensee

You could be forgiven for thinking you were in a time warp - transported into the late 19th century, the heyday of a traditional Edinburgh drinkers' bar - all glass mirrors, mahogany panelling, gas fires, and barmen in long white aprons; even the beer pumps are over 90 years old. Over 12 well-kept ales at any one time, chosen from the 80 which are tried during the year. Well over 100 malt whiskies and a choice of gins, rums and vodkas. Cheap and cheerful bar snacks of the filled rolls, pies and bowl of soup variety.

OPEN: 11 - 11.15.
Real Ale. Lunchtime snacks.
No children. No dogs.

EDINBURGH

Café Royal Circle Bar   Tel: 0131 556 1884

17 West Register Street, Edinburgh
Scottish & Newcastle. Graham Bell, manager

If you want to catch up with the daily news in congenial surroundings - enjoy a drink and perhaps a quick snack - the circle bar is just the place. Refurbished in the Victorian style, but far more comfortable than the original, it has marble floors, handsome light fittings and a big central bar counter with interesting Doulton tile portraits of famous Scotsmen - whose inventions changed the world. Filled rolls: cheese & tomato and slices off the hot roast are available at lunchtime only. Marstons Pedigree, McEwans 80/-, Youngers No.3 and Theakstons Best. Nearly 50 malt whiskies.

OPEN: 11 - 11 (midnight Thurs; 1 am Fri & Sat; closed Sun).
Real Ale. Restaurant. Snacks lunchtime only.
No children. No dogs.

EDINBURGH

Kay's Bar
Tel: 0131 225 1858

39 Jamaica Street West, Edinburgh EH3 1HF
Scottish & Newcastle. David Mackenzie, manager

Choice of nine different ales at any one time, 70 malt whiskies
and nearly a dozen blended ones. One malt a night and you can
book yourselves in for two and a half months! Small, intimate bar
with lots of Victoriana associated with the brewing and licensed
trade as decoration. Bar snacks include: filled baked potatoes,
omelettes, haggis, steak pies and other traditional dishes. The
ales could include Marstons Pedigree, Smiles Exhibition,
McEwans 80/- and six others. Lager is kept for the uninitiated
tourist.

OPEN: 11 - 12.45 (12.30-11 Sun).
Real Ale. Lunchtime snacks.
Children in back room. Dogs on leads.

EDINBURGH

Starbank
Tel: 0131 552 4141

64 Laverockbank Road, Edinburgh EH5 3BZ
Free House. Valerie West, licensee

If you want to sample a selection of the beers brewed in Scotland,
this is the place to come. The pub keeps approximately ten on
hand pump which change frequently, but you can be assured of a
well chosen range. There is also a good choice of bar food: soup,
ploughmans, steak and kidney pie, fish, a chicken dish or two and
daily specials. Wines by the glass and a selection of malt

whiskies. Views over the Firth of Forth from the pub and seats on the terrace out of the prevailing wind.

OPEN: 11 - 11 (11 - midnight Thurs - Sat; 12.30 - 11 Sun).
Real Ale. No smoking restaurant.
Children welcome. Dogs on leads.

ELIE

Ship Inn   Tel: 01333 330 246

The Toft, Elie, Fife KY9 1DT
Free House. Richard & Jill Philip, licensees

Very near the Watersports Centre, so you will be surrounded by people who do energetic things and recover in the Ship Inn. Windsurfing, water-skiing and sailing in the Bay, the pub also organises its own cricket fixtures and even Rugby matches on the sandy beach beyond the beer garden. When you are totally exhausted even thinking about it, be assured that the whole family is welcome here to relax. Licensed since 1838, they have perfected the art of catering for the traveller. Big downstairs bar, three dining areas - one upstairs. They serve lunchtime and evening bar food, and a three-course lunch or an à la carte dinner. There is also a children's menu. A barbecue area comes into operation during July and August. Bar food could include mushrooms stuffed with stilton cheese, deep-fried North Sea prawns served with garlic butter and home-made bread, seafood pancakes, breast of chicken coated with oatmeal and stuffed with paté in a port sauce, steak & Guinness pie, extremely hot chilli on a bed of brown rice, lots of steaks and a roast Sunday lunch. Courage Directors, Belhaven 80/- and Boddingtons. Choice of wines and malt whiskies. The big beer garden overlooks a sandy bay and the Firth of Forth.

OPEN: 11 - midnight (12.30 - 11 Sun).
Real Ale. Restaurant (not Sun eve).
Children in restaurant and lounge bar. Dogs on leads.
Occasional jazz outside.

GLASGOW

Babbity Bowster   Tel: 0141 552 5055

16/18 Blackfriars Street, Glasgow, Strathclyde G1 1PE
Free House. Fraser Laurie, licensee

===

A fine renovated Adam town house in a quiet pedestrianised
street in the business centre of the city. Understandably popular
with journalists, businessmen and students. Breakfast is served at
8.30 and bar snacks from 12 until 9 at night. More a café/bar with
a restaurant and hotel attached, than a pub. Bar food includes
filled baguettes, spicy chicken, haggis, neeps and tatties. Specials
from the blackboard include lots of fish dishes: langoustines,
oysters, prawns, fresh fish - all with home-baked bread.
Barbecued dishes in the summer. Maclays 80/-, 70/-, Cains
Amber Ale and a guest beer. This is the only pub in the city centre
which has an outside drinking area. There are seats and tables on
the small terrace.

Open: 8 - midnight.
Restaurant.
Real Ale.
Children in restaurant.
No dogs.
Bedrooms.

GLASGOW

Three Judges   Tel: 0141 337 3055

141 Dumbarton Road (Partick Cross) Glasgow G11 6PR
Maclay-Alloa. Helen McCarroll, manager

===

Very much a down-to-earth, no-nonsense sort of local, which has
for the last couple of years won awards for the best pub and
landlord in Glasgow. In Partick Cross, which is the place to go if
you want to hear Gaelic. They say more Gaelic is spoken here

than in the Western Isles. Only bar snacks are available - toasties, ploughmans - that sort of thing - a crisp or nut goes without saying. Maclays 80/-, Oat Malt Stout and guest beers plus a draught farm cider. 750 different beers have been brought in as guests over the last two years; they fully expect to offer their 1000th ale early next spring or summer. Range of whiskies: they feature a "malt of the month". Very near the University and the Kelvin Grove Art Gallery; the Botanical Gardens are 200 yards away and the Transport Museum just 100 yards along the road.

Open. 11 - 11 (11 - 12 Sat); (12.30 - 11 Sun).
Real Ale.
No children. Dogs on leads.

GLASGOW

Ubiquitous Chip   Tel: 0141 334 5007

12 Ashton Lane, Glasgow G12
Free House. Ronnie Clydesdale, licensee

On good authority this is "the trendy place to hang out". Situated in a cobbled lane in the very heart of Glasgow, it was originally a Victorian coach house, but is now a well-known restaurant, with the addition of an upstairs bar serving imaginative bar food. There is a daily changing menu, but food could include: home-made soup, smoked fillet of mackerel, beef and ham terrine with Dijon mayonnaise, char-grilled shark in a lime/ginger parsley marinade, Scotch mutton creole style, a choice of salads and home-made puddings. The wine selection is reputed to be the best in Scotland (they have their own wine shop). 120 malt whiskies and, last but not least, real ales: Caledonian 80/- and Deuchars IPA. Bulmers cider and Furstenberg lager.

OPEN: 11 - 11 (11 - 12 Fri & Sat; 12.30 - 12 Sun).
Real Ale. Restaurant.
Children welcome.
Dogs on leads in bar.

INNERLEITHEN

Traquair Arms Hotel   Tel: 01896 830229

Traquair, Innerleithen, Borders EH44 6PD
Free House. Hugh Anderson, licensee

Innerleithen was reputedly the model for "St Ronan's Well" in Sir
Walter Scott's Waverley novels. The Traquair Arms is a good,
solidly dependable stone inn, with a comfortable main bar serving
generous portions of popular bar food and an interesting range of
ales. Food includes soups, sandwiches, omelettes, filled baked
potatoes, baked smoked haddock with cream and cheese,
chicken and pasta, vegetarian dishes and steak & ale pie. There
is a greater variety of dishes during the evening. Broughton
Greenmantle Ale, Theakstons Best and Traquair House and
sometimes Traquair Bear Ale. The 18th century brewery is
situated in a wing of Traquair House. They resumed brewing in
1965 with the original equipment which hadn't been used since
the middle of the last century. Traquair House itself, dating back to
the 10th century, is one of Scotland's oldest inhabited houses.
The iron gates have remained closed since 1745 and will do so
until the Stuarts return.

OPEN: 11 - midnight (12-12 Sun).
Real Ale. Restaurant.
Children welcome. Dogs on leads.
Bedrooms.
(1st Sun in month Scottish music and story telling.)

KILBERRY

Kilberry Inn   Tel: 01880 770223

Kilberry by Tarbert, Strathclyde PA29 6YD
Free House. John & Kathy Leadbeater, licensees

This inn is halfway round the single track road from Tarbert
(overlooked by the stronghold of Robert the Bruce) and

Lochgilphead (B8024) and well worth the trip. Feast your eyes on the spectacular views across the loch to Gigha and work up an appetite for the delights on offer at the Kilberry Inn. Formerly a croft, it is now a "dining pub" offering interesting home-cooked food - you can even buy the marmalade and chutneys. They have a constantly changing menu but favourites can always be found: layers of sausage stuffing and apple in a pie, beef cooked in Old Peculiar Ale, venison in red wine, salmon fish pie, not forgetting soups, ploughmans, all with home-baked bread. Desserts include apple pie, lemon meringue pie and shortcakes. Scottish bottled beers, Jennings Oatmeal Stout and Broughton Old Jock Strong Ale. A choice of malt whiskies.

OPEN: 11 - 2; 5 - 10 (closed Sun).
Children in no-smoking family room. No dogs.
Bedrooms.

KILLIECRANKIE

Killiecrankie Hotel   Tel: 01796 473220

Killiecrankie, Nr Pitlochry, Tayside PH16 5LG
Free House. Colin & Carole Anderson, licensees

In four acres of its own land, overlooking the River Garry and the Pass of Killiecrankie, this fine hotel occupies an enviable position in a beautiful area of Perthshire. It has a panelled bar where they provide bar lunches and suppers, and there is a table d'hôte menu in the elegant dining room. Bar food includes the stalwarts: soups, ploughmans, paté, sandwiches, but also hot dishes such as braised pheasant in red wine, grilled fish, venison casserole, local trout and salmon and a choice of puddings. Good wine list and a selection of malt whiskies. You are surrounded by lovely countryside with lots of things to see. The 17th century mill at Blair Atholl is still working and the smallest distillery in Scotland is north east of Pitlochry. Pitlochry also has a theatre festival every year. Go at the right time of the year and you can watch the salmon struggle up a "fish ladder" at the southern end of Loch Faskally.

OPEN: 11 - 2.30; 6 - 11 (closed Jan - Feb).
No-smoking evening restaurant.
Children welcome.
Dogs not where food is served.
Bedrooms.

KIPPEN

Cross Keys Hotel   Tel: 01786 870293

Main Street, Kippen, Central FK8 3DN
Free House. Angus and Sandra Watt, licensees

Small well-run pub situated in the centre of a small village not far
from Stirling. Food is served in either the lounge bar or the newer
restaurant. It has a family room, also a simply furnished public bar
with the pool table and dreaded juke box. Home-cooked bar food
includes soup, smoked salmon and prawn cornets, lasagne, steak
pie plus daily specials which could include poached Scottish
salmon in lemon sauce, breast of chicken in mushrooms and
cream sauce plus vegetarian dishes and traditional puddings.
Children's portions. An evening restaurant offers a more elaborate
menu. Broughtons Green Mantle and Youngers No.3, lots of malt
whiskies. Seats outside in the garden.

OPEN: 12 - 2.30; 5.30 - 11 (5.30 - 12 Sat).
Real Ale. Restaurant.
Children in restaurant/family room only.
Dogs on leads.
Bedrooms.

MOUNTBENGER

Gordon Arms Hotel   Tel: 01750 82232

Yarrow Valley, Mountbenger, Selkirk TD7 5LE
Free House. Harry Mitchell, licensee

Situated in the remote rolling Border hills near St Mary's Loch and the River Yarrow, next to a well-positioned 'stop' sign at the junction of the A708 and B709. Ideally placed for any traveller on the Southern Upland Way or on the direct route between Land's End and John O'Groats. Friendly, accommodating, with open fires in the bars in cold weather, and a range of home-cooked meals and choice of real ales. Breakfast is served all day. Bar snacks include soups, sandwiches, filled baked potatoes, grills, fish and traditional puddings. Children's portions, and in summer high tea in the lounge. Particularly geared up to the walker/cyclist/bird watcher with a cleverly converted bunkhouse which offers clean, warm, basic accommodation. So not only big boots and hairy socks, but back-packs the size of a Wendy House too. Broughtons Greenmantle ales, one guest and Scottish Oatmeal Stout. Lots of malt whiskies. Trout and salmon fishing can be arranged. Fantastic, wild scenery.

OPEN: 11 - 11 (midnight Sat); 11 - 3; 6.30 - 11 winter weekdays.
Real Ale. Restaurant (not Sun eve). Closed Tuesday mid Oct - Easter.
Children in eating area lounge & dining room until 8 pm.
Dogs on leads.
Accordion & Fiddle Club 3rd Wed each month.

SHEILDAIG

Tigh an Eilean Hotel   Tel: 01520 755251

Sheildaig, Strathcarron, Ross-shire.
Free House. Mrs E Stewart, licensee

The village was only created in 1800 by the Admiralty who offered grants to entice people to live here and work for the Navy.

Spectacular scenery surrounds this small village and its hotel, built on the edge of the sea, with views towards the National Trust "Island of Pines". The non-residents side has no more than a small bar, whose windows look out to sea. Well chosen bar food ranges from sandwiches, soups and salmon salad to hot weekly specials which could include chicken in white wine, rabbit or game casserole and a choice of fish. There is a comprehensive wine list. Tables and chairs in a side courtyard. Excellent walking country.

OPEN: 11 - 11 (11 - 2.30 Sun). Winter: 11 - 2.30; 5 - 11; closed all day Sun.
Evening restaurant summer only.
Children until 8 pm. No dogs.

SKEABOST

Skeabost House Hotel   Tel: 01470 532202

Skeabost Bridge, by Portree, Isle of Skye IV51 9NP
Free House. Iain McNab, licensee

North west of Portree, in the wild landscape of the Island of Skye, the Skeabost Hotel was built in 1870 as a hunting lodge. It lies in 12 acres of its own lovely wooded grounds, which have glorious views over Loch Snizort. One main and one public bar. Bar food includes the usual soups and sandwiches, paté, steak and ale pie and also game casseroles, salmon and trout. A buffet menu with lots of cold meats and salads is available in the no-smoking conservatory. In the dining room there is a daily changing table d'hôte: roast leg of Skye lamb with coriander and baked salmon with fennel and cream are just two of the dishes frequently available. Choice of wines and over 80 malt whiskies.

OPEN: 12 - 2; 6 - 11 (6 - 12 Sat). Public bar closed Sun.
No smoking evening restaurant.
Children welcome. No dogs.
Bedrooms.
(Hotel closed Oct - March.)

ST MARYS LOCH

Tibbie Shiels Inn   Tel: 01750 42231

St Mary's Loch, Selkirk, Borders TD7 5NE
Free House. Jack & Jill Brown, licensees

Named after Isabella Shiel, landlady for 55 years, it was originally a tiny inn built on the finger of land that separates St Mary's Loch and the Loch of the Lowes. After her husband died, she supported herself and six children by taking in "gentlemen lodgers". Thirteen beds were somehow distributed between what is now the bar and the attic - increasing to 35 in the shooting season! The inn has been somewhat extended since then so there is a little more room to move around. Bar food includes: soups, ploughmans, spicy chicken, fresh local trout and salmon, vegetarian dishes and a variety of puddings. Broughton Green Mantle and Belhaven 80/- on hand pump. Selection of wines and over 50 malt whiskies. Lots of walks, the Southern Upland Way is close by - too energetic? Tables and chairs at the front of the pub.

OPEN: 11 - 11 (11 - 12 Sat). Closed Mon Nov - March.
Real Ale. Restaurant.
Children welcome.
No dogs.
Bedrooms.

SWINTON

Wheatsheaf Hotel   Tel: 01890 860257

Main Street, Swinton, Berwickshire TD11 3JJ
Free House. Alan Read, licensee

Popular with everyone, locals, tourists, fishermen - not far from the River Tweed - and between Coldstream (Battle of Flodden Field, 1513) and Duns. Food is an important feature: the landlord is a dedicated chef and offers a daily changing menu which, as well as the usual lunchtime favourites, could include spinach and pesto pancake in cheese sauce, fillet of pork with parma ham, smoked haddock and cheese rarebit topped with crisp bacon, medallions of Scotch fillet steak in oyster, mushroom and brandy sauce. Imaginative puddings. Broughton Green Mantle ale and one guest beer. Good wine list and choice of malt whiskies.

OPEN: 11 - 2.30 (11 - 3 Sat); 6 - 11. Tues - Sun, closed Monday.
Closed Sun eve Nov - March. Closed 2 weeks Feb.
Real Ale.
Restaurant.
Children welcome. Dogs on leads.
Bedrooms.

TAYVALLICH

Tayvallich Inn   Tel: 015467 67282

Tayvallich by Lochgilphead, Strathclyde PA31 8PR
Free House. John Grafton, licensee

More a restaurant and bar than a conventional inn. It was built on a natural harbour on Loch A'Bhealaich and in good weather the glass doors in the bar are opened onto the terrace from where you can sit and admire the view. Wonderful variety of shellfish on the menu: mussels, scallops, oysters and prawns prepared in many ways; not forgotten, though, are chicken, steaks, burgers and vegetarian dishes for those without fishy leanings. Choice of wines and malt whiskies plus keg beers. There are walks along the edge of the loch, and to Knapdale Forest.

OPEN: 11 - midnight (11 - 1am Sat). Closed Mon Nov - March.
Restaurant.
Children in eating areas.
Dogs on leads.

TWEEDSMUIR

Crook Inn

Tel: 0189 97272

Tweedsmuir, Nr Biggar, Borders MLR 6QN
Free House. Stuart Reid, licensee

Built in 1604 and situated on the scenic route between Moffat and Edinburgh, this was originally a drovers' inn, now a welcoming, friendly pub in the lovely Tweed Valley. Simply furnished bars with cosy fires on colder days. Traditional bar food with the addition of local trout with almonds, poached salmon with dill sauce, steaks, mixed grills and vegetarian dishes - they also serve high tea. Broughton Green Mantle and McEwans 80/- on hand pump - good range of wines and malt whiskies. Seats and children's play area in the garden. Daily trout fishing permits are available from the inn.

OPEN: 11 - midnight.
Real Ale.
Restaurant.
Children welcome.
Dogs on leads.
Bedrooms.

WALES

ABERDOVEY

Penhelig Arms Hotel   Tel: 01654 767215

Aberdovey, Gwynedd LL35 0LT
Free House. Robert & Sally Hughes, licensees

Beside Penhelig Harbour and near the mouth of the River Dyfi, this delightful hotel has everything you could wish for: comfortable bars, imaginative lunchtime and evening bar menus, an excellent restaurant, above average accommodation, fantastic views over the harbour and last but not least, good ales. From the Fishermen's Bar, the bar food could include seafood vol-au-vent grilled with cheese, omelettes with a variety of fillings, chicken cooked in cream sauce spiced with ginger and cardamon served with rice, a choice of fish, salads, sandwiches and a variety of puddings. A slightly shorter evening bar menu, but no less imaginative. A reasonably priced three-course dinner is available in the restaurant; also a three-course Sunday lunch. Champagne by the glass if you want to be indulgent. Well chosen wine list. Felinfoel Double Dragon, Morlands Old Speckled Hen, Smiles Best, Tetleys and Brains SA ales. In warm weather you can sit outside on the sea wall and admire the view or tuck yourself up near the fire in the bar if the Welsh winds blow. Good walks along the sea front in both directions.

OPEN: 11 - 3; 6 - 11.
Real Ale. Restaurant (not Sun eve). No bar food Sun lunchtime.
Children in restaurant. No dogs.
Bedrooms.

BANGOR

Union Hotel   Tel: 01248 362462

Garth Road, Bangor, Gwynedd LL57 2SF
Burtonwood. John Duggan, tenant

They say they are open all hours here - all permitted hours, that is. Adjoining the local boatyard - "Dickies"- and the yacht basin, the Union Garth, as it is known, claims to be the only quiet pub in this cathedral city. Certainly anyone wanting to hire a room for a party goes through the third degree, and his DJ has to promise that any music played is sotto, sotto voce. It has a distinctly nautical atmosphere - the view of Snowdonia from the small garden at the back of the pub is viewed through a forest of yacht masts, accompanied by that evocative slap of rigging on main masts that is the only music you need on a summer's evening. Good, reliable, traditional bar food: soups, ploughmans, paté, smoked mussels and salads, omelettes, grilled gammon, steaks, filled baked potatoes and steak and kidney pie. Burtonwood Ales. Seats in the small garden.

OPEN: All permitted hours. Real Ale. No food Tues evenings.
Children welcome.
Dogs on leads.
Bedrooms.

BEAUMARIS

Ye Olde Bulls Head   Tel: 01248 810329

Castle Street, Beaumaris, Anglesey LL58 8AP
Free House. David Robertson, licensee

An attractive small town which is dominated by the castle built by Edward I in the 13th century. The pub is a little younger than the Castle, but still of venerable age, dating back to the 15th century. The interior of the Bulls Head reflects its long history: panelled, beamed, with open fires and full of interesting artefacts which include the town's original ducking stool - a use for which could be found I'm sure. There is a daily changing menu, but bar food is only available at lunchtimes: sandwiches and ploughmans (with local cheeses), soups, omelettes, braised chicken in wine and mustard sauce, crab or smoked trout salad among other dishes. A three-course Sunday lunch is served in the no-smoking restaurant. Bass, Worthingtons and a guest beer. Good choice of wines.

OPEN: 11 - 11 (no bar meals & snacks Sun lunchtime).
Real Ale. Restaurant.
Children until 8 pm (none under 7 in restaurant).
No dogs. Bedrooms.

CILCAIN

White Horse   Tel: 01352 740142

The Square, Cilcain, Flintshire CH7 5NN
Free House. Peter Jeory, licensee

Near Mold, a busy market town, two country parks and the River Alyn, the creeper-covered White Horse is in an enviable position. This old stone pub has several bars, one with an inglenook fireplace - go into the back one if you have your dog with you. Mostly local produce - including free range eggs and organically grown vegetables - is used to create a varied selection of home-made bar food: filled rolls, omelettes, the ham is home-baked, various casseroles, steaks, seasonal game dishes, plus a variety of puddings. Marstons Pedigree and changing guest beers. Selection of wines, farm ciders. Seats at the side of the pub.

OPEN: 12 - 3.30 (12 - 4 Sat); 7 - 11.
Real Ale.
No children inside pub.
Dogs on leads.

CLYTHA

Clytha Arms   Tel: 01873 840206

Clytha, Nr Abergavenny, Gwent NP7 9BW
Free House. Andrew & Beverley Canning, licensees

On the Abergavenny/Raglan road, not far from Clytha Castle, this nice old country inn, which has only re-opened in the last few years, has a good-sized country bar and a smaller, lounge bar. The blackboard menu lists dependable, reasonably-priced, country dishes: the usual sandwiches and ploughmans, faggots and peas, venison sausages, potato pancakes and laver bread are just a selection of those available. The restaurant (with napkins, candles and fresh flowers) has a separate, more expensive menu featuring regional specialities. They have a set Sunday lunch. Hook Norton, Theakstons XB and Hancocks HB ales plus an interesting selection of guest beers. There are wonderful walks along the banks of the River Wye and also through the grounds of Clytha Castle.

OPEN: 11 - 3.30; 6 - 11 (11 - 11 Sat).
Closed Mon lunchtimes except Bank Hols.
Real Ale. Restaurant.
Children welcome until 8 (not in bar).
Dogs if well behaved.
Bedrooms.

CRESSWELL QUAY

Cresselly Arms   Tel: 01646 65121

Cresswell Quay, Kilgetty, Dyfed SA68 0TE
Free House. Maurice and Janet Cole, licensees

Not far from Carew, its ruined 13th century castle and the only 19th century Welsh tidal mill on the Carew River, the Cresselly Arms is a timeless place, little changed since early this century. You can arrive by car, or by boat (depending on the tide), to enjoy your pint - still served from the cask into large jugs, and from there into your glass. A friendly, traditional pub serving good beer plus, no doubt, a crisp or a nut. Flowers IPA, also Heineken or Guinness. Seats outside from which to watch the tides and the boats.

OPEN: 11 - 3; 5 - 11.
Real Ale. No food.
No children. No dogs.

LLANGATTOCK

Vine Tree Inn   Tel: 01873 810514

The Leager, Llangattock, Crickhowell, Powys NP8 1HG
Free House. I S Lennox, licensee

This village of old weavers' cottages with its tiny paved square and 16th century church, is fortunate to be so near the lovely Monmouth Brecon Canal and the River Usk. Food is all-important here; fast, efficient service in a very busy pub. Freshly cooked, using local produce and fish from Cornwall. There is an extensive menu: home-made pies, casseroles, steaks, salmon, also Sunday roasts. Even the bread is home-made. Boddingtons, Flowers Original and Whitbreads West Country. Seats outside overlook the river and there are wonderful walks along the canal.

OPEN: 12 - 3; 6 - 11.
Real Ale. Restaurant (not Sun eves).
Children welcome. Dogs on leads (well behaved).

LLANFIHANGEL CRUCORNEY

Skirrid Inn   Tel: 01873 890 258

Llanfihangel, Crucorney, Gwent NP7 8DH
Ushers. Heather Gant, lease

It is surprising that there are no mournful ghosts at the Skirrid. Dating back to 1110 AD it was not only the local alehouse; it was also a place of execution. The beams at the bottom of the stairs were used as a makeshift gallows, from which over 180 people were hanged between the 12th and 17th centuries. Scorch and drag marks made by the ropes can still be seen. It was a combination of public meeting place, court and alehouse for over 600 years - resuming its role as an inn in about 1689. Stone-built, with medieval windows - the ancient timbers and panelling in the dining room are reputed to be from a 16th century Man-o'-War. Outside, the mounting block is contemporary with the inn and Owen Glendower is said to have rallied his troops, used the block to mount-up, and led his men on the march to Hereford. To sustain you after the history lesson, you will find a good selection of bar food ranging from home-made soup, ploughmans with Welsh cheeses, beef in ale pie, wild rabbit with mushrooms, cream and garlic, local lamb with apple and rosemary jelly and other specials. Ushers Best and Founders, four other changing ales on hand pump. A range of malt whiskies. The pub has a lovely garden with seats on the terrace at the back of the pub.

OPEN: 12 - 3; 7 - 11.
Restaurant.
Real Ale. No food Tues eve.
Children and dogs if well behaved.

LLANTHONY

Abbey Hotel   Tel: 01873 890487

Llanthony, Nr Abergavenny, Gwent NP7 7NN
Free House. Ivor Prentice, licensee

Ruins set amid the quiet beauty of the Vale of Ewyas. And among the ruins, in a truly magical setting, is the Abbey Hotel which incorporates parts of the Prior's house, and includes an atmospheric vaulted crypt bar. Simple furnishings in the main flagstoned bar where the food is plain and traditional: home-made soups, sandwiches, ploughmans and burgers; in the evening

dishes include casseroles, local lamb, pies and vegetarian dishes.
Ruddles County, Draught Bass, Flowers Original and farm ciders.
Glorious setting with wonderful walks.

OPEN: 11 - 3; 6 - 11 (11 - 11 Sat & Summer hols).
Closed weekdays end Nov - end March.
Open Christmas & New Year week.
Real Ale.
No children inside.
No dogs.
Bedrooms.

LLANWNDA

Goat Hotel   Tel: 01286 830256

Llanwnda, Caernarvon, Gwynedd LL54 5SD
Free House. Anne Griffith, licensee

The walled town of Caernarvon, full of lovely old buildings and
dominated by the ruins of Edward I's castle, is in a prominent
position overlooking the Menai Strait. It is also your nearest
point of contact when searching for this tiny hamlet. Well worth
finding for the friendly welcome you get when you arrive. Polish
up your Welsh so that you can greet the landlady and the
villagers. The Goat has a fair-sized main bar and a no-smoking
parlour. On high days and holidays an impressive, very
reasonable buffet is available, with a choice of starters, many
fish dishes, cold meats and pies; otherwise there are home-
made soups, interesting sandwiches, ploughmans with local
cheeses, home-cooked ham and salads - good substantial fare.
Draught Bass, Whitbread and Boddingtons Bitter. Tables on the
terrace at the front of the pub.

OPEN: 11 - 4; 6 - 11.
Real Ale. (No lunchtime food Sun.)
Children welcome.
Dogs on leads.
Bedrooms.

MAENTWROG

Grapes   Tel: 01766 590208

Maentwrog, Blaenau Ffestiniog, Gwynedd LL14 4HN
Free House. Brian & Gill Tarbox, licensees

Built in an attractive alpine-like valley with cottages clinging to its
sides and from where there are magnificent views of the
mountains, is The Grapes - a popular old coaching inn with
comfortable pine-panelled bars and big fires, serving well
presented, generous bar food. This could include lunchtime
soups, sandwiches, ploughmans, seafood pancakes, steak and
kidney pies, salads, rack of Welsh lamb and vegetarian dishes.
There are lots of fishy specials. The restaurant is no-smoking and
there is a children's menu. Bass and Worthingtons Best plus a
guest beer and farm cider. Seats on the verandah which look over
the garden to the mountains beyond. Nearby is the Vale of
Ffestiniog and the Ffestiniog Railway. Using 1860 locomotives it
travels through 14 miles of breathtaking scenery, and is well worth
a ride.

OPEN: 11 - 11.
Real Ale. Restaurant (not Sun eves).
Children in family room.
Dogs on leads.
Bedrooms.

MENAI BRIDGE

Liverpool Arms   Tel: 01248 712453

St George's Pier, Menai Bridge, Anglesey, Gwynedd, Wales
Greenalls. Tony Thickett, tenant

Overlooking the Menai Bridge - the graceful suspension bridge
Thomas Telford built in 1826 to link the Welsh mainland to the
Island of Anglesey - the Liverpool Arms, a brick-built early 19th
century pub, is full of nautical artefacts. It has two comfortable

bars, dining room and a conservatory seating 38. The food in the restaurant and the bar is all home-made and could include: leek and ham mornay, cod and prawn mornay, baked ham salad, sirloin steak, salmon, prawn and fresh Cromer crab salads. Thomas Greenalls Original, Greenalls and Tetleys Bitters. No garden, just a patio.

OPEN: 11 - 11 (12 - 3; 7 - 10.30 Sun).
Real Ale. No food Sunday.
Children welcome. No dogs.

NANTGWYNANT

Pen-y-Gwryd Hotel   Tel: 01286 870211

Nantgwynant, Gwyneth LL55 4NT
Free House. Jane Pullee, licensee

The Pen-y-Gwryd is in a wooded valley at the start of Watkin Path, a 3,300 ft climb to the summit of Snowdon. This is serious climbing country here: never mind the big boots and hairy socks, you'll need all-weather gear, with ironmongery and ropes attached to various parts of your body. The Hotel even has a climbers' bar which also serves as the headquarters of the local Mountain Rescue team. There is an interesting collection of boots that have made famous (accompanied) climbs, and this was where the successful 1953 Everest team based itself. A jolly, friendly inn serving hearty bar food, including special pies which change daily, casseroles in winter, as well as soups, sandwiches and home-made bread with the ploughmans. No bar food in the evening, just meals in the no-smoking restaurant. Bass and Theakstons ales.

OPEN: 11 - 11 (closed Nov - New Year;
open weekends only Jan - Feb).
Real Ale. Evening restaurant.
Well behaved children welcome, not in residents' bar.
Dogs on leads.
Bedrooms.

PENRHYNSIDE

Penrhyn Arms
Tel: 01492 540809

Pendre Road, Penrhynside, Llandudno, Gwynedd LL30 3BY
Free House. Mick Morris, licensee

"No music, no food and no customers!" was how the owners of the Penrhyn Arms introduced themselves. The first two statements are correct, but not the third. Near the slate quarries, and now part of Llandudno, the village of Penrhynside and the Penrhyn Arms were built at the turn of the century to cater for the quarry workers. A small pub, just one bar and a pool room. The treasured bagatelle board is nearly as old as the pub; they also play bar skittles and the next purchase is going to be a shove-ha'penny board so they can join the Welsh league. Bought off the brewery, the landlord is hoping to put back some of the character previous owners have removed; the garden is due some attention too. "Vast range of food," says the landlord, "three types of crisps and two of nuts. Occasionally things get really exciting and I change the flavour of the crisps." This is a traditional ale house, with the sort of friendly, ebullient landlord you would wish for all village pubs. Marstons ales from the cask, lagers and cider from the pumps. Water and biscuits under the counter for the dog.

OPEN: Mon - Fri: 12 - 2.30; 5.30 - 11ish. Sat - Sun: 12 - 11ish.
Real Ale. Crisps and nuts.
Children if well behaved.
Dogs very welcome.

PRESTEIGNE

Radnorshire Arms
Tel: 01544 267406

The High Street, Presteigne, Powys LB8 2BE
Free House. Aidan Treacy, manager

This small, Welsh market town has an interesting part-Saxon church, which the Normans, Tudors and Georgians have all added to, or altered during their times. In Elizabeth I's reign, the Radnorshire Arms was a private house, complete with secret passages and a priest's chamber; it became a coaching inn in 1792 and since then has perfected the art of looking after the needs of the traveller. A wonderful example of Elizabethan timbering outside, with oak beams and panelling inside; it has been successfully modernised without losing its age old charm and welcoming atmosphere. The bar menu, served in the oak-panelled bar, is all home-made, offering a choice of both local and regional specialities. They have a no-smoking restaurant. Draught Bass and Ruddles County plus wines by the glass. Seats outside in the sheltered garden.

OPEN: 11 - 11.
Real Ale. Restaurant (not Sun eves).
Children welcome.
No dogs.
Bedrooms.

ST ASAPH

Farmers Arms   Tel: 01745 582190

The Waen, Nr St. Asaph, Clwyd
(on the B5429 between the Expressway A55, and Tremeirchion)
Free House. B Seaman, licensee

A delightful country pub which leans more towards a restaurant than a pub. There is a public bar with all the noisy bits, situated well away from the bar in the main lounge; a small snug and a room for parties, which is also used for meetings by the Rotary Club and local Young Farmers. Fractionally borderline in our case, there certainly isn't any piped music but early in the evening when the bar is still fairly empty, there could be very quiet "cocktaily" music on tape, this is turned off as the pub fills up, and the landlord, a classically trained musician, can sometimes be persuaded to play the grand piano in the lounge bar. The home-cooked food ranges from simple bar food to an elaborate à la carte menu in the dining room. Theakstons is the main ale, and two others are chosen by the landlord.

OPEN: 12 - 3; 7 - 11 (12 - 3; 7 - 10.30 Sun).
Real Ale.
No Children.
No Dogs.

STACKPOLE

Armstrong Arms   Tel: 01646 672324

Stackpole, Pembroke, Dyfed SA71 5DF
Free House. Senga & Peter Waddilove, licensees

Just three miles south of Pembroke - which boasts the largest Norman castle in Britain and is reputed to be the birthplace of Henry VII in 1457 - the Armstrong Arms is a mere 400 years old and has only been a pub for a few years. In this short time it has nevertheless created a niche for itself as one of the few pubs with a deserved reputation for serving imaginative and interesting home-cooked food. Friendly and welcoming, the pub is spacious with well-spaced tables and chairs. Usual pub standards: soups, sandwiches, ploughmans, jacket potatoes, and changing specials; a choice of fish dishes, crab salad, loin of pork with apple sauce, game pie and chicken supreme with apricot sauce are just a selection of the dishes frequently available. Impressive home-made puddings. Worthingtons Best, Hancocks HB, Adnams plus guest beers and over 40 malt whiskies. Seats outside in the flowery garden.

OPEN: 11 - 3; 6 - 11.
Real Ale. (No meals/snacks winter Sun eves.)
Children welcome.
Dogs in bar.

TUDWEILOG

Lion Hotel Tel: 01758 770244

Nefyn Road, Tudweilog, Gwynedd LL53 8ND
Free House. Andrew Lee, licensee

Popular, 300 year old village inn not far from the sandy beaches
and windsurfing sea on the Lleyn Peninsula. Comfortable and
friendly, it has a good-sized main bar, no-smoking family dining
room and a public bar filled with games machines - including a
juke box (not used much we hope). Satisfying bar menu includes:
home-made soups, sandwiches, ploughmans, baked potatoes
with various fillings, lasagne, steaks, Spanish style chicken and
several vegetarian dishes. Children's portions and a choice of
puddings. Theakstons Best, Dark and Mild, Boddingtons,
Marstons Pedigree and a guest beer during spring and summer. A
number of malt whiskies. Children's play area and tables in the
front and back gardens.

OPEN: 11 - 3; 5.30 - 11 (12 - 7; 7 - 11 winter). Closed Sun.
Real Ale. Restaurant (not Sun).
Children in family dining room.
No dogs.

WINE BAR AND PUB GROUPS

DAVYS

Lunching on a slice of traditional English pie taken with chilled champagne from a pewter tankard is an experience you won't easily forget. Of course, to savour it to the full, it helps to be surrounded by old oak barrels and freshly sawdusted floors, which evoke an atmosphere of times gone by. This cellar imagery is one Davys have cultivated successfully since they opened *The Boot and Flogger* wine bar in 1965. Today, they own 54 establishments, of which all but seven are in London. This year Davys celebrated 125 years as one of Britain's major wine shippers. While other establishments fall out of favour, Davys remains constantly popular, distinctive and welcoming.

LONDON

Bangers
12 Wilson Street
London EC2
Tel: 0171 377 6326

Bangers Too
1 St Mary-at-Hill
London EC3
Tel: 0171 283 4443

Bishop of Norwich
91/93 Moorgate
London EC2
Tel: 0171 920 0857

Bishops Parlour
91/93 Moorgate
London EC2
Tel: 0171 588 2581

Bottlescrue
Bath House
53/60 Holborn Viaduct
London EC1
Tel: 0171 248 2157

Bung Hole
57 High Holborn
London WC1
Tel: 0171 242 4318

Bung Hole Cellars
Hand Court
57 High Holborn
London WC1
Tel: 0171 831 8365

Burgundy Bens
102/108 Clerkenwell Road
London EC1
Tel: 0171 251 3783

Champagne Charlies
Villiers Street
London WC2
Tel: 0171 930 7737

The Chiv
90/92 Wigmore Street
London W1
Tel: 0171 224 0170

Chopper Lump
10c Hanover Square
London W1
Tel: 0171 499 7569

City Boot
7 Moorfields High Walk
London EC2
Tel: 0171 588 4766

City Flogger
Fenn Court
120 Fenchurch Street
London EC3
Tel: 0171 623 3251

City F.O.B.
Below London Bridge
Lower Thames Street
London EC3
Tel: 0171 621 0619

City Pipe
Foster Lane
off Cheapside
London EC1
Tel: 0171 606 2110

City Vaults
2 St Martins-le-Grand
London EC1
Tel: 0171 606 8721

Colonel Jaspers
161 Greenwich High Rd
London SE10
Tel: 0181 853 0585

Colonel Jaspers
190 City Road
London EC1
Tel: 0171 608 0925

The Cooperage
48/50 Tooley Street
London SE1
Tel: 0171 403 5775

Crown Passage Vaults
20 King Street
St James's
London SW1
Tel: 0171 839 8831

Crusting Pipe
27 The Market
Covent Garden
London WC2
Tel: 0171 836 1415

Davys at Creed Lane
10 Creed Lane
London EC4
Tel: 0171 236 5317

Davys Wine Vaults
161 Greenwich High Rd
London SE10
Tel: 0181 858 7204

Dock Blida
50/54 Blandford St
London W1
Tel: 0171 486 3590

Grapeshots
2/3 Artillery Passage
London E1
Tel: 0171 247 8215

Guinea Butt
White Hart Yard
Borough High Street
London SE1
Tel: 0171 407 2829

Gyngleboy
27 Spring Street
Paddington
London W2
Tel: 0171 723 3351

The Habit
Friary Court
65 Crutched Friars
London EC3
Tel: 0171 481 1131

Lees Bag
4 Great Portland Street
London W1
Tel: 0171 636 5287

The Mug House
1-3 Tooley Street
London SE1
Tel: 0171 403 8343

The Pulpit
63 Worship Street
London EC2
Tel: 0171 377 1574

Shotberries
167 Queen Victoria Street
London EC4
Tel: 0171 329 4759

Skinkers
42 Tooley Street
London EC1
Tel: 0171 407 9189

The Spittoon
15/17 Long Lane
London EC1
Tel: 0171 726 8858

Tappit-Hen
5 William IV St
Strand
London WC2
Tel: 0171 836 9839

Tappit-Hen Cellars
5 William IV St
Strand
London WC2
Tel: 0171 836 9839

Tapster
3 Brewers Green
Buckingham Gate
London SW1
Tel: 0171 222 0561

Truckles of Pied Bull
Yard (Ale & Port House)
off Bury Place
Bloomsbury
London WC1
Tel: 0171 404 5338

Truckles of Pied Bull
Yard (Wine Rooms)
off Bury Place
Bloomsbury
London WC1
Tel: 0171 404 5334

Tumblers
1 Kensington High St
London W8
Tel: 0171 937 0393

Udder Place
Russia Court
Russia Row
1/6 Milk Street
London EC2
Tel: 0171 606 7252

Udder Place
(Wine Rooms)
Russia Court
Russia Row
1/6 Milk Street
London EC2
Tel: 0171 600 2165

The Vineyard
International House
1 St Katherine's Way
London E1
Tel: 0171 480 6680

The Vineyard Coffee House
International House
1 St Katherine's Way
London E1
Tel: 0171 480 5088

COUNTRY
ESTABLISHMENTS

Bottlescrue Bills
66 South Street
Exeter
Devon
Tel: 01392 437511

Colonel Jaspers
3 Beacon House
Queen's Avenue
Clifton
Bristol
Tel: 01272 731289

Colonel Jaspers
15B Longbridge Road
Barking
Essex
Tel: 0181 507 8481

The Crypt
Frewin Court
off Cornmarket
Oxford
Tel: 01865 251000

Spotted Dog
15 Longbridge Road
Barking
Essex
Tel: 0181 594 0228

White Hart Hotel
66 South Street
Exeter
Devon
Tel: 01392 79897

The Wine Vaults
122 North End
Croydon
Tel: 0181 680 2419

GALES

In the 148 years since George Gale & Co Ltd was founded, it has become Hampshire's major brewery, producing a very popular range of real ales for its tied houses and other outlets. Twenty-five out of its 131 pubs are free of piped music and are listed below. Some of these are delightful old establishments, but they were brought to our notice too late to receive the full QUIET PINT descriptive treatment, which they will get in the next edition.

BERKSHIRE

The Bull Inn
High Street
Sonning, Berks
Tel: 01734 693901

DORSET

The Red Lion Hotel
Broad Street
Lyme Regis
Dorset

St Peters Finger
Lychett Minster
Poole
Dorset
Tel: 01202 622275

HAMPSHIRE

The Castle
1 Finchdean Road
Rowlands Castle
Hants
Tel: 01705 412494

The Cricketers Inn
Church Road
Steep
Petersfield
Hants
Tel: 01730 251035

The Golden Lion
High Street
Fareham
Hants
Tel: 01329 234061

Hogs Lodge
London Road
Clanfield
Portsmouth
Hants
Tel: 01705 591083

The Kings Arms
19 Havant Road
Emsworth
Hants
Tel: 01243 374941

The Milkmans Arms
55 North Street
Emsworth
Hants
Tel: 01243 373356

The Old House at Home
62 Love Lane
Romsey
Hants
Tel: 017945 131175

The Red Lion
High Street
Southwick
Fareham
Hants
Tel: 01705 377223

The Rising Sun
Milland
Nr Liphook
Hants
Tel: 01428 676347

The Roebuck
Kingsmead
Wickham
Fareham
Hants
Tel: 01329 832150

The Temple Inn
82 Forest Road
Liss Forest
Liss
Hants
Tel: 01730 892134

The Three Horseshoes
Bighton
Nr Arlesford
Hants
Tel: 01962 732859

The White Horse
Priors Dene
Nr Petersfield
Hants
Tel: 01420 588387

SURREY

The Prince of Wales
Hammervale
Haslemere
Surrey
Tel: 01428 652600

SUSSEX

Berkeley Arms
Delling Lane
Old Bosham
Chichester
Sussex
Tel: 01243 573167

The Limeburners
Newbridge
Billingshurst
Sussex
Tel: 01403 782311

The Murrell Arms
Yapton Road
Barnham
Sussex
Tel: 01243 553320

Park Tavern
11 Priory Road
Chichester
Sussex
Tel: 01243 785057

The Royal Oak
Pagham Road
Lagness
Chichester
Sussex
Tel: 01243 262216

The Royal Oak
Pook Lane
East Lavant
Chichester
Sussex
Tel: 01243 527434

The Spotted Cow
Selsey Road
Hunston
Chichester
Sussex
Tel: 01243 786718

The Woodman
Hammpot
Angmering
Littlehampton
Sussex
Tel: 01903 871240

WILTSHIRE

The Poplars
Wingfield
Nr Trowbridge
Wiltshire
Tel: 01225 752426

The Saracens Head
Market Place
Highworth
Wiltshire
Tel: 01795 762284

WETHERSPOONS

J D Wetherspoons specialise in the conversion of high street outlets into popular pubs - ex-betting shops, shoe-shops, post offices and banks - all have a character of their own. Wetherspoons commitment to music free pubs serving reasonably priced beer and food, served by friendly professional staff, is a formula that is hard to beat. One of the capital's top radio stations voted "The Moon under the Water" in Leicester Square the most popular pub in London. You can draw your own conclusions from that vote of confidence.

WETHERSPOONS
LONDON

The Bankers Draft
36-38 Friern Barnet Road
New Southgate
London N11
Tel: 0181 361 7115

The Bankers Draft
80 High Street
Eltham
London SE9
Tel: 0181 294 2578

The Beaten Docket
50-56 Cricklewood B'way
Cricklewood
London NW2
Tel: 0181 450 2972

The Beehive
407 Brixton Road
Brixton
London SW9
Tel: 0171 738 3643

The Bird in Hand
35 Dartmouth Road
Forest Hill
London SE23
Tel: 0181 699 7417

The Camdens Head
456 Bethnal Green Road
Bethnal Green
London E2
Tel: 0171 613 4263

The Coliseum
Manor Park Road
Harlesden
London NW2
Tel: 0181 961 6570

Crown & Sceptre
2 Streatham Hill
Streatham
London SW2
Tel: 0181 671 0843

The Dog
17-19 Archway Road
London N19
Tel: 0171 263 0429

The Drum
557-559 Lea Bridge Road
London E10
Tel: 0181 539 6577

The Elbow Room
22 Topsfield Parade
Crouch End
London N8
Tel: 0181 340 3677

The Elbow Room
503-505 High Road
Tottenham
London N17
Tel: 0181 801 8769

Fox on the Hill
Denmark Hill
London SE5
Tel: 0171 738 4756

The Gatehouse
North Road
Highgate
London N6
Tel: 0181 340 8054

The George
High Street
Wanstead
London E11
Tel: 0181 989 2921

The Golden Grove
146-148 The Grove
Stratford
London E15
Tel: 0181 519 0750

The Grid Inn
22 Replingham Road
Southfields
London SW18
Tel: 0181 874 8460

The Half Moon
749 Green Lanes
Winchmore Hill
London N21
Tel: 0181 360 5410

Hamilton Hall
Unit 32
The Broadgate Centre
Liverpool Street Station
London EC2
Tel: 0171 247 3579

J J Moons
80-82 Chiswick High Road
Chiswick
London W4
Tel: 0181 742 7263

J J Moons
553 Kingsbury Road
Kingsbury
London NW9
Tel: 0181 204 9675

J J Moons
56A High Street
Tooting
London SW17
Tel: 0181 672 4726

J J Moons
397 High Road
Wembley
Tel: 0181 903 4923

The Lamb
52-54 Church Street
Edmonton
London N9
Tel: 0181 887 0128

Man in the Moon
40-42 Chalk Farm Road
London NW1
Tel: 0171 482 2054

The Masque Haunt
Old Street
London EC2
Tel: 0171 251 4195

The Millers Well
419-421 Barking Road
East Ham
London E6
Tel: 0181 471 8404

Moon & Sixpence
183 Wardour Street
London W1
Tel: 0171 734 0037

Moon & Stars
164-166 High Street
Penge
London SE20
Tel: 0181 776 5680

Moon on the Green
172-174 Uxbridge Road
Shepherds Bush
London W12
Tel: 0181 749 5709

Moon under Water
28 Leicester Square
London WC2
Tel: 0171 839 2837

Moon under Water
194 Balham High Street
Balham
London SW12
Tel: 0181 673 0535

Moon under Water
1327 London Road
Norbury
London SW16
Tel: 0181 765 1235

Moon under Water
10 Varley Parade
Colindale
London NW9
Tel: 0181 200 7611

The New Moon
413 Lordship Lane
Tottenham
London N17
Tel: 0181 801 3496

Old Suffolk Punch
10-12 Grand Parade
Green Lanes
London N4
Tel: 0181 800 5912

The Outside Inn
314 Neasden Lane
London NW10
Tel: 0181 452 3140

The Railway
202 Upper Richmond Road
Putney
London SW15
Tel: 0181 788 8190

The Red Lion & Pineapple
281 High Street
Acton
London W3
Tel: 0181 896 2248

Rochester Castle
145 High Street
Stoke Newington
London N16
Tel: 0171 249 6016

The Spotted Dog
72 Garratt Lane
Wandsworth
London SW18
Tel: 0181 875 9531

The Tally Ho
749 High Road
North Finchley
London N12
Tel: 0181 445 4390

Three Horseshoes
28 Heath Street
Hampstead
London NW3
Tel: 0171 431 7206

The Toll Gate
26-30 Turnpike Lane
London N8
Tel: 0181 889 9085

179 Upper Steet
179 Upper Street
Islington
London N1
Tel: 0171 226 6276

Wetherspoons
Unit 5
Victoria Island
Victoria Station
London SW1
Tel: 0171 931 0445

The White Lion of
Mortimer
256-8 West Hendon B'way
West Hendon
London NW9
Tel: 0181 202 8887

The White Lion of Mortimer
125-127 Stroud Green Road
Finsbury Park
London N4
Tel: 0171 281 4773

The Whole Hog
430-434 Green Lanes
Palmers Green
London N13
Tel: 0181 882 3597

WETHERSPOONS
COUNTRY

BERKSHIRE

The Monks Retreat
163 Frier Street
Reading
Berks
Tel: 01734 507592

The Old Manor
High Street
Bracknell
Berks
Tel: 0134 304490

BUCKINGHAMSHIRE

The Falcon
9 Cornmarket
High Wycombe
Bucks
Tel: 01494 538610

The Last Post
77 The Broadway
Chesham
Bucks
Tel: 01494 785622

DORSET

Moon on the Square
4-6 Exeter Road
The Square
Bournemouth
Dorset
Tel: 01202 314940

ESSEX

The Barking Dog
61 Station Parade
Barking
Essex
Tel: 0181 507 9109

The Elms
London Road
Leigh on Sea
Essex
Tel: 01702 74687

The Great Spoon of Ilford
114-116 Cranbrook Road
Ilford
Essex
Tel: 0181 518 0535

The Last Post
Weston Road
Southend on Sea
Essex
Tel: 01702 431682

Lord Denman
270-2 Heathway
Dagenham
Essex
Tel: 0181 984 8590

Moon & Stars
99-103 South Street
Romford
Essex
Tel: 01708 730117

New Fairlop Oak
Fencepiece Road
Barkingside
Essex
Tel: 0181 500 2217

The Playhouse
4 St John Street
Colchester
Essex
Tel: 01206 571003

HERTFORDSHIRE

Hart & Spool
148 Shenley Road
Borehamwood
Herts
Tel: 0181 953 1883

Moon under Water
148 High Street
Barnet
Herts
Tel: 0181 441 9476

The Railway Bell
13 East Barnet Road
New Barnet
Herts
Tel: 0181 449 1369

KENT

The Paper Moon
55 High Street
Dartford
Kent
Tel: 01322 281127

Sovereign of the Seas
109-111 Queensway
Petts Wood
Kent
Tel: 01689 891606

The Wrong 'Un
234-236 The Broadway
Bexley Heath
Kent
Tel: 0181 298 0439

MIDDLESEX

Blacking Bottle
122-126 High Street
Edgware
Middx
Tel: 0181 381 1485

The Good Yarn
132 High Street
Uxbridge
Middx
Tel: 01895 239852

J J Moons
12 Victoria Road
Ruislip Manor
Middx
Tel: 01895 622373

J J Moons
3 Shaftesbury Parade
Shaftesbury Circle
South Harrow
Middx
Tel: 0181 423 5056

J J Moons
Terminal 4 - Airside
Unit CU3 - South Hall
Heathrow Airport
Hounslow
Middx
Tel: 0181 759 0355

J J Moons
19-20 The Broadwalk
Pinner Road
North Harrow
Middx
Tel: 0181 424 9686

Man in the Moon
1 Buckingham Parade
Stanmore
Middx
Tel: 0181 954 6119

Moon & Sixpence
250 Uxbridge Road
Hatch End
Harrow
Middx
Tel: 0181 420 1074

Moon & Sixpence
1250-1256 Uxbridge Road
Hayes End
Middx
Tel: 0181 561 3541

Moon on the Hill
373-375 Station Road
Harrow
Middx
Tel: 0181 863 3670

Moon on the Square
Unit 30
The Centre
Feltham
Middx
Tel: 0181 393 1293

Moon under Water
116/7 Chase Side
Enfield
Middx
Tel: 0181 366 9855

Moon under Water
10/11 Broadway Parade
Coldharbour Lane
Hayes
Middx
Tel: 0181 813 6774

Moon under Water
53-57 London Road
Twickenham
Middx
Tel: 0181 744 0080

Moon under Water
84-86 Staines Road
Hounslow
Middx
Tel: 0181 572 7506

The New Moon
25-26 Kenton Park Parade
Kenton Road
Harrow
Middx
Tel: 0181 909 1103

The Sarsen Stone
32 High Street
Wealdstone
Harrow
Middx
Tel: 0181 863 8533

The Sylvan Moon
27 Green Lane
Northwood
Middx
Tel: 01923 820760

The Village Inn
402-408 Rayners Lane
Pinner
Middx
Tel: 0181 868 8551

Wetherspoons
Terminal 4 - Landside
Heathrow Airport
Hounslow
Middx
Tel: 0181 759 2906

NORFOLK

The Bell
5 Orford Hill
Norwich
Tel: 01603 630017

SURREY

The Foxley Hatch
8-9 Russell Hill Road
Purley
Surrey
Tel: 0181 671 0843

The George
17-21 George Street
Croydon
Surrey
Tel: 0181 649 9077

Moon on the Hill
5-9 Hill Road
Sutton
Surrey
Tel: 0181 643 1202

The Regent
19 Church Street
Walton on Thames
Surrey
Tel: 01932 243980

Whispering Moon
25 Ross Parade
Woodcote Road
Wallington
Surrey
Tel: 0181 647 7020

White Lion of Mortimer
223 London Road
Mitcham
Surrey
Tel: 0181 646 7332

SUSSEX

The Red Lion
International
Departures Lounge
North Terminal
Gatwick Airport
West Sussex
Tel: 01293 569874

BIRMINGHAM

The Square Peg
Units 1,2 & 3
115 Corporation Street
Temple Court
Birmingham
Tel: 0121 236 6530

THE QUIET PINT

AUGMENTING THE DIRECTORY

This FIRST edition of QUIET PINT does not list all Britain's piped-music-free pubs. There are hundreds we have not yet tracked down, or which no one has told us about. If you come across any we have not listed, please send us the details on the adjacent forms.

You can get most of the information from the publican or his bar staff, but make sure they understand that an entry in THE QUIET PINT is absolutely FREE. Most will be only too pleased to tell you about their pub, its history, the ales and food they serve, many other fascinating details and, of course, themselves.

Descriptions are up to you. Just report what you see and feel about the pub you are nominating. There are plenty of examples to go by in THE QUIET PINT.

Many thanks.

THE PIPEDOWN CAMPAIGN

The Pipedown Campaign is solely against piped music in all public places, not just in public houses. Music on the telephone is another irritant some members are protesting about. Pipedown may, in some ways, be a crusade, but their aim is to convert, not to exterminate. The world is full of shrill, fanatical, single-issue protesters. Pipedown is not among them.

Everyone who supports their aims should join them. The more support they have, the more they will be able to accomplish.

NOMINATION FORM

1. Name of Pub ....
2. Telephone Number ....
3. Postal Address, including Post Code ....
   ....
   ....
4. Is pub Free House or Tied House? *[Please delete as appropriate.]*
5. If Tied, please name the Brewery or Group it belongs to.
   ....
6. Name of Publican and Status..
   e.g.Tenant(s)/Licensee(s)/Manager(s). *[Please delete those which do not apply.]*
   Name and Address of Investigator ....
   ....
   ....

Please use the space overleaf to describe the pub and its surroundings in your own way. THE QUIET PINT is full of examples of the kind of descriptions we are seeking. The pub may have a brochure and/or menu: if so, please send them with this form to:

The Quiet Pint, FREEPOST, Sandwich, Kent CT13 9BR

PIPEDOWN SUBSCRIPTION FORM

Annual subscription is £10.00, overseas £15.00 payable to:

Pipedown, 6 Kingsley Mansions, London W14 9SG

Tel/Fax 0171 385 5811

Name ....

Address..

....

DESCRIPTION OF PUB/WINE BAR

NOMINATION FORM

1. Name of Pub ....
2. Telephone Number ....
3. Postal Address, including Post Code ....
   ....
   ....
4. Is pub Free House or Tied House? *[Please delete as appropriate.]*
5. If Tied, please name the Brewery or Group it belongs to.
   ....
6. Name of Publican and Status...
   e.g. Tenant(s)/Licensee(s)/Manager(s). *[Please delete those which do not apply.]*
   Name and Address of Investigator ....
   ....
   ....

Please use the space overleaf to describe the pub and its surroundings in your own way. THE QUIET PINT is full of examples of the kind of descriptions we are seeking. The pub may have a brochure and/or menu: if so, please send them with this form to:

The Quiet Pint, FREEPOST, Sandwich, Kent CT13 9BR

PIPEDOWN SUBSCRIPTION FORM

Annual subscription is £10.00, overseas £15.00 payable to:

Pipedown, 6 Kingsley Mansions, London W14 9SG

Tel/Fax 0171 385 5811

Name ....

Address..

....

DESCRIPTION OF PUB/WINE BAR

NOMINATION FORM

1. Name of Pub ....
2. Telephone Number ....
3. Postal Address, including Post Code ....
   ....
   ....
4. Is pub Free House or Tied House? *[Please delete as appropriate.]*
5. If Tied, please name the Brewery or Group it belongs to.
   ....
6. Name of Publican and Status..
   e.g.Tenant(s)/Licensee(s)/Manager(s). *[Please delete those which do not apply.]*
   Name and Address of Investigator ....
   ....
   ....

Please use the space overleaf to describe the pub and its surroundings in your own way. THE QUIET PINT is full of examples of the kind of descriptions we are seeking. The pub may have a brochure and/or menu: if so, please send them with this form to:

The Quiet Pint, FREEPOST, Sandwich, Kent CT13 9BR

PIPEDOWN SUBSCRIPTION FORM

Annual subscription is £10.00, overseas £15.00 payable to:

Pipedown, 6 Kingsley Mansions, London W14 9SG

Tel/Fax 0171 385 5811

Name ....

Address..

....

DESCRIPTION OF PUB/WINE BAR

NOMINATION FORM

1. Name of Pub ....

2. Telephone Number ....

3. Postal Address, including Post Code ....

   ....

   ....

4. Is pub Free House or Tied House? *[Please delete as appropriate.]*

5. If Tied, please name the Brewery or Group it belongs to.

   ....

6. Name of Publican and Status...

   e.g.Tenant(s)/Licensee(s)/Manager(s). *[Please delete those which do not apply.]*

   Name and Address of Investigator ....

   ....

   ....

Please use the space overleaf to describe the pub and its surroundings in your own way. THE QUIET PINT is full of examples of the kind of descriptions we are seeking. The pub may have a brochure and/or menu: if so, please send them with this form to:

   The Quiet Pint, FREEPOST, Sandwich, Kent CT13 9BR

PIPEDOWN SUBSCRIPTION FORM

Annual subscription is £10.00, overseas £15.00 payable to:

Pipedown, 6 Kingsley Mansions, London W14 9SG

Tel/Fax 0171 385 5811

Name ....

Address...

....

DESCRIPTION OF PUB/WINE BAR

NOMINATION FORM

1. Name of Pub ....

2. Telephone Number ....

3. Postal Address, including Post Code ....

   ....

   ....

4. Is pub Free House or Tied House? *[Please delete as appropriate.]*

5. If Tied, please name the Brewery or Group it belongs to.

   ....

6. Name of Publican and Status..

   e.g.Tenant(s)/Licensee(s)/Manager(s). *[Please delete those which do not apply.]*

   Name and Address of Investigator ....

   ....

   ....

Please use the space overleaf to describe the pub and its surroundings in your own way. THE QUIET PINT is full of examples of the kind of descriptions we are seeking. The pub may have a brochure and/or menu: if so, please send them with this form to:

   The Quiet Pint, FREEPOST, Sandwich, Kent CT13 9BR

PIPEDOWN SUBSCRIPTION FORM

Annual subscription is £10.00, overseas £15.00 payable to:

Pipedown, 6 Kingsley Mansions, London W14 9SG

Tel/Fax 0171 385 5811

Name ....

Address...

....

DESCRIPTION OF PUB/WINE BAR